RUSSIAN JOURNEY

Russian

Journey

BY WILLIAM O. DOUGLAS

DOUBLEDAY & COMPANY, INC., GARDEN CITY, NEW YORK, 1956

405442

TO MERCEDES

PHOTOGRAPHS BY WILLIAM O. DOUGLAS
AND MERCEDES H. DOUGLAS

Library of Congress Catalog Card Number 56–7945

FOREWORD

It took a long time to get my Russian visa. Every February for five consecutive years I applied for one. I was finally rewarded in the spring of 1955 when the Soviet Embassy telephoned to say my request was granted.

My desire to see Russia sprang from various interests. I was anxious to see what socialism under a totalitarian regime had done to a people and a nation. I was curious about the impact of the police state on individual freedom. I was particularly interested in Russia's Central Asia. I had seen most of the other regions of Central Asia. They and the Russian part shared much history and were steeped in the same tradition. Most of the Central Asian areas I had traveled were still feudal. I wondered what changes Russia had made.

I managed my trip so as to enter Russia through Iran. The plains and hills of south Russia are as dry as Iran's, and as Morocco's too, for that matter. The rainfall in Soviet Central Asia is between ten and fifteen inches a year. But though Soviet Central Asia is dry, dusty, and windblown, it has a strong attraction, traceable perhaps to associations of my youth.

Samarkand—hot in the sun but comfortable in deep shade—reminded me very much of Paso Robles, California, where I spent a few early years.

The hot winds and the dust storms of Baku are linked in memory with those of Bickleton, Washington, which was my home after my family moved north from California.

One afternoon at a milk farm near Frunze I looked up to feel for a second that I was once more at the base of barren but majestic Mt. Clemens near Yakima, Washington.

Ashkhabad, which sits on a barren plain not far from the Iranian border, is a larger version of Pasco, Washington. It, too, has an intense, dry heat. The day I arrived there the temperature was over 120° F. The summers are so warm in Ashkhabad that hotels and homes have double windows to keep out the heat. I drove out of Ashkhabad in late afternoon to visit Nissa, an empty crater on a low peak, where ages ago the Parthians held off their foes. So far as the low hills and valleys were concerned, I might have been en route from Pasco to Walla Walla.

I also felt strangely at home in the barren spot on the east side of the Caspian Sea where the city of Krasnovodsk, built in 1860, is located. It's a hot, wind-blown place with no grass and hardly a bush or tree to adorn it. Yet I was taken with the place. The houses, painted blue, are neat, the streets are clean, the Russian Orthodox Church is well kept up, the railroad station is rather pretty, and the new apartments made of stone are quite attractive. But most impressive of all are the barren, bluish hills that rise like a rampart from the sea, reminding me of the cliffs below Wallula, Washington, a small town now submerged by the backwaters of the McNary Dam on the Columbia.

The Tien Shan Mountains of southwest Russia, where one reaches the conifers at 5100 feet, reflect all the beauties of our

Rocky, Sierra, and Cascade Mountains. When I first came across the plains toward them at Frunze, it seemed I was once more a young lad headed for high adventure, for they looked very much like the mountains of eastern Washington that had been my challenge as a boy. And when I reached Siberia, it seemed I was back on the Great Plains, not far from my Minnesota birthplace.

Perhaps it was because I felt at home in the physical environment of Central Asia and Siberia that I came to their problems with more of an understanding heart than I otherwise might have had.

The entire Russian journey was a rich experience. Russia is a world so different from our own that comparisons are difficult. One who loses himself in the limitless expanses of Russia for some weeks comes out a different man. He need not like what he saw to have more understanding. If he gets only one lesson, it is this: that war can never settle the differences between the two nations —that Russia, like the United States, is too powerful, too vast, too far flung, ever to be conquered and garrisoned by a victorious army. A trip to Russia emphasizes the great differences and cleavages between the two peoples. But it teaches that the only settlement is a political one. That problem is, indeed, the great challenge of this, the last half of the twentieth century.

I had three companions who greatly helped me on this Russian journey. For the last three weeks Frederick W. Flott, Jr. of Chicago was with me. Robert F. Kennedy of Hyannis, Massachusetts, entered Russia with me, and apart from one side trip in Siberia we were together almost a month before we reached Moscow. My wife, Mercedes H. Douglas, met me in Moscow, and she was with me for the last two weeks of my journey. In Russia I met other Americans who were of great assistance. At Tashkent, my trail crossed that of the American Farm Delegation, headed by Dean William V. Lambert of the University of Nebraska. Dean Lambert gave me a clearer understanding of Russian agriculture.

In Moscow I met our foremost authority on Soviet law, Professor Harold J. Berman of Harvard, who helped me put together the strange pieces of the Russian jigsaw puzzle. Each of the five enriched my trip.

I thought I would be greatly disadvantaged if I traveled Russia with only an interpreter furnished me by Intourist, the Soviet travel bureau. It would be preferable if one could speak the language or have his own interpreter along. Yet one needs the official interpreter to open many doors. Without the official interpreter my journey would have been much less illuminating. Moreover, the idea that the official interpreter will keep one from learning the true facts is not valid. Too much of life is open and exposed to be kept secret, both here and in Russia. One recognizes slums wherever he is. And the picture of women praying at an altar tells the same story the world over.

I am indebted to the Soviet Government for permission to bring my own interpreter with me. Fred Flott, whom Selden Chapin, one of our distinguished ambassadors, loaned me from his American Embassy staff in Teheran, speaks Russian fluently and is one of our Russian authorities. There was a delay in getting his visa. So Fred did not catch up with me until my trip was half finished. But his presence for the last part of the journey gave me understanding and insight that otherwise I would not have had. One episode will illustrate what I mean.

At Petropavlovsk I had a long talk with Chief Justice B. F. Anushin of the Regional Court, a tall, thin man about forty, with a noble demeanor and an aristocratic face. I will mention him later as the judge who lost a leg fighting the Nazis. He is indeed a fine human being—warmhearted, alert, curious about the world, and a person with a fine sense of humor. There were several other people in the room, including two young Tass news reporters, a man and a woman. After questioning the Chief Justice for an hour or more about the workings of the Soviet courts I said, "Pardon me for keeping you on the witness stand so long. Now it's your turn to cross-examine me."

The man from Tass started by inquiring into the trial of the eleven Communists in this country—the famous case of *Dennis* v. *United States*, 341 U.S. 494, which reached the Supreme Court in 1951. I did not stop to develop the differences in American law between free speech, advocacy, incitement, and conspiracy. Rather, I opened by saying,

"Suppose all the people in this room have a meeting and decide to overthrow the Bulganin-Krushchev government. I assume, Mr. Chief Justice, that that conspiracy would be a crime under Russian law." At that point Fred Flott heard the lady reporter from Tass say to her colleague in a loud whisper, "This is getting embarrassing. Let's change the subject."

Some areas in Russia are still restricted. Two places I asked to visit were barred to me—Leninabad in Uzbekistan and Karaganda in Kazakhstan. Yet once I was allowed to enter a region or city, nothing was kept from me. Some questions were, of course, evaded and others not answered. Thus, the power of Russian radio stations, i.e. the number of watts, was never disclosed. At Baku the Minister of Culture in charge of that town's famous station said, "Only the engineer knows how many watts the station has." At Tashkent the engineer said, "Only the minister knows." But by and large I found the Russians eager to give me the answers I sought; and they were always patient under long periods of cross-examination. I left Russia with high respect for most of the people I had met. And for many of them I developed a genuine affection.

Seeing Russia was, of course, a moving experience. But for me the seminars where I explained the American way of life to the Russians were equally stimulating. I always told them the truth, even when the truth was a minus rather than a plus. Only once did I not tell the whole truth. It happened at Alma Ata when I had a long discussion with the Rector of the university concerning freedom of expression. The Rector—Darkanbaev is his name—is a Kazakh nearing middle age. He is a biochemist; and a scholar of distinction. He had shown me many technical magazines published in the United States, including chemical journals. He asked me if colleges and universities in America subscribed to Soviet technical magazines. I asked him the reason for his question. He said he had just read an American article in his field of chemistry and was astonished that there was not even a footnote reference to Soviet literature on the subject.

"Don't your schools take our chemical magazines?" he asked.

It was so late and I was so tired that I made an evasive reply. I did not tell him that, while there is a great flow of American technical literature to Russia, the reverse flow is not large. I did not tell him that beginning in 1950 and 1951 his government stopped the export of many Soviet technical journals to this country. Nor did I tell him that, while many Russians can speak and read English, few of us can speak and read Russian. Perhaps I should have informed him that in spite of Soviet restrictions we obtain many Soviet journals, that our scientists are alert to the nuggets of wisdom that Soviet research often turns up, and that they have a program to translate into English the important Soviet scientific contributions, especially in chemistry, physics, and mathematics. He would have been pleased at that. But I am sure that this Kazakh scientist would have been as much disturbed, as I was amused, to learn what one Soviet physics journal, translated here, said on the occasion of Einstein's death. The editorial maintained that, brilliant as Einstein was, he deserved little credit for his theory of relativity, since that had been pretty well forecast by Karl Marx.

WILLIAM O. DOUGLAS

CONTENTS

ILLUSTRATIONS

Illustrations

RUSSIAN JOURNEY

CHAPTER 1

THE SOVIET PEOPLE

I entered Russia with misgivings. Russia, under Stalin, had become a sinister force—cold, aloof, and ominous. It was the police state where people disappeared overnight, never to be heard of again. Its slave labor camps were notorious. The police were ever present. Trials were secret. There was no due process in Russia. The foreigner who traveled Russia did so at his own risk. It was never safe to travel alone. I remembered the Turkish courier who had no companion on his journey from Ankara to Moscow. The pouch in which he carried confidential documents was found slit open; he was never seen again. Businessmen, newsmen, and other travelers from the outside world were often arrested, tried, and convicted of offenses which seemed to be manufactured or imagined. Russia under Stalin was Russia under Ivan the Terrible. It was even worse, for while Ivan the Terrible was friendly to the West, Stalin conspired against the world as well as against Russians.

These were my thoughts as I stood on the dock at Pahlevi, Iran, watching a fiery red sun sink into the Caspian Sea. It was a hot, humid evening with not a breath of air stirring. I had spent two days along the Caspian visiting one of the Shah's model villages at Zeit, the famous resorts at Babolsar and Ramsar, and the silk mills at Charlous. A lighthearted, heavy-set Iranian by the name of Henri had driven me in his DeSoto car across the Elburz Mountains from Teheran and then along the whole stretch of the Caspian. It had been cool from the ten-thousand-foot pass over the Elburz down to five thousand or four thousand feet on the north side of that rough mountain range. But as we dropped lower onto the slopes where the famed Hyrcanian tiger lives, the air was hot and soggy, even in a moving car. During the night there was no relief from the heat even in the spacious hotel at Babolsar. The Caspian looked cool and refreshing from the broad, white beaches at that resort; so I bought some bright red trunks and went swimming. But I found the Caspian disappointing. Its slightly saline water turned out to be almost tepid under the hot Central Asian sun.

There had been short stretches of macadam road along the Caspian. But the highway was mostly dirt. We were in swirling dust throughout most of the three hundred miles. When the dust was not being churned by passing cars, it was sucked up through the floor boards or in through the windows. The result was that I arrived at Pahlevi miserably hot and filthy.

The Grand Hotel had one room left, thanks to a telegram from the Shah. It was in fact the one and only remaining room in Pahlevi. The town was packed with visitors—Iranians for vacation on the Caspian, Russians to catch the boat with me to Baku. My room at the Grand echoed all the noise of the street, which was directly below it. Its coarse lace curtains flapped outside the window when I kept the hall door open. The ancient iron bed, though clean, drooped in the middle. The bathroom was almost as decrepit. It had a nineteenth century, rickety tub with one end of a rubber hose attached to the nozzle and the other to the head of a shower. But the pressure was so low that only a trickle of water came through. I took nearly an hour for the shower, using that trickle not only to wash the dirt and sweat from my body but also to get some relief from the heat. Greatly refreshed, I put on clean clothes and headed for the water front. For I heard that my Russian boat had arrived and would leave in the morning for Baku.

The heat was so oppressive that I was once more drenched by the time I had walked the few blocks to the estuary where all boats dock. The sun was setting. Boys with boats seating four or five people and propelled by a long, polelike paddle were shouting for customers. For fifty cents I hired one for an hour. My skipper, a young man in his teens, pointed the craft downstream, keeping up a continuous conversation with his friends along the water front. We slipped by a number of tankers and barges tied to the wharves. We passed two ancient freighters that once plied the Caspian but now looked no more than relics. A quarter mile below them was the Russian boat I sought, bearing the name *Pioneer* on its bow. We pulled alongside. Henri jabbered in Russian to some members of the crew who leaned over the rail in their undershirts. The sun was now down; and the *Pioneer*, dark and gloomy, seemed to me as ominous as Stalin himself. Tomorrow night, somewhere in the Caspian, I would be on this evil-looking boat bound for mysterious Russia.

A breeze had come up when I was on the estuary; but it was stifling hot by the time I returned to the Grand. The restaurant of the hotel is in an open courtyard, shaded by pepper trees. The courtyard this night was filled with an oppressive heat; and hundreds of determined flies crawled over the tables. The flies, the heat, the thoughts of Russia robbed me of any desire for food. So I said good night to the waiter as he brought me Pahlevi's best shishkebab, and retired for the night. I rolled and tossed on my squeaky bed for an hour or more. Then a strong west wind came up and I went to sleep to the tune of my old lace curtains flapping out of the window.

It was clear and hot in the morning. But the west wind still blew, bringing some relief from the heat. The *Pioneer* was scheduled to leave at 10 A.M. It actually left at noon. It had been unloaded the day before of the sugar and steel beams brought down from Russia. This morning it was being loaded with tea and cotton from Iran by miserable-looking stevedores recruited from Pahlevi's water front. When the last bale was on the forward deck, the Iranian pilot came aboard, the lines were cast loose, and the diesel-powered *Pioneer* moved down the estuary. My Iranian friends, who had gathered to say farewell, became blotches on the wharves, the town of Pahlevi fast receded, and soon we were between two fingers of land at the narrow mouth of the estuary. The pilot boat pulled alongside to take off the Iranian officer. The pilot boat was a small twenty-footer that bobbed like a canoe in the rough water. The pilot saluted the Russian captain and jumped from the side of the *Pioneer* into the pilot boat. As he landed, a huge wave broke over the bow of the small boat, drenching him. He was nonchalant and full of dignity, acting as if nothing had happened. But the Russian captain and crew, watching from the upper deck, broke into uproarious laughter and shouted raucous advice to the unfortunate man. They reminded me of Americans when a policeman in the movies slips on a banana peel.

The drenching of the Iranian pilot and the laughter of the Russian crew broke a tension within me. My thoughts carried me back to an evening in New Delhi. My wife, Mercedes Douglas, Josephine Black, and I sat at dinner with Nehru and his daughter, Mrs. Indira N. Gandhi at the Prime Minister's home. Nehru talked a lot about his Russian journey, reliving the experience with obvious excitement. He had been royally received in the Soviet Union by hundreds of thousands of people. He mentioned to us the farms he had seen, the schools he had visited, the Baptists, Russian Orthodox, Catholics, and Moslems of Central Asia he had met. He spoke most affectionately of the small children who clapped their hands and called him "Uncle."

"You liked the Russian people?" I asked.

"Very much," he replied. And then he added rather wistfully, "The Russians remind me of you Americans. Both of you are friendly and outgoing."

The words of Nehru came back to me on the deck of the *Pioneer*. The silly episode of laughing at the drenching of the Iranian pilot bridged a gap between me and the Russian people. I now felt that they were like Americans, an impression that grew as I traveled Russia.

We had no sooner cleared the buoys at the mouth of the estuary than the captain—Simonoff was his name—came out of the pilot house to greet me. He is a huge six-footer, about thirty-five, with a round face and shaved head. He said, "Welcome," in broken English, as he squeezed my hand in a crushing clasp. Then he switched to Russian and spoke with great gusto and emphasis. I did not understand much that he said except to know it was friendly discourse. Shortly he tipped his hat and returned to the pilot house.

In the late afternoon I had a longer conversation with Simonoff. I sat with him by the hatch leading to the engine room and taught him English. We were there perhaps an hour. Word apparently spread through the boat, for soon there were a dozen crew members gathered around. I had my Russian-English dictionary with me and drilled the class over and again with simple words and expressions: good morning (*dobroye ootro*), tomorrow (*zavtra*), I love you (*yellow blue vaze*), thank you (*spasibo*), please (*pojalusta*), comrade (*tovarisch*), hot weather (*zhara*), moon (*loona*), caviar (*ikra*), egg (*yaitso*), sugar (*sakhar*), apple (*yabloko*), water (*voda*), beer (*piva*).

I went around the circle asking for individual pronunciations. Soon the class was reciting in unison. Their faces were serious, their eyes intent. They acted as if their lives depended on pronouncing correctly, "I want my hair cut," "Americans are good." Yet when anyone made an obvious mistake like putting an American and Russian word together in the same sentence, the crowd roared.

This camaraderie of the captain and crew was carried to the dining room. The combination freighter and passenger was clean, neat, and well run, comparing favorably with our vessels on the Great Lakes. The meals (served on the American plan) were excellent. A large bowl of grapes, apples, and peaches was always present. Several different kinds of cheese and cold meats were served with every meal, in addition to dark bread, preserves, caviar, and smoked fish. There were eggs, cucumbers that were as sweet as the Persian species, and tea for breakfast. For the other two meals, lamb (or beef), rice, tomatoes followed borsch or a clear soup. The boat had good refrigeration, for the melons were cold. This delicious food was served by a gentle, middle-aged lady who had a mouth full of steel-filled teeth. Her hands were coarse and gnarled, marking a lifetime of manual labor. Her smile was always present. Her great reward came when I ate something of everything and left my platter clean. This waitress was the prototype of many Soviet women I was to meet on my long journey. The warmth of welcome which she and the captain of the *Pioneer* gave me during my first hours under Russian authority dispelled the fears I had had. There was much in Russia that I was to see which was grim and ugly. But I never lost the affection for the people that I acquired aboard the *Pioneer*.

When we tied up at Baku, twenty-six hours after leaving Pahlevi, it was time to say farewell. My baggage was placed on the dock by the crew, and the captain came down from the bridge to shake my hand. I had a gift for him. Bob Kennedy and I took with us to Russia a generous supply of American ball-point pens to use instead of gratuities. When I offered one to Captain Simonoff, I learned at once another aspect of the average Russian. He had been under a police system so long that he was fearful of accepting any favor from a foreigner. The captain at once stepped back, holding up his hand and saying, "No, thank you." I persisted in my effort to reward him. He continued to say "No," each time more emphatically. Soon the crew gathered around; and when they saw the gift and heard the captain refuse it, they all shouted, "Take it, take it." The Russian crew, indeed, overruled their captain. Captain Simonoff blushed and finally, at the command of his crew, extended his hand and took the pen. Tipping his hat, he disappeared into a cabin.

In Baku I had two interpreters—Elizabeth Alexjeva, an attractive blonde in her thirties, who speaks English with an Austrian accent, and Ivan Nesterovish, a tall, thin man in his late twenties, who had been recently assigned to Baku from White Russia. They followed the example of the captain and crew of the *Pioneer* and were most friendly and helpful.

One day I went with Ivan to a state farm nearly ninety miles north of Baku. We traveled a macadam road all the way, passing a steel tube plant about thirty miles out of Baku. A few miles from the plant was a military air base where sixty-four jet fighter planes were lined up, ready to take off against any bombers coming from Turkey. Far to the west were the Little Caucasus, indistinct against the horizon. The road wound through wheat land and dry pastures where sheep and camels grazed. In about an hour the Little Caucasus, as green as the Bitterroot Mountains of Montana, were close at hand. We took a dirt road leading toward one of their canyons and traveled perhaps ten miles before we came to orchards and vineyards lying against the foothills. The road crossed several dry arroyos that are swollen rivers in springtime and turned into a narrow lane lined with poplars. Behind the poplars were apple orchards stretching far on each side. In a quarter mile we came to a cluster of wooden buildings marking the administrative headquarters of state farm No. 12. This farm of 4500 acres was managed by a heavy, dark Azerbaijani with black receding hair, by the name of Melikov. Statues of Lenin and Stalin overlooked a large flower garden. On its far side was a two-story stucco building housing the public school that ran through the tenth grade. Facing it was the administration building.

A neat village was laid out here. Five hundred men and women work the orchards. There is a cinema on the farm, a recreation hall, and a sixty-bed hospital. But, like all other state farms and collectives in Russia, it has no church.

The homes of the farmers are four-room wooden houses, neat and tidy. Each family has an acre and a quarter of land that is its own. Most of them grow only vegetables; some raise pigs and chickens. The produce from these private tracts is the family's own and can be sold for any price obtainable.

It was late afternoon and all the workers were in from the orchards, many of them cultivating their gardens. They all stopped to see the first American who had come this way. The buzz of excitement at my arrival brought many people, young and old, into the dirt roadway. A stout, bald-headed man, over seventy, and his gray-haired, plump wife invited me into their home for tea. They owned their own home; and the husband, though well beyond the retirement age, continued to work in the orchards, making 600 rubles ($48) a month. The living room had coarse lace curtains at the windows, pictures of Lenin and Stalin on the wall, and a high-backed, decrepit divan. Green tea was served in glass tumblers set in metal holders.

This was my first contact with Russian farmers. This first experience was vivid and took the shape of dozens to come. The greatest interest of these simple peasant folk was America—her people, how they lived, the wages they received, the kind of farms they had.

Then came the question I was to hear most frequently of all—the question of peace. Did the American people want peace as much as the Russian people? I assured this elderly couple, as I did all Russians I met, that the American people were as eager to avoid war as any people in all the world. The old man beamed; his wife clapped her hands.

There were married children and grandchildren to meet and pictures to take. Finally when it came time to depart, this old lady squeezed my hand in a hearty grasp and told me what I was to hear over and again on my Russian journey, "Give our kind regards to all your people."

Word of our presence spread to Kabu, a village six miles distant. The head of a collective farm on the far side of Kabu raced down in his Zim, the equivalent of our Buick, to extend an invitation to dinner. His name is lost in my notes, but his face and personality are fresh in my memory. He was an Azerbaijani of Turkish stock, dark, short, wiry, with a pointed head and sharp, friendly eyes. I even lost the name of the collective farm he manages. It has 2500 acres in fruit and 10,000 acres in pasture and grazing lands for beef cattle. It's a prosperous collective, the chairman himself making last year 40,000 rubles or roughly $3200, which by Russian standards is very high.

We drove something like fifteen miles to the collective and climbed outside stairs to the second floor of the chairman's home. I went out on the second-floor porch to wash up. There was soap in a dish on the porch rail and a towel hanging on a post. A large can of water with a valve at the bottom was fastened to the post. An upward thrust of the valve brought out a half cup of water. I was to see this type of washstand all through rural Russia.

After each had had his turn at soap and water, some eight of us sat down at a table for what turned out to be my first twenty-one-course Russian feast. This was strictly a stag affair, none of the women of the family putting in an appearance.

The dinner started with cold cuts, grapes, and nuts. Then came a long series of single dishes adding up to twenty-one. Their Russian names were all unknown to me at the time. Some, like borsch and lamb on a skewer, were familiar. Most were new: small meat balls wrapped in dough, boiled and served with a white sauce (*pelmeny*); meat wrapped in dough the size of a biscuit and cooked in deep fat (*belyashi*); meat balls wrapped in cabbage leaves (*farshirovanny perets*). There were also strange dumplings and the well-known Persian rice dish, pilaff. The dishes came too fast for me to keep complete track. The dish I relished most was lamb kidneys cooked on a skewer over charcoal. Juicy peaches and sweet apricots ended the feast.

The dinner continued almost three hours with toasts too many to count. My hosts offered vodka, brandy, and wine. Vodka is the customary drink on these occasions. It is served straight, not mixed; and it's downed in a gulp, not sipped. Pieces of bread or meat are eaten after each drink to provide a brake on the inebriation which three or four dozen toasts are likely to produce. That much I knew. I also knew that in Russia it is a breach of etiquette for a guest not to respond to a toast in spirits. But the guest, I had been told, could choose his own weapons; he need not go the vodka route.

I had but an instant for a decision. I looked at the glasses. Some of the men had small tumblers; some had medium wine glasses. Even the smallest, which held at least three jiggers, could become formidable when filled with vodka (or brandy) over and again. I looked from the glasses to the men. They were all men of the soil—hands calloused from toil, faces tanned from outdoor work, muscles firm. They looked to me as if they were in excellent condition. Their faces were charged with excitement. There was the light of competition in their eyes. Nehru's words came back to me—that Russians were very much like Americans. I imagined what would happen if a group of Oregon farmers had a prominent

Russian for the evening. They would, I felt sure, be dedicated to the cause of making him a casualty of the evening. Maybe I judged the Russians and Azerbaijanis gathered around this country table unjustly. But their eagerness for the first toast warned me. So I chose wine—my choice for toasts throughout the 8000-mile journey.

The first toast of the host was to friendship. Then it was my turn. The words of the Russian grandmother I had seen on the state farm came back to me; and I remembered her spontaneous reaction when I said Americans wanted peace. So I proposed a toast to peace between Russia and the United States. Before drinking, the men put down their glasses and applauded with gusto. And as they applauded they kept shouting, "Peace, peace."

At the Bajir collective farm out of Ashkhabad, I sat on a dark red Turkmen rug under a grape arbor and had one of the most delicious meals I can recall having eaten anywhere. It was cooked by an attractive Turkmen lady, Ogul Taganova, who is chairman of that collective farm. We had lamb on a skewer served with large slabs of hot, dark, unleavened bread about a half inch thick. Ogul also gave us broiled onions so tender they were almost sweet, dark red tomatoes at the peak of ripeness, the sweetest white grapes I ever did taste, and a delicious melon that was the closest I found in Central Asia to our honeydew. With the meal we had a native dry white wine with a delicate bouquet. Afterwards we were served a green Georgian tea that was as good as any I ever drank on my Himalayan journeys. Here too were toasts to peace and friendship.

Peace (*mir*) and friendship (*drujba*)—these were the toasts that brought rousing cheers all across Russia. More often than not the Russians would put down their glasses before drinking and applaud, just as they did at Kabu. When they didn't do that, they cheered loud and lustily. And once, at a collective near Stalinabad, capital of Tadzhikistan, a grizzled old farmer, wearing a black

Tadzhik skullcap with a white border, grabbed me and gave me a squeeze that could have broken a few ribs.

I had even a more dramatic experience at Petropavlovsk in northern Kazakhstan, a region like North Dakota where the land rolls to the horizon without a break and one can see a train coming for fifty miles. There I lunched with B. F. Anushin, Chief Justice of the Regional Court. He is a Great Russian in his forties who lost a leg under German artillery fire. When I proposed a toast to peace this reserved judge broke into tears.

This response to toasts to peace and friendship was the same in city and in country. It was always spontaneous and vigorous. I learned before I left Russia that the Soviet press and radio had dinned peace into the minds of the people so effectively that the desire for peace had become a deep and powerful force. The peace offensive that I had assumed to be beamed primarily abroad was in fact for home consumption. The Russian people had slaved and sweated for decades without getting many of the good things of life. Moscow's peace offensive was to convince them that in spite of its emphasis on armaments, the central government was for peace. Moreover, Moscow had in mind the ease of converting this longing for peace into a burning resentment against any foreign power if war came.

In every way the Soviet people were generous and spontaneous in their expression of friendliness to America. I traveled like any tourist, paying my own expenses, and without official status. No state delegation met me. There were no official functions in my honor, except the luncheon tendered by the Supreme Court when I reached Moscow.

One night in Tashkent I attended the opera house to see an Uzbek play. The downstairs, which seats 1000, was packed with Uzbeks who, like Timur the Lame of ancient fame, have Mongol antecedents. As I entered the theater the audience rose to the man and clapped. They had no idea who I was, apart from the fact that I was an American. Perhaps the applause in the theater was inspired by the officials. But I knew from the spontaneity of the reactions that most of what I experienced was natural, not staged.

I learned on my Russian journey that America still has a deep reservoir of good will in Russia. In World War II, the Germans razed much of Russia, killing or causing the death of nearly eight million Russians. Leningrad alone lost about a million during a 900-day siege. It was our military might that was decisive in the ultimate Russian victory. The Russian people remember that. They also know President Eisenhower as the victorious general. In Russia, Eisenhower is indeed a great symbol of American friendship. That is one reason why the smiles at Geneva had powerful reactions in the villages of Russia, releasing feelings long suppressed. I traveled Russia a month after Geneva and found evidence of friendship for America in every village. Under Stalin, a Russian could not even smile at an American without fear of retaliation. After Geneva he was under no such restraint. And the response of the average Russian I met was so spontaneous I knew he acted beyond the line of duty.

Whenever I stopped to take a picture on a city street, someone would come up to talk. Twice these strangers froze with fright after a few words. That happened on a main street of Stalinabad when a forty-year-old man spoke to me in English. After a word or two he broke out into a cold sweat. Perhaps he saw an MVD trailing him; perhaps he had memories of Stalin's terror. Anyway, he turned abruptly and almost ran. Once in Frunze, a twenty-year-old, English-speaking girl—an attractive brunette—came up to me on the street, touched my arm, and said in perfect English, "I would like to talk to you. You see, I like America very much." I suggested we leave the busy street corner and walk down the shaded avenue to a bench under the trees. We started down the street, when she turned to see a man following. She whispered to me, "I can't go on. I'm frightened. I must leave." And she left.

There was another episode in Petropavlovsk. I was out with my Leica hunting pictures. I came to a state store in a ramshackle wooden building where a queue of women extended a half block. There has been no food rationing in Russia since 1947. These women were lined up for milk which was being unloaded from wagons in the rear. The waiting women were dressed in short skirts and quilted coats; shawls covered their heads; and their knee-high boots were thick with mud from Petropavlovsk's unpaved streets. They were the colorful pictures I had been seeking. After I got the few I wanted and started to leave, I was accosted by a young lady about thirty years old who was obviously upset at my performance. I could not understand a word she said; but from her voice and gestures I gathered she was angry at me for photographing Russian women who were so poorly dressed. Her voice was shrill and her gestures dramatic. In a few moments I was completely surrounded by women who seemed to hang on her words.

I could not speak enough Russian to make an explanation. So in my predicament I reached in my pocket for my small dictionary that had not only Russian-English words, but phrases and sentences as well. I turned page after page, anxiously looking for a helpful expression. I passed over sentences like "I don't feel well," "I feel dizzy," "This jacket is too small," "I want to speak to the manager," "Bring me some hot water," and dozens of like tenor. I ran my finger down another page and stopped on the Russian words:

"Pozvoltye vas priglasti na etat tanyets?"

I held the book so my female accuser could read from it. She read it slowly, out loud. Having finished it she fairly shouted it to the crowd of women. Then she and they broke into loud and hilarious laughter. In their excitement I escaped. What she read meant in English:

"May I have this dance with you?"

All of my other street contacts were completely friendly. Once a single person stopped to talk with me, a crowd gathered. In a few minutes I was surrounded by fifty or a hundred people. It happened over and again. Then speaking through my interpreter, I would hold a seminar on the American way of life. The longest and the most typical street seminar was held in Petropavlovsk. I had visited the railroad yards, taking pictures. As I left, a huge crowd gathered. There were Russians, Mongols, and Kazakhs in this crowd. The people were railroad workers, farmers, clerks. No ugly question was asked; there was no unfriendly demeanor or critical voice in the entire crowd.

Many people took part in this conversation. The leader was a young Russian agronomist in his late twenties who had come out of Moscow to one of the new state farms that was raising wheat on the virgin lands of Siberia. Nick Nikolaev, my Russian interpreter, who was with me all the way from Baku to Moscow, was busy this morning making transportation arrangements. On this occasion Fred Flott and I were alone; and through Fred I talked with the crowd for an hour.

The first question concerned segregated public schools in America. I explained our Court's decisions and went on to give a discourse on the increasingly prominent role the Negro plays in American life. I referred particularly to the fact that the president of the Borough of Manhattan in New York City is a Negro, that over twenty major municipal posts in Chicago are held by Negroes, that we have many distinguished Negro judges, lawyers, etc.

The next question related to women in America, whom many Russians think of as a persecuted minority. I gave an account of the achievement of women in this country and closed by telling of the vast control through stock ownership they have over American business.

Someone asked if the Communist party would win the next election in the United States. The impression in Russia is widespread that the Communist party here runs nip and tuck with the Republicans and Democrats. I told the crowd that in all of America there were not even 100,000 Communists, that they were the most unpopular, suspect group in the land, and that they could not hope to elect one of their members to any office in the nation. The crowd was astounded, for what I told them exploded a myth they cherished.

"What happens to the poor, unemployed people in America?" a factory hand asked. I explained employment problems in America, the function of private enterprise, the role of public works, and the vast unemployment insurance schemes we have.

Then came medical care; old-age pensions; Sacco-Vanzetti (for whom a street is named in Akmolinsk); the trial of Communists in this country; the refusal of a passport to Paul Robeson; lynching; wheat, cotton, and corn production in the United States; the use of machinery on American farms; what people eat in America; and the wages of American workers.

American wages are astronomical compared with Russian wages. In Russia, the maximum yearly salary of the most skilled industrial worker is equal to about 36,000 rubles (which in purchasing power in Russia are worth about eight cents each). The average annual factory wage is close to one fourth that amount, or $700. The average unskilled laborer makes around $400 a year. There are a few farmers who make $7500 a year. But the average agricultural worker makes closer to $600 a year; and there are many who make a mere pittance.

Some of the crowd did not at first believe me when I told them what American auto workers, coal miners, bus drivers, mechanics, and farm hands earn. When I repeated the answers, incredulity turned to amazement. Then came questions about homes for workers, refrigerators, sewing machines, vacuum cleaners, washing machines, toasters, electric plates. These are all in short supply in Russia and usually priced beyond the reach of the average family.

BAKU

Baku is the petroleum center of Russia, the foremost port on the Caspian Sea, and one of Russia's most modern cities.

The wall of the old city of Baku is now fully restored as a historical relic.

At Baku a brass band plays every afternoon and evening in a city park.

The Girl's Tower in Baku was the locale of an ancient tragedy.

BAKU

The Armenian church in
Baku is active, but
the congregations are sparse.

Farmers' private plots
on farms near Baku furnish
that city with most of its
fruits and vegetables.

An old lady at a state farm
near Baku said,
"Give our kind regards
to all your people."

When I described their abundance in America, the crowd was transfixed. Though they were all raised on the materialistic philosophy of life, they still have few of the good things to substantiate the Communist creed.

Finally the discussion got around to automobiles; and this was the topic that broke up the gathering. Russia has three types of cars—the Zim, which resembles our Buick; the Pobeda, which is like our Ford or Chevrolet; and the Moskvitch, which resembles the Austin. Few people except government officials own a car. When I told the crowd at Petropavlovsk that in America there was in 1954 one passenger car to about three people, they shook their heads in amazement. I am sure that when I finished with this street crowd there was not one of them who did not believe that Detroit was, indeed, the Heavenly City.

At Alma Ata, down in southeast Russia not more than two hundred miles or so from the Chinese border, some of the Kazakh artists gave Bob and me a dinner—Kuklina, the soprano, Omarova, the alto, and Serkebaev, the baritone. These talented artists sang their Kazakh songs and also songs from Russian, German, and Italian operas. Then we had another twenty-one-course dinner. When the first main course was served (lamb on a skewer), I was introduced to an ancient Central Asian custom.

The head of the lamb from whom this meat was taken was placed before me on a platter. In the Arab and Persian worlds I had seen whole sheep served on the table. I had been the honored guest who was offered one of the eyes. The memory of the eyes came back to me as this sheep's head was served; and I vividly recalled how, after I swallowed the eye, it went up and down like a bobbin before my stomach finally agreed to accept it. I looked anxiously at this sheep's head and was relieved to see that the eyes were not there. But the rest of the head in all its ugliness was present. It was seared and shrunken, as repulsive a dish as I ever faced. As I sat looking at the sheep's head, trying to conceal

33

my feelings, a local Kazakh told me through Nick that his people always presented the sheep's head to the honored guest. The guest, it seemed, is supposed to cut off the left ear and present it to his favorite lady. Then he is to keep the right ear for himself. With due deliberation I severed the left ear and presented it on a plate to Kuklina, the lovely Kazakh soprano. Then I severed the right ear and placed it on my own plate. Kazakh custom then calls for the honored guest to carve a piece of meat from the head of the sheep and pass the head around the table. To my surprise I found a very thin layer of meat below the fat that covers the cranium. Carving a small piece for myself, I passed the head along.

That left me with a bit of cranium meat and the right ear of the sheep. The cranium meat was surprisingly good. The ear, however, was different. It was a gruesome thing on my plate. There is, of course, nothing inherently objectionable about an ear. It is clean and neat and wholesome. But somehow or other I rebel at the thought of swallowing one. Perhaps I have too many pleasant associations with ears to enjoy eating them. Perhaps an influence, deep in the subconscious, raises a rebellion at the thought. Perhaps as one Kazakh suggested, I have not developed the taste for them that would be acquired if I ate one every day. In any event, for good reasons or for bad, I don't like sheep ears. But all eyes at the table were on me. I was under the Kazakh spotlight. Taking my knife, I carved out the central portion of this horrible-looking ear—the part that contains the inner ear and secretes the wax in time of trouble—and put it in my mouth. The next few minutes were as awkward as any I have known. What I had was a mouthful of tough gristle. If I had not seen the ear but had to guess, I would have ventured that I had a rooster's comb or over-cooked leather shoelaces in my mouth. But I knew what was in my mouth and was on the edge of nausea. I tried to swallow the gristle; but up it came and I had to chew some more. I put on a brave front, for I had the feeling that this night America was on trial in Kazakhstan. With a final valiant effort, the mouthful of sheep ear, quickly washed with red wine, went down a second time. This time it stayed down; and I could see signs of pleasure along the whole table. Now I was free from surveillance and in a second got the waiter to take the rest of the sheep's ear away. But I had only a short respite. As soon as the waiter removed the plate holding the ear, he placed in front of me another plate containing a queer glob of food. "They are the brains of the sheep," a Kazakh host explained.

I dislike brains. Calves' brains are bad enough. Sheep's brains are beyond the pale. But here they were—a whole cup of them— in front of me.

"And what is my duty, Nick?" I asked.

"Your duty is to sample them and pass them around the table."

I took a few, washed them down so quickly with wine that they hardly touched my tongue, and thankfully passed the rest.

I had avoided camel's milk on all my Middle Eastern journeys. But it finally cornered me in Soviet Turkmenistan. Near Ashkhabad, capital of that republic, I visited the village Kurtly and a collective farm by that name. The chairman of this farm was a middle-aged Turkmen by the name of Hangeldiev. I spent most of the day with him and came to know his problems and concerns. I had always thought of *kulaks* as the absentee landlords who are so notorious in Asia. But I learned in Russia that a *kulak* was not necessarily that type of man. A *kulak* includes anyone who owned even ten acres of land. I learned that Hangeldiev himself had been one. He had owned thirty acres of land that was confiscated by the government and placed in a collective farm. I was to learn that hundreds of thousands of Central Asians revolted at these measures. Not so Hangeldiev. He bowed to the inevitable and joined the collective which had absorbed his land. Today he is chairman of that collective and better off than he ever was. Today he makes $2500 a year and, as chairman, gets a Zim car to drive. He supervises 227 families and 190,000 acres of land. Thirty-six hundred acres are in fruit, grapes, melons, and vegetables. The rest are grazing land for sheep and camels. The sheep, which number 6000, were high in the mountains to the west. So I never saw them. But I saw most of the 150 camels owned by the collective, for they take the place of trucks and haul produce to Ashkhabad. They also go as pack trains into the hills where the sheep are grazed. These Central Asian camels are more than transport; they are an important source of milk and meat to the Turkmens.

This is mostly hot, treeless country like the Imperial Valley in California and the Inland Empire in Washington. The life of the area is irrigation; and much of the water comes from subterranean streams tapped by wells. Hangeldiev delighted in showing me his wells and in having me sample the water. He also had to show me the school (ten grades), the hospital, and the adobe stores that sell everything from potatoes to canned fish and salt pork.

After this hot, dusty tour of the farm, Hangeldiev insisted I visit his home. It was a simple, four-room house with little furniture. The bedding, in the Persian custom, was on the floor at night and rolled up on a shelf during the day. We sat barefooted on an open veranda, level with the ground and covered with beautiful red Turkmen rugs woven by the women of Kurtly. Lamb, tomatoes, melons, and sweet white grapes were served betwixt many toasts. But before any food was served, a large metal bowl of camel's milk was passed.

The host with true Turkmen hospitality offered it to me first. I took it with misgivings, for I had a gastric upset caused in part from some poor meat I had eaten the day before and in part by the heat, which was dry but fierce, hovering around 120° Fahrenheit.

When the camel's milk was passed, I almost rebelled. But I realized that guests have responsibilities and that I, a guest from a nation so at odds with Russia, should be meticulous in my relations with these people. So I raised the bowl of camel's milk to my lips and swallowed some, quickly passing the bowl along. I thought the milk would be repulsive. Though warm, it had a therapeutic effect I felt almost instantly. It seemed to soothe and settle my stomach. So when the bowl came round again I drank deeply. I learned at Kurtly that I have an affinity for camel's milk. In fact, it cured my upset stomach and made the meal of lamb, tomatoes, and melons a most pleasant one.

It is not enough to say that the Soviet people are friendly and hospitable to the American visitor. That is one facet of their character, easier to divine than many of the others. In some respects they are complicated personalities. When one touches politics, foreign policy, economic planning, and the like he is on a different footing. I found that it is useless to talk politics, economics, or sociology with any official or with a party member. They do not bend. They are committed to one doctrine and one theology; and they defend it savagely. They see no good in any competing system. Theirs is the one and only true faith. It is in fact a matter of religion with them—a religion based on an atheistic, materialistic creed. I will not recite my arguments and debates with the officials and the party members. Each traveled the same monotonous route, going in a circle. Those debates were so dull and repetitive that I soon discontinued them, resolving not to be drawn into another.

But the party is relatively small in number—about 7,000,000 people out of Russia's population of 210,000,000. The masses must have views that are not necessarily the views of the bureaucracy. After all, the people of Russia have all the idiosyncrasies of other races. The monolithic state can produce the appearance of unanimity. But it is a mask that undoubtedly conceals large disagreement. I do not speak from personal knowledge, for it would take years to know what really goes on in the minds of the Russian people. I only surmise, drawing inferences from casual, disconnected episodes. I clearly sensed that such disagreement as does exist is not building up to a counterrevolutionary force. Russia is not about to fall apart. It is strongly held together not only by a network of party cells and a thorough police system, but by loyalties, pride, history, racial and national consciousness, a feeling of achievement, a competitive urge, and a host of other subtle influences. One would have to spend a lifetime to put them all together into a composite of the Russian character. I was there only long enough to sense them and feel their power.

Russia has had nearly forty years of Communist rule. That means that everyone under fifty has few memories other than those under communism. The great bulk of the people are products of the system. They and their children were mostly born under the red star. They know nothing different; and they have been taught through schools, newspapers, and radio that theirs is the best of all possible systems. Those who have been advanced and now enjoy the perquisites of position, power, or prestige, owe it all to the regime. They respect the system that benefited them. They have, indeed, a vested interest in the *status quo*.

Russia, a nation of many races, has known the vicissitudes of war and famine. She has been invaded by Poland, Sweden, Mongolia, Turkey, France, Germany. Those wars have helped give her solidarity and a keen sense of nationalism. The Communists have not overlooked the power of these influences. For the glorious deeds of the heroes of those wars are today made the symbol of patriotism. Communist literature and the Communist stage teach that the peoples of Russia are first, last, and always Russian.

The Russian people are highly competitive. They love the race and the contest. I listened—as all Russia did—to the radio accounts of the game between Russia's soccer team and the world champions from West Germany. I was in Alma Ata at the time. The Russians with me were as excited as the most rabid collegiate fans in America. They were depressed when Russia missed a goal and out of their chairs shouting when Russia scored and finally won. All over Russia great stadiums are either built or under construction. Baku has a lovely bowl that seats 50,000 people. Novosibirsk plans one that will hold 80,000. Every town has a playing field for soccer. A factory usually has its own gymnasium and athletic grounds. Some factories boast their own stadiums. The greatest ambition of every Russian, big and small, is to win the Olympic games.

The five-year plan suits the Russian character. It suits the competitive urge and helps create a sense of a national effort. I sensed it in every factory I visited. Each has its annual quota, which in turn is broken down into months and days. Large charts show whether yesterday was short of the quota or beyond it. Honor rolls are prominently displayed, usually in the form of large bulletin boards carrying pictures and the names of the men and women who lead. Bonuses are paid for exceeding the quota. There are instances where the system breaks down, due to mismanagement or inefficiency. But by and large it seems to work.

The Soviet people today are making an energetic, enthusiastic, united effort in building up their country. What all the compulsions may be is difficult to analyze. I went to Russia feeling that fear was one of the chief ones. I left Russia with a different viewpoint. Fear may play a part; but it is not the paramount one. Fear of the government, fear of the police, fear of the invader, fear of the foreigner have left their impact over the ages. There are Russians who are cunning and devious persons. Those qualities appear among people of all ranks—the peasant selling his private produce in the market, the city official, the MVD. But the Russian these days is also influenced by more generative and constructive forces. People move and act with enthusiasm. They are not docile, subdued persons. They have smiles and a spring in their walk. The people of Russia are always going somewhere in a hurry. They have bounce and bustle. That is, indeed, the most prominent single observation my notebook records. Everywhere, night and day, the Russian people are moving fast. Every factory, farm, and street gives the same impression.

Bukhara down in Central Asia furnished a striking example. Bukhara is the ancient seat of Islamic learning. For centuries Bukhara's religious schools turned out fanatics who carried the word of the Prophet to the farthest reaches of Central Asia. Bukhara was in the "golden triangle" with Samarkand and Merv—three oases in a hot and torrid land. The day I arrived in Bukhara the thermometer showed 145° Fahrenheit in the sun. The air was so hot I dared not take a deep breath. I could find no relief in my hotel room, for Bukhara has no electric fans. I left the hotel and crossed the street to a park that was deep in shade. I sat on a bench watching young boys dive and splash in a spacious pool of dirty, tepid water. It was four o'clock in the afternoon and the temperature in the shade was 120°. A breeze came up; but it was as hot as a furnace's breath. I sat on this bench a half hour, watching the people pass. A Persian or Arab would curl up in the shade on an afternoon as hot as this. He would wait until evening to run his errands and do his chores. There were, indeed, few Uzbeks moving about the streets this afternoon. But the Russians were abroad in great numbers. A squad of Russian soldiers marched by singing a lusty army song, their uniforms soaked through with perspiration. Russian women in cotton prints scurried along with shopping baskets. Russian men in their short-sleeved shirts breezed by as if they were late for an appointment. Dozens of Russians were on the street, all of them practically on a dog trot.

As I sat there reflecting on their movements, the radio came on. In every public park in Russia there's a radio receiver that broadcasts the news and the "culture" to the people. These radios are tuned so loud that anyone can hear them. They go with a blast for most of the day and half of the night. For some reason the park radio had been off when I sat down on the bench. Now it came on with a blare, perhaps for my benefit. For the program started with Paul Robeson singing "Ol' Man River":

> *Ol' man River, dat ol' man River,*
> *He mus' know sumpin',*
> *But don't say nothin',*
> *He just keeps rollin',*
> *He keeps on rollin' alon'.*

Everywhere I went in Russia I had precisely that impression of the Soviet people—a great force moving incessantly and dynamically toward some unknown destiny. There is unity, determination, and eagerness in the drive that I have found nowhere else except in America.

CHAPTER 2

THE OLD AND THE NEW

The U.S.S.R. is a strange mixture of old Czarist Russia and communism. Czarist Russia is, of course, the past, with its capitalism, middle class, and landlords. But it's also a past of great literature, great art, great minds and great deeds, and a powerful sense of nationalism. Today Moscow is seeking to preserve the memories of that past.

Everywhere I went in Russia I saw old monuments, memorials, castles, palaces, and churches being renovated, restored, and redecorated. The past is very much on display.

Tretyakov was a rich nineteenth-century merchant who was a connoisseur of art. His old home in Moscow is now an art gallery. It contains two galleries that are rich storehouses—one containing prerevolutionary paintings, the other, Soviet paintings. The latter was closed when I was in Moscow. I spent several hours in the gallery that holds the paintings of the Russian artists of all time. There on canvas after canvas are Russian mountains, lakes, valleys, old palace scenes in all their splendor, stolid faces of Russian peasants, Russian armies in victorious battles, czars, queens, members of the royal families, Peter the Great interrogating his son who plotted against him. Some paintings are rich in Russian folklore. Some are designed to illustrate a Russian saying. Some suggest the theme of a ballad. Others are Biblical accounts, many of Christ. The largest picture of all is by Alexander Ivanov. It takes up the entire end of one large gallery. It shows John the Baptist seeing the apparition of Christ walking on clouds above a valley. The one of Russian life and history that I liked the best was done by I. E. Repin. It records a historic clash between Turks and Cossacks. The Turks had demanded tribute from the Cossacks who were penning their reply. The one Cossack who could write was made the penman. He is sitting, while the other Cossacks stand and kneel around him, giving advice. They are shouting gleefully. One can almost hear the coarse and challenging message they are sending the Turks.

West of Moscow about fifteen miles is the former home of Prince Yusupov, now converted into the Archangel Museum. It's a large estate of 1000 acres sloping down to the Moskva River. The mansion has been fully restored and decorated. The formal gardens are neat and trim. The woods are threaded with paths. A large sanatorium has been erected at one corner of the estate, where invalids and those who are convalescing may rest.

The mansion is a two-story affair. The downstairs has an inlaid oak floor highly polished. All visitors as they enter must put on large felt slippers over their shoes, so as not to mar the floor. The walls hang with the works of French and Dutch masters. Exquisite china fills the cupboards, china baked in Yusupov's own kilns. A graceful glass chandelier, as pretty as any I have seen, adorns the room where the dances were held.

The Sunday I visited Yusupov's palace was a clear and bright day. The house was fairly swamped with visitors, each group with its own guide. My interpreter was a young lady from Intourist in

Moscow. She bubbled with information about the place. It was built in 1790, burned in 1820, and rebuilt shortly thereafter. Yusupov, she related, lived in the eighteenth century. He made a fortune in silk. He had 31,000 serfs working for him on his various projects. He symbolized the oppression of the rich against the poor. He and his ilk were fine people but they exploited the masses, who at last have come into their own inheritance. A part of that inheritance is the castle itself. It now belongs to the common people, who visit it and enjoy it as they wish.

As this Russian lady droned on, I watched the faces of the people crowding the rooms in Yusupov's palace. They were clerks, railway workers, waitresses, streetcar conductors, and farmers—a true cross section of the new Russian society. They walked slowly and quietly with hardly a murmur in the whole crowd. They roamed from room to room with awe. They were at last in the master's shoes; and they enjoyed their new status. They had no resentment toward the capitalist Yusupov. He was but a name. He lives today only as a symbol of the past—a Russian who in his own way was great and brought glory to the nation.

Old mansions of this character are scattered all over Russia. And they are mostly put to use as museums, parks, recreational centers. Down in Bukhara, the oasis near the border of Uzbekistan and Turkmenistan that is watered by canals from the Amu Darya (Oxus) River and from the river known as Zeravshan, stands a less austere relic of the olden days. Bukhara was long the stronghold of Moslem orthodoxy and fanaticism. It was ruled by emirs, the last of whom was Abdul Said Mir Alim who lost the city to Communist troops in 1920 and fled first to Stalinabad and then to Afghanistan to become a merchant in a Kabul bazaar. When the Communist army under the command of General Frunze captured Bukhara, it plundered the ancient city. Some of the loot was several wagons of gold and precious stones from the treasury of the Emir. The worst destruction was the burning of the library, an event my local Uzbek guide refused to discuss. For the library that was burned contained probably the most valuable collection of Moslem books and tracts in all the world. The conquering army also set fire to many of the 100 religious schools (*medresses*) for which Bukhara was famous. But it left untouched the country palace of the Emir.

I drove three miles out of the city to see it. I had no desire to visit it this day but was persuaded to go by Nick. As I have said, it was 145° Fahrenheit in Bukhara. The fiery heat made the Uzbekistan Hotel (already a miserable place) practically unbearable. The local guide told Nick of a swimming pool on the grounds of the Emir's palace. Nick passed the word along and transferred to me some of the great eagerness he felt for a swim. So out we went on a fearfully hot Sunday morning.

The Emir's palace was built about 1914. I imagine it once had beauty. Certainly the tall, graceful columns across the front make a good start. But the blue paint is peeling and the windows have fallen out. The front of the palace faces the largest swimming pool I have seen. It is roughly 75 by 150 feet, lined with rock slabs. I imagined it would contain clear, cool water. I could practically feel it against my body as the car pulled up into the driveway. But my dream was soon shattered. The pool contained as dirty water as can be found. It was so dirty one could not see one's hand a few inches under the surface. Moreover, it was as warm as soup. Nick went in; but I refused. Instead, I found a shower of fairly cool, clear water that had been rigged up in bushes near the pool. I stripped and stood under this shower for at least half an hour, seeking relief from the heat.

Then we sat for a while in the shade discussing the Emir. The Uzbek guide told how dissolute the old man had been. He had 450 wives; and still he was not satisfied. For he would send emissaries into Bukhara, searching the town for pretty girls. One emissary would pose as a peddler, going from door to door. When he saw an unusually pretty girl, he would make a note of the address and send soldiers for her that night. The next day she would be bathed, oiled, and anointed by ladies in waiting and sent naked into the pool. The Emir, so the guide said, had a hiding place in the bushes by the pool. There he would secretly watch the newly found damsel. If she seemed to be the choice morsel he desired, he would have her sent to his harem.

"The older women hated the Emir," the Uzbek told me. "He was a monstrous person—dissolute, lascivious."

The guide went on to tell how communism had saved the people from characters like the Emir.

A group of a dozen Russians—men and women—shortly appeared by the pool. They were vacationists. The lower floor of the palace has been turned into barracks. Here people on vacation from the factories can stay free of charge. A radio high in a tree blares on hour after hour. There are benches in the shade; and outdoor tables for writing. An old greenhouse, badly in disrepair, will be restored. Soon the old palace of the Emir will be fully rebuilt. Clean, cool water will be in the pool. The old estate will be made a comfortable resort for the workers. And when they come here to stay, they will be told how evil the old khans and emirs were. This swimming pool will be used to illustrate why it was that no young girl was safe in the olden days.

Then the guide told me of the Emir's three sons. They remained behind when their father fled. They studied in Russian institutes and came to know the sins of their father. They came to understand the virtues of socialism. "They made a public statement praising Soviet Russia," the guide said. "They want to make Russia their home and work with the people for the new order."

In Central Asia, old palaces are sometimes used to teach the non-Russians, whose fathers lived under khans and emirs, that the old regimes were evil and exploitive. That tells, however, only part of the story. Moscow has had tremendous nationality problems on her hands. Central Asia is composed not of Russians but of Uzbeks, Turkmens, Tadzhiks, Kirgiz, and Kazakhs. Central Asians are Turkish, Persian, and Mongol. They are tied together by religion and customs and to a degree by race and language. Central Asia was, indeed, a proud part of the Moslem world, with great schools, famous libraries, outstanding mosques. It was a rich storehouse of art, literature, and learning. It was the center of astronomy. It had distinctive and delicate architecture. Its poets and playwrights were known throughout Asia. Soviet Central Asia was no paradise. It had its seamy side as well. It was a feudal economy with about 6 per cent of the people literate and with most of the wealth in the hands of a few families. Moreover, Islam developed a fanaticism in Central Asia that violated some of the important teachings of the Prophet. Non-believers were not only barred from the region; if apprehended visiting its holy places, they were executed. As a consequence, places like Samarkand and Bukhara remained practically sealed from the outside world. The chronicles say that between A.D. 1404 and 1841, Samarkand was visited by only two foreigners. Two visitors in nearly four and a half centuries! No wonder Central Asia has an aura of mystery and romance about it.

The Russians conquered the region in a series of engagements extending over the latter half of the last century. Their moves in Central Asia were partly countermoves to the British in India, Afghanistan, and Persia. They were in part an effort to annex to Russia a cotton belt that would make her no longer dependent on America. Czarist Russia, having conquered Central Asia, left it pretty much alone. Army garrisons were, of course, maintained. Each emir had a Russian resident agent to advise him. There were efforts to make Central Asia dependent on Russia by increasing its cotton production and decreasing its food production. But Czarist Russia did not disturb the social and economic order; and

47

it bent the political regime only enough to keep the area subservient.

Last century Bukhara had 360 mosques and 100 *medresses*. Today one *medresse* is left, a two-story school built around a small courtyard and housing 100 students. I did not take an inventory of all the mosques in Bukhara. Most of them are closed or used for warehouses. A few are open. All are in a state of neglect. But the Uzbek guide assured me that Moscow had a program to restore many of these religious buildings and make them great museums.

The Great Minar, or Tower of Death, which was built 700 years ago, is now the show place of Bukhara. It is a huge brick tower, round in design, 45 meters high, with narrow slits for windows at the top. An interior winding staircase leads to those windows from which in earlier days screaming prisoners were pushed to their death. I asked my Uzbek guide when the tower was last used by the Soviets for an execution. He quickly denied that the Communists ever used it, saying it was an institution of the khans and emirs. Then he qualified that statement by adding that once at the behest of a murderer the Communists had allowed the execution to take place there.

"Only once?" I asked. He nodded.

I asked permission to climb the tower stairs.

"They are in disrepair," my guide answered. "But soon the government will have them safely restored."

The Great Minar is at one end of a large square lined with mosques. The most beautiful to me was the Blue Dome because of the delicate hue of its color. There are others, however, that have tiles better preserved. One of these was built by Ulug Beg, the famous astronomer who was grandson of Timur. Near the Great Minar is the famous Ark, historic city palace of the Emir. Many of its buildings are in partial or complete ruins. Close by is the Zindan, a famous dungeon. The dungeon has two compartments—upper and lower. The upper dungeon is a walled-in court, with cells on all sides. These cells are open at one side and covered by an iron grille. Today the Communists have a dummy of an aged Uzbek in one of these cells for all to see. The lower dungeon is a pit about eighteen feet deep. Today it has a ladder; but in olden days prisoners were lowered by ropes.

As I looked into the bug pit, I thought about Jeremiah:

Then took they Jeremiah, and cast him into the dungeon of Malchiah the son of Hammelech, that was in the court of the prison: and they let down Jeremiah with cords. And in the dungeon there was no water, but mire: so Jeremiah sunk in the mire (38:6).

Pits using ropes instead of ladders were common types of prisons throughout Asian history.

In 1843 Emir Nasrullah held two British officers—Colonel Stoddart and Captain Conally—for two months in the bug pit of Bukhara before beheading them. They had come to interest the Emir in British assistance against Russian cunning. They were beheaded for their intrigues and because, after having embraced Islam at the insistence of the Emir, they returned to the Christian faith. The two months they spent in the pit must have been horrible ones. They were kept bound, hand and foot, and given nothing to eat or drink. As they lay there helpless, they were chewed and mutilated by vermin. For this was the bug pit famous in Central Asian history where ticks, scorpions, and other insects were raised specially to torture prisoners. The Soviets have dramatized this bug pit. In it today are two dummies tied hand and foot, representing the two benighted Britishers.

Bukhara was once surrounded by a mud wall, twenty-five feet high, ten feet thick with a circumference of fifteen miles. Eleven gates opened into the city. A hundred years ago the walls were crumbling. They and the gates are today decrepit; but for the most part they still stand.

"They will be restored in all their glory someday soon," the guide told me.

The domes and minarets of Bukhara rise above a great expanse of flat roofs. The houses today, as a century ago, are built of mud, the rooms facing a courtyard. Most of them are one-story buildings with few windows on the streets. A block up Lenin Street from my hotel I found the ancient Street of the Jews where the Jewish community still lives as it did centuries ago. Its single synagogue is there, made of mud, with no plaque or sign to identify it. The street has no mark of change on it.

The bazaars of Bukhara, nine in number and marked by cupolas, are still the same as in days of old—except in one respect. Today they are state stores where employees of the government offer soft drinks, cotton cloth, shoes, and Communist literature for sale.

Bukhara will someday be restored. A new city will rise alongside of it, with plumbing, pure water, paved streets, shaded boulevards, and parks. The old city will be beside it, resplendent in ancient glory. And that glory will be used to remind the people of the cruelty of their old rulers and the oppressive feudal character of their regime.

There are names to conjure with in Central Asia—and great glory too. Bukhara is not the only one. There is Samarkand also. The Golden Road to Samarkand was immortalized in poetry by James Elroy Flecker:

> *We travel not for trafficking alone:*
> *By hotter winds our fiery hearts are fanned:*
> *For lust of knowing what should not be known*
> *We make the Golden Journey to Samarkand.*

Samarkand lay on the ancient Silk Road leading from China to Europe. Alexander the Great reached here in the great push that marked the zenith of Greek Empire.

The poet Hafiz placed a high value on Samarkand:

Belle of Shiraz, grant me but love's demand
And for your mole—that clinging grain of sand
Upon a cheek of pearl—Hafiz would give
All of Bukhara, all of Samarkand.

The chronicler of Genghis Khan had called Samarkand "a delicious place." Samarkand, like Bukhara, had fallen to Genghis Khan without a serious battle. Samarkand, like Bukhara, had been looted by the Mongols. It was from Samarkand that Genghis Khan headed his hordes towards Afghanistan and Persia, a campaign that led to the conquest of the Middle East and that brought Genghis Khan pounding at the doors of Europe. Genghis Khan had become interested in trade and in the year 1218 sent a caravan of 500 camels laden with gold and silk south to the markets of Baghdad and Damascus. The Emperor of Khorezm had the caravan seized. Genghis Khan sent an ambassador to protest. The Emperor of Khorezm beheaded the ambassador and burned off the beards of his assistants. The person of an ambassador was sacred to the Mongols. The insult could be wiped out only by war. So Genghis Khan laid his plans carefully and soon let loose a thundering horde of warriors who laid waste to Central Asia.

Here Marco Polo visited on his historic journey from Venice to Peking. Marco Polo said: "Samarcan is a noble city, adorned with beautiful gardens, and surrounded by a plain, in which are produced all the fruits that man can desire." It is all of that today. But now, as in Marco Polo's day, it has other treasures too.

Samarkand was the city selected by Timur for his home. Timur, who came to power in 1369, and his grandsons made of Samarkand an oasis of grandeur. Pieces of the old wall of Samarkand with its six gates still stand. Timur lies buried in a beautiful blue-domed mosque, called Gur Emir. In a side room his grave is marked by a well-polished, dark green stone bearing a crack, which the Uzbek guide said was made by Nadir Shah of Persia who after sacking Delhi, India, came north to Samarkand for further conquests.

Timur defeated the remnants of the hordes of Genghis Khan, uniting under one regime all of Central Asia from the Caucasus to China. He then turned south and conquered Afghanistan and Persia. He crossed the Khyber and poured into India. On the west he laid Baghdad, Aleppo, and Damascus low; and his army poured on to the Bosporus, leaving no Turk in Asia. This lame man brought beauty to Samarkand but waste and sorrow to the world of his day. He was, like Genghis Khan before him, the embodiment of war.

Soviet scientists opened his tomb in Gur Emir to make measurements of the skeleton with a view of attempting a facial reconstruction of the legendary figure. That was on June 15, 1941. On June 22, 1941, the Germans invaded Russia; and soon the Nazis were broadcasting to the Middle East that the Russians had brought on the conflict by opening Timur's tomb and "setting loose" the spirits of war.

Samarkand has another beautiful, blue-domed mosque called Bibi Khanum, built by Timur for one of his wives who was a Chinese. According to my local guide, it was built by a Persian architect who fell in love with Timur's Chinese wife. Timur sent soldiers to kill him. The Persian climbed to the highest minaret and just before capture produced a pair of wings and flew south to Persia. Bibi Khanum has suffered much from time and earthquakes; it is largely in ruins. My guide did not promise that it would be restored by the Soviets.

Farther out of town on the edge of a melancholy stretch of empty land is Shakh Zinda. A flight of thirty-nine steps leads up to a gate in a square façade. At the top of the steps are several mosques with brick walls faced with clay and glazed in delicate hues of blue. Many members of Timur's family, including a nurse, are buried here. Beyond the tombs lies the sepulcher of Shakh Zinda, the military saint who, the guide said, will rise some day and preach the Islamic faith. This shrine is perhaps the holiest place in Central Asia—a Mecca to which Moslems make pilgrimages. Shakh Zinda is in fair condition. It, too, will be a show place for the world, the guide assured me.

Samarkand's greatest relic is the Registan, which takes up a large block. One side is open to the street; the other three are enclosed by beautiful brick buildings faced with glazed tiles of blue, turquoise, green, and orange (all baked in Persia, it is said) and adorned by lofty, arched façades. Round, graceful minarets, some of which seem not quite perpendicular, mark the corners of the square. Each of these buildings is a *medresse* (religious school) with a long history. Each *medresse* is built around a central courtyard with cloisters on each side. In the old days the living quarters of the Moslem students were upstairs, the classrooms downstairs. No religious students are there today. These ancient *medresses*, built by Timur and his grandson, Ulug Beg, are now living quarters for townsfolk and tourists.

The Registan stands in intense sunlight, undecorated by trees or shrubs or fountains. But its sheer beauty, its graceful lines, the rich color of its tiles give it great majesty. I do not think it is as lovely as the Taj Mahal, which Timur's descendants built in India. But it is more magnificent than any other structure I have seen in Asia or Europe. The Registan finds grandeur in mass and in simple lines rather than in ornament. It represents Persian and Arab genius at its best in the medium of brick and tile. It is a place where I could sit for hours. I did in fact seek out a shaded doorway opening into the main courtyard. But I no sooner sat down than I heard shouts from above. My guide came running with the message that workmen were replacing bricks high on the archway and feared that I would get hurt. As I wandered through the buildings I saw that much restoration was under way. Many scaffolds were up. Bricks and tiles were being replaced; arches strengthened; windows replaced; floors repaired.

"This too will be a great museum," the guide advised me.

Samarkand and Bukhara, indeed the whole region, are exciting places for historians and archaeologists. The Russian scholars are there in numbers—digging, exploring, looking for new ruins. Samarkand, an oasis irrigated principally by the river Zeravshan, is deep in shade. But once its limits are passed there is nothing but barren, rolling land that is bright, dusty, and torrid under an August sun. It had a dazzling heat the day I traveled it. I went out near the former site of the ancient city of Maracanda, founded by Alexander the Great. There is hardly a trace of it left. But there are many diggings going on there. And the greatest treasure of all is Ulug Beg's astronomical observatory built partly underground. It has a track in the shape of a crescent, along which the observer could travel as he followed the arc of a planet or star. My Uzbek guide was in ecstasy at this point. It was to him the prized discovery of the ages. It proved that in the fifteenth century, the Uzbeks had been people not only of culture but of scientific genius as well. Ulug Beg did, indeed, make a notable catalogue of 992 stars from his own observations, the first since the time of Ptolemy in the second century.

Over in Baku—the great petroleum city located on the Caspian Sea—I found the same emphasis on history and historic relics. Baku is the capital of Russian Azerbaijan, a country seized from Persia and Turkey near the beginning of last century. The people around Baku and to the south are mostly Turkish in race and tongue. The Persian cultural influence is still strong.

The wall of the old city of Baku is being completely restored. Elizabeth, my Baku interpreter, took special pride in pointing out how faithful the restoration is to the old design. The restoration of the old wall looked, indeed, like a substantial job; and it was well along when I was there.

In Baku the Soviets place great emphasis on Nizami, the Persian poet who was born about 1140. Nizami, a Persian romanticist greatly honored by the khans of his day, is a hero in modern Baku. His statue is in a small park which faces a museum bearing his name. The side of the museum that faces the park has tall, graceful pillars adorned with blue tile, and in the recesses are statues of famous Azerbaijanis, including some women. In design and color the building is Persian. Inside are treasures from the Persian world, including rich rugs, delicate paintings, and rare books and tracts written in beautiful Arabic.

The Russian Communists use these statues, museums, and shrines to memorialize history that will appeal to the races which they must rule in Central Asia. These historic relics, which I found everywhere in Central Asia, are a part of Russia's concession to the nationality problem within her borders. They are devoid of current political significance. But they are part of the mucilage used to hold the diverse cultures within Russia together.

The pride of Russians in their history is notably displayed in Leningrad. About fifteen miles out of town on Neva Bay stands Peterhof, built by Peter the Great in accordance with the plans of Leblond, a French architect. It's the old summer palace. It stands at the top of a terrace fifty feet or so high that overlooks the Finnish coast. Down the terrace are a series of basins, each laid with colored marble and spouting many fountains. There is the fountain of Samson opening the jaws of a lion and causing a jet of water to shoot sixty feet into the air. There are fountains of sea gods, tritons, horses, dolphins, all spouting water. There are fountains in the shape of gigantic vessels. There are statues of women pouring water. Seen from below, the spouting water, the basins, and the statues form as beautiful a scene as the famous Versailles. Seen from above, the gardens and water cascades of Peterhof are even more impressive than Versailles. For the water from the dozens of fountains and spouts gathers at the bottom into a long, narrow canal flanked by trees and fountains and running to the sea about a half mile distant.

This spot during World War II was held by the Germans who looted the palace and destroyed the fountains and the statues. By the time the Russians reclaimed it, Peterhof was in ruins. The palace was still under repairs when I visited it. But most of the statues of Peterhof had been replaced and freshly gilded and the fountains were spouting in a symphony of light and music. Most of the former glory of the place is now restored. It is a show place that has few equals in Russia.

Leningrad is a veritable storehouse of relics, art, and historic symbols. While under the long siege during World War II, it lost about a million people, many from starvation. Then its treasures were in packing cases underground. Today the packing cases have been emptied and the walls and shelves and cases of Leningrad's many museums refilled. The Hermitage, built by Catherine the Great, is a storehouse of art treasures. It always adjoined the Winter Palace where the czars stayed during the cold months. Today it has merged with the Winter Palace, so to speak, or rather overflowed into it. One walks from the Winter Palace into the Hermitage. They are connecting museums of art, containing the works of not only Russian masters but of French, Dutch, Italian, Spanish, and British masters too. In a special room, carefully sealed and open only by appointment, is the famous collection of Scythian gold from southwest Russia. It dates back as far as 700 B.C. Here are bracelets, rings, and pins of exquisite design; many small gold tigers as graceful as life; and ancient gold coins almost too numerous to catalogue.

One could spend weeks in the Hermitage alone, the collections are so rich and so numerous. Leningrad is packed with show places. The old, white-pillared Stock Exchange on the Neva River (converted into a museum) still stands. The Admiralty, now a school, still dominates the scene. The Stroganov Palace, the Tauride Palace, the Imperial Library, the National Museum, the Alexandra Theater, the Cathedral of the Virgin of Kazan and the

Cathedral of St. Isaac (both anti-religious museums), are living reminders of the greatness of Russian art and architecture. The whole city is in a sense a museum, the most beautiful in Russia. There is a stateliness and grandeur in Leningrad one does not see elsewhere.

The Communists are, of course, memorialized there. There is, for example, a great plaque on the building where Lenin and Stalin worked during the days they were managing the campaign of the Bolsheviks against the White Russians. Statues of the two men and other Soviet heroes are common in Leningrad. But the greater emphasis in Leningrad is on Russia's luxurious past and the nobility of her czars and the might of her armies. Peter the Great is prominent in Leningrad. So are Catherine and Nicholas. Wherever one turns in that noble city there are reminders that it was Russian might that turned back the French last century and the Germans this century.

The Kremlin in Moscow is also being made a show place of Russian greatness. The Kremlin was the nucleus of old Muscovy; it was to Russia what the Acropolis was to Greece and the Capitolium was to Rome. When the Tartars invaded, the Kremlin was only a village surrounded by a wooden stockade. But here the Russians made their stand. It has evolved under the influence of many czars and architects into its present condition. It is still a medieval citadel on the banks of the Moskva River, basically unchanged since the Communists came to power. It is now being renovated and restored; and since the death of Stalin its gates are open to sight-seers who throng there by the thousands. Apart from one short spell after the Revolution, the Kremlin was tightly shut to the public until 1955.

The walls of the Kremlin, flanked by nineteen towers, are shaped into an irregular pentagon. The walls are sixty feet high in some places and twelve feet to sixteen feet thick. The Kremlin was built for defense before gunpowder was invented. It now is the administrative headquarters of government. The offices of the ministries and the Praesidium are there, located in an office building erected after the October Revolution on sites which until then had been occupied by two monasteries—the Ascension and the Miracle.

The Kremlin after a lapse of two centuries again became the capital of Russia in 1918, when Leningrad seemed to be in an exposed position. The Kremlin is our White House, Capitol, and Supreme Court all combined. But it is more than that. The Kremlin contains most of the great monuments of Russia's past.

Within its walls are seven cathedrals and churches (not to mention towers and palaces that contain shrines): the Cathedral of the Annunciation, the Cathedral of the Assumption, the Cathedral of the Archangel Michael, the Church of the Saviour in the Forest, the Cathedral of Our Saviour Behind the Golden Grille, the Church of the Twelve Apostles, the Church of the Consecration of the Priests.

In these cathedrals are icons painted by Russian masters, images of the Saviour and of the Virgin Mary encased in gold and precious stones, images of saints with breast plates of precious jewels, frescoes, paintings of Biblical scenes and holy figures, many great chandeliers, floors of marble, jasper, and agate. Here are tombs of czars and princes. None of the cathedrals inside the Kremlin is used for services. They are museums, pure and simple. And now that the gates are open the crowds flock to them.

The Tower of Ivan the Great, with a cross 270 feet high, stands in the center of the Kremlin, commanding all the cathedrals. This tower has thirty-three bells, hung in three tiers. Certain bells are used for some occasions; others, for different occasions. For holidays or special days of celebration all the bells go into action.

Today's sight-seers gather about the King of Bells that lies on the ground near the Tower. The beam holding it broke when it was damaged by fire. The bell fell and was shattered. It was recast and once more hung. In 1937 a fire broke out again and the streams of water used to put out the fire cracked the hot metal, causing a huge piece to split off. The defective bell now on display has a sign saying that it weighs 200 tons.

Inside the Kremlin is the Grand Kremlin Palace erected beginning in 1839 and absorbing some units of older palaces of the Russian czars. It covers a large part of the hill of the Kremlin; its dome-shaped belvedere in bright gold seems to dominate the scene. Its rooms are now open for special tours. The halls and salons are filled with crystal chandeliers, marble columns, alabaster, rare woods. The salons are dedicated to different orders of chivalry and ornamented with heraldic motifs. Some halls are filled with military memorials. Two have recently been combined into one large auditorium seating 2500 people and fully air-conditioned. Here sits the Supreme Soviet.

One passes through the private apartments of the czars—where they slept, ate, and prayed. The innermost privacy of the past is now open to the proletariat. And they love it.

One of the greatest attractions of all is the display of art treasures in the Oruzheinaia Palata in the Kremlin. The art objects— both sacred and secular—are mostly encased in glass. There are ancient vestments, manuscripts, books, censers, crowns, icons, armlets, crosses, staffs, chalices—each with a special history associated with some czar or some religious patriarch. The ecclesiastical jewelry is dazzling. Bibles are in covers heavily studded with jewels.

There is a great array of Russian arms from the thirteenth to seventeenth century. This collection represents every branch of the service and every rank.

Another hall shows the coronation robes, crowns, and thrones of the czars. The day I visited this hall, the crowd seemed greatly interested in the White Ivory Throne of Ivan the Terrible. There are gloves, boots, jewels, goblets, tankards, flasks, flagons, horns, helmets, gowns, maces, swords used by the czars. There are emeralds as big as eggs; robes with pearls weighing on the aggregate sixty pounds; gold plates weighing nine pounds.

Luxury tea service sets are on display. There are golden and silver plates, clocks, incense burners, stage coaches, harnesses for horses (including a headpiece that contains 1000 diamonds), saddles, sleds, golden stirrups, silver shoes for horses. Trophies of all the wars are on display. Gifts from foreign potentates, celebrating historic events, fill large rooms.

What the crowd on my visit liked the most was the section devoted to Peter the Great, the man nearly seven feet tall whose boots look as if they were made for a giant and whose skills ranged through fourteen professions, including shipbuilding and shoemaking.

Outside the west wall of the Kremlin is Red Square—a large oblong rectangle. In front is the Lenin Mausoleum; on the east the big Soviet department store called GUM (the initials for Government Department Store), comparable to our own; on the north is the Historical Museum; and on the south the Church of St. Basil the Blessed. Today St. Basil's is being repaired; its eight cupolas are being gaily painted in Christmas red and green. Red Square is, indeed, one of the busiest places in Russia.

It serves Moscow much like the Roman Forum once served Rome. Here is the low, flat-topped rostrum called the Lobnoe Mesto where the czars delivered messages to the people, where priests gave their blessings, where news and edicts were announced. Once the Red Square was a place of execution. Here until 1727 were scaffolds, iron cages for burning prisoners, wheels to stretch and break them, hooks to tear the victims to pieces. Here also was a famous market place.

When Lenin died, a mausoleum was erected in Red Square outside the Kremlin wall and his body placed there. It is a rectangular, low, and flat-roofed building, made of red granite and black-gray labradorite. Two armed guards are on constant duty, changing every four hours. When Stalin died, he was placed alongside Lenin in the mausoleum. Only their heads and hands are visible above the black cloth of the tomb. (Some say that their hands and heads have been severed from the bodies.) There they lie in state with separate spotlights shining on them and a soldier at the foot of each bier.

For some hours each day the tomb is open to the public. During my Moscow visit I saw thousands of people lined up waiting to get in. The line passes through a garden where lesser Communists are buried and then out into the street leading to Red Square. Some days when the line started to move the people were in double file for six blocks; and for hours the line remained that long, as the people slowly shuffled by the biers. The crowd moves continuously; but it takes about two hours to go through. Some of my friends found it to be a macabre experience. On my visit I kept watching the crowd trying to figure out why, day after day, they pour silently by these biers. Some doubtless go for sheer curiosity. Some, I think, go out of a feeling of awe and respect. In America, we are familiar with the sentiment that if only Roosevelt, Truman, Eisenhower, or whoever the President is, really knew what was going on, he would take steps to remedy the evil. In Russia there is also a feeling that somewhere in Moscow a just ruler sits, an attitude that extended even to Stalin. Moreover, in Russia it has long been customary to look to authority for leadership. The czar was always the Little Father. The Little Father is now the top man in the dictatorship. None in recent history symbolizes total power better than Lenin and Stalin.

Today the political motif of Russia features the Great Russian. Stalin the Georgian was an interloper. Political power is now back in the hands of the Great Russians. Of the eleven-man Praesidium there are only two outsiders—Anastas I. Mikoyan, an Armenian, and Lazar M. Kaganovich, a Jew. Stalin, though having an honored place in the mausoleum, is second to Lenin. It is Lenin who is being quoted these days. Stalin is being quietly forgotten. I discovered that even the literature prepared for kindergarten children is now being rewritten to exclude Stalin and to extol only Lenin.

In Soviet Russia the new is also old. In Leningrad, I saw that theme dramatized on the stage of the Marinsky Theater. We attended the opera *Ivan Susanin*. It is built around old folklore from the time when the Poles invaded Russia. Ivan, a Russian peasant, was forced by the Poles in dead winter to be their guide to Moscow. Ivan, loyal to Russia, led them astray so they were hopelessly lost in the woods. The Poles killed Ivan for his treachery. When Ivan sang his last song saying he was glad to die for Russia, the entire theater broke forth into a thundering applause. The applause was so great that Ivan had to appear many times to take a bow. This night Communists, bureaucrats, engineers, workmen, lawyers, all honored patriotism to country in a great emotional outburst.

Russia today is different than it was under Stalin. But it is, if anything, more Russian.

3

THE STATE AND FREE ENTERPRISE

I looked everywhere in Russia for a barber who owned his own shop. Now and then I was told that there were such people. I came across doctors who have private patients on the side. But I could find no private barber. I left Russia satisfied that if there is one, he is the most elusive character in the world. I had several haircuts on my 8000-mile journey. But the barbers were either employees of the state or members of a barbers' co-operative society organized under Soviet law. Some were men; some were women—all very skilled. They used hand clippers (I saw no electric ones), sharp scissors, and well-honed razors. And when they finished, they consistently sprayed me with a delicate perfume. Each haircut cost me five rubles, which at the foreign exchange rate amounts to $1.25 but which to the Russian amounts to about 40 cents. No barber I met would take a tip, probably because some jealous or suspicious person would notice it and involve the recipient in a dubious relationship with a foreigner. These Soviet barbers are a taciturn lot. They do not talk politics, the weather, soccer, crop prospects, fishing, or hunting. I could not get a word out of them on any subject. They bent to the task and had it over and done with in a hurry.

The barber who works for the state gets a monthly salary. It may be sent him by check; more often it is deposited in his account. For there are savings banks in Russia, all owned by the central government and having checking accounts and savings accounts. They are widespread. They are, indeed, in every city and town of any size. The barber who works in a hotel is under the manager who is fiscal agent for the state. The manager has charge of the bank account for the hotel. All hotel receipts are deposited in that account and out of it all disbursements, including salaries for barbers and other people who work in the hotel, are made.

Like the barbers and other workers, all engineers, architects, doctors, dentists, nurses, bacteriologists, physicists, and scientists also work for the state. They have attended an institute or college after ten years in public schools. Engineers and most other scientists spend five years in their specialty; doctors spend six years. All professional people (apart from lawyers) are assigned on graduation by some ministry to a post. Engineers are assigned to institutes, laboratories, oil fields, construction jobs, or ministries. Doctors and dentists are assigned to hospitals that may be in factories, on farms, or in cities. The assignment may be to remote villages or to far-off construction camps. One goes where he's told to go. Like in our Army or Navy, preferences may be stated. But the assignment comes down from on high without recourse.

Soviet law prohibits the hiring of labor for profit. Trade unions, however, are one exception to the rule. Some pushcarts selling soft drinks, ice cream, cigarettes, cough medicines, and contraceptives are owned by trade unions. Such is the case in Petropavlovsk where these pushcart vendors receive their monthly wages from the union, the union retaining all the profits from the business.

Co-operative societies are another exception.

KRASNOVODSK

Krasnovodsk is opposite Baku on the Caspian Sea.

The port of Krasnovodsk is the rail head of the Turkish-Siberian railroad.

Public-school teachers and the principal at Krasnovodsk are all Turkmens.

In Central Asia camels are used as transport by collective farms.

SAMARKAND

The family's bed is placed
under a grape arbor at
a collective farm
near Samarkand.

Uleg Beg's observatory
near Samarkand
is a popular museum.

The agricultural implement
factory at Frunze supplies
much of Central Asia.

Most Russian dairy farms
use milking machines.

As I have said, a barber may be a member of a co-operative. If so, he gets his salary each month from the fiscal officer of that society. Most barbers belong to these co-ops. So do men who shine shoes and most of the old women and men who manage the white pushcarts on the streets. Moreover, repairmen for sewing machines, typewriters, and watches are organized into co-ops.

There are not many lawyers in Russia by our standards. In Novosibirsk, a city of 800,000, there are only eighty lawyers. In Petropavlovsk, a town of 125,000, there are only twelve. But such as do practice law are organized into a form of co-operative society, known as the College of Advocates.

The co-ops also cover a wide range of industrial activities. They are found in textiles, leather goods, metal work (including the making of cots), glassware, porcelain, and in many other light industries. Of the many co-operative societies, industrial co-operatives are the most numerous.

Soviet producer co-ops play a very important role in the economy. They produce, for example, about 50 per cent of Russia's wagons, 40 per cent of her furniture, and 35 per cent of ready-to-wear clothing. They run about 126,000 enterprises and shops; and they employ about 2,000,000 people.

There is a Central Council of Co-operatives in Moscow, which has its counterpart in each republic. A group that wants to form a producer co-op applies to the local council. The members contribute a capital fund and pay annual dues. These amounts may or may not be sufficient for their working capital. If not, the co-op, once licensed, can get loans from the Trade Bank, one of the four banks which the Soviet government created to make long-term loans to industry and agriculture. The co-ops pay their members a monthly salary. They pay the state an income tax on net profits. The tax ranges from 5 per cent to 20 per cent, being graduated according to amount.

The members pay an income tax on their salaries and dividends. This income tax, the same that every worker pays, is graduated from 1½ per cent to 13 per cent. It starts at 260 rubles (roughly $21) a month. One reaches the 13 per cent bracket when he makes 1001 rubles (roughly $80) a month.

In Soviet ideology neither business nor farming need be state owned, if the means of production are owned by all those who participate in the joint enterprise. These co-ops do that; and they have a few aspects of private enterprise too. For example, they have their own retail stores. I saw them everywhere. But the essence of private enterprise is squeezed out of these stores, for they sell only at such prices as the state directs. Much of their production goes directly to the state-owned stores with which the co-op stores compete. The state, in substance, requisitions the production of the co-ops, according to its needs. Moreover, the industrial co-ops are laced tightly into the state planning machinery, being allotted annual production quotas.

A textile co-op in Tashkent is typical of the ones I saw. I found this co-op in the old part of the city, off a narrow, winding street lined with mud walls on both sides. A gate opened into a courtyard. This had once been a rather spacious home with rooms on the four sides of the yard. All the rooms are now occupied by the co-op. The old parlor is the office of the president who is an extra-large middle-aged Uzbek woman. The other rooms around the courtyard are filled either with women working with sewing machines or women doing needlework. The rooms filled with machines were packed with women on the day of my visit. The machines set up such a roar I could hardly hear the Uzbek lady president speak. This co-op, organized in 1935 by 16 people, now has 405 members. Of these, 100 work at home in the manner of garment workers of other countries. Most of them are women; and practically all are Uzbeks. They turn out shirts, blouses, and dresses—some of them extremely attractive. They also produce tablecloths and curtains. About 50 per cent of their products go to state stores, the rest to their own stores. There are over 300 co-operatives of all types in Uzbekistan and about 80 in Tashkent, its capital.

These women textile workers fairly itched with curiosity at the visit of my party. They apparently had orders to work hard when I went through their little factory, for they were bent over their machines in concentrated work while I was there. But as soon as I left the rooms and entered the courtyard, the hum of machines stopped. I looked around and saw most of the women looking out of the windows and crowding the doorways. By the time I had entered my car to drive off they had spilled into the courtyard, filling it. There were female giggles and whispers and then, as the car started, I was showered with cheers in the Uzbek language.

The collective farm is another species of the co-operative. It took the place of the individual farmers or *kulaks* about a quarter of a century ago. Many of the collective farms were formed peace-fully, without bloodshed or terror. Others were the products of great violence. Today they are deeply rooted in Russia and ap-parently there to stay. They are the most common type of farm. The other is the state farm. In Russia the state owns 5000 farms. Those state farms have 15 per cent to 18 per cent of the agricul-tural lands of Russia. Most of the rest (approximately 76 per cent) are farmed by the collectives which number 90,000.

In Russia, all land is owned by the state; the collectives are mere lessees. Each collective has a charter from the government which describes its lands by metes and bounds, grants it the ex-clusive right to use them, prohibits it from selling or leasing the property, and guarantees that the agricultural unit will remain permanently inviolate. The members of a collective farm are elected. They choose a committee of from five to nine persons who run the farm between meetings of the members. New members are recommended by the committee and voted on by the mem-bers. A majority vote is needed for election. A majority vote is all that is necessary for expulsion also, provided two thirds of the members are present at the meeting. Expulsion, however, is an extreme measure applicable only to persons who are "incorrigible, subversive, and disruptive to the collective farm." Expulsion may not take effect until the executive committee of the local soviet has approved.

The members are not partners. All that can be devised by will, or obtained if a member withdraws, is his share of the profits already earned during the preceding accounting period.

The restrictions and restraints under which the collective operates rob it of most of the independence it is theoretically supposed to have. The controls and restrictions placed over it by the state have made it a tool of the state planners.

The charter of the collective obligates it to operate pursuant to the state's agricultural program. The collective is also frequently tied to the state by loan agreements. The government has created the Agricultural Bank to finance collective farms in the construction of buildings, the purchase of livestock, the erection of irrigation works, and the like. In case of these loans, the state exercises a close surveillance over the collective.

Each collective owns its livestock, mills, buildings, seed, water, fodder, and the other means of production, with one exception—the large machinery necessary to operate the farm. They include tractors, cultivators, thrashers, combines, well digging outfits, etc. Those implements are all owned by an agency of the state called the MTS (Machine Tractor Station), which was first introduced in 1929–30. They are used on the collective, pursuant to an agreement with the local MTS, which, in substance, makes the MTS a co-manager of the farm. A schedule of fees for the services of the machinery is included in the contract. Some fees are payable in crops, some in cash, payment being made to the Ministry of Requisitions, a state agency performing wholesale functions. The following is an illustration of the fees collected by an MTS from a beef and dairy farm I visited near Moscow. The fees were paid in kind, 75 per cent in milk, 25 per cent in meat. This farm has 300 milk cows. I give only the payments to MTS for servicing the dairy cattle for one year.

Transportation of forage........132.28 lbs. of milk or meat
Harrowing .... 1,349.22 ·· ·· ·· ·· ··
Cultivation for sowing ....286.60 ·· ·· ·· ·· ··
Sowing clover ....553.36 ·· ·· ·· ·· ··
Plowing .... 762.79 ·· ·· ·· ·· ··
3,084.25

I learned on my travels that for cotton, the MTS over-all charge is usually 11 per cent of the crop; for wheat 12½ per cent; for corn 10 per cent to 12 per cent.

The crops and cash fees which the MTS collects from the collectives may be only a disguised tax levied by the state. They are truly a tax once they exceed the value of the services. The extent to which they do is hard to compute. Certainly the MTS is a powerful instrument of state control over the collective; and many are convinced it is a means of levying hidden taxes on it. That MTS was orginated as a coercive device is indicated by the fact that in its early years all of its officials were armed.

The agreement governing the annual crop production program obligates the collective to deliver designated quantities of produce to the state at specified prices. This obligation covers only a part of the total production—usually an eighth or a sixth; and the deliveries are made to the Ministry of Requisitions. To the extent that the prices to be paid the collective by the state are lower than fair value, they again are a hidden tax. The state buys from the collectives at prices which will give a profit to its retail stores. Students of the subject, notably Harry Schwartz in *Russia's Soviet Economy*, are convinced that the prices to the collectives are placed so low as to levy in substance a tax.

After the obligatory deliveries are made to the state and after MTS is paid for its services, the collective usually has between two thirds and a half of its crop left. Out of this, it sets aside what it needs for its operations until the next crop comes in. This includes seed requirements, feed requirements, and other reserves. Furthermore, the collective usually will have invalids and aged people too old to work but who are a responsibility of the collective. Reserves will be set aside to meet their needs.

After all these requirements have been met, the collective has from 25 per cent to 40 per cent of the crop left; and in addition, it has cash on hand, less expenditures, from the sale of its quota to the government. At this point the collective makes a distribution to its members. The distribution is pursuant to a complicated formula.

In the first place each worker is given a workday classification. The least exacting work is given a partial workday, the most exacting work a workday of two or three days. Thus some who work eight hours for one day will be credited with a half day's work, while others will get credit for three days' work. At Kurtly collective farm near Ashkhabad I went over the workday classifications with the lean Turkmen chairman. This collective raises grapes as well as sheep. The worker in grapes has three times as many workdays as the sheepherder. In other words, for an eight-hour day the worker in the vineyard gets three times the wage of the sheepherder. The schedule governing these workdays is very complicated and involved. For example, an Uzbek dairymaid, in charge of from 8 to 14 cows, gets 2.4 workdays for every 100 liters (105 quarts) of milk produced. Drivers of tractors and operators of machines get from 4 to 7 workdays per shift, dependent on the type of machine operated. Cotton cleaners get 5 workdays per shift.

A second element in determining the workday concerns the norm. Each job has a defined norm. The norm for plowing may be 10 acres a day (dependent of course on the nature of the plow). If a person plows more than 10 acres, his workday is increased; if he plows less, it is decreased. Like norms are figured for every job—number of cows milked, pigs fed and pig pens cleaned, apple trees sprayed, apples picked, etc. The norms are set in advance and represent the work of the most efficient units.

A third element in determining the amount of the workdays earned is the failure or success of the worker (or the group of which he is a member) in filling the requirements of the plan. If the plan is 40 bushels of wheat per acre and the production is 40.4 bushels (or 1 per cent increase), the total workdays are increased 1 per cent. If the production falls off 1 per cent, the total workdays are decreased 1 per cent. But there can be neither an increase nor a decrease of more than 25 per cent in the workdays.

There are variations in the computations of workdays. But these are the main features.

Then there is the task of setting the value to the workday. A workday usually has two values—one expressed in rubles, and the other in kilograms of grain, meat, or other produce. Near Ashkhabad, cotton pickers get 18 rubles and 2.5 kilograms of grain per workday. A diversified collective in Kazakhstan pays 10 rubles and 3 kilograms of grain per workday. Near Frunze, the workers on a collective farm get 3 rubles, 4 kilograms of wheat, and half a kilogram of potatoes per workday. Workers in animal husbandry get paid in rubles plus meat, milk, butter, or cheese, or a combination of them.

During the year the workers can draw down on their accounts, being allowed as an advance 50 per cent of the estimated annual earnings. At the end of the year the dividend in cash and in kind is determined and paid to the members.

There is still a balance of produce retained by the collective. That balance can be sold by the collective on the free market at whatever price it can obtain, or the collective may enter into special contracts for sale of the produce to the state. Usually the collective does both.

These auxiliary contracts with the state are attractive. The state pays bonuses for deliveries to it over and above the obligatory deliveries. For example, the state paid one collective about $1.00 per 220 pounds of wheat for obligatory deliveries. But it paid ten times that amount, or $10 per 220 pounds of wheat, for deliveries above the quota. The state may offer other inducements to the collective to make extra sales to it. It may, for example, offer quantities of scarce food to the collective at low prices, if the collective will make bonus deliveries of produce to the state. These contracts for delivery of produce over and above the obligatory deliveries appeal to the profit motive. So does the tax schedule. If the collective sells produce on the free market, it pays a 15 per cent income tax on those sales. If it sells produce to the state over and above the quota called for by its obligatory deliveries, it pays only a 9 per cent income tax on the proceeds.

The bonus sales to the state and the sales by the collectives on the free markets probably account for no more than 5 per cent to 10 per cent of all the produce of the collectives. But it is from these small sales that the collective receives the great bulk of its cash income.

The members of the collective need most of the produce they receive in kind from the collective to live on or to feed their pigs or chickens on their private plots. Some may sell part of it on the free market. But the great percentage of the members' sales on the free market is from their private plots.

These private plots are present on every farm in Russia that I saw. They vary in size from a quarter acre to an acre or more. The size varies with the quality and classification of the land; and it averages one-half acre. The amount is specified in the contract with the collective. There is also specified in that contract the number of livestock that may be privately owned. A cow and a calf are commonly permitted. Small numbers of sheep and of pigs are usually allowed. No restriction on the number of chickens, geese, and ducks is usually imposed. These private plots are a form of community property, undivided into shares. No member of the household may transfer his interest in them. If the household is dissolved (as when one leaves to get married or to form a new household), the property is divided or distributed either pursuant to an agreement or to the custom that prevails in the locality.

Private plots are found not only on collectives but on most state farms as well. Alamedin State Farm near Frunze is typical. It has 1070 head of cattle, half of them beef, half dairy. It raises various grasses and hay and a lot of corn, pigs, and chickens. The milk cows have the eleventh best record in the U.S.S.R. and the first in Kirgizia. One cow produces 10,000 liters a year and the average is 4950 liters to 5200 liters a year, with a butterfat content of 4 per cent.

These cows were cared for by the biggest woman I ever saw—a warm-hearted Ukrainian in a frame suited for a huge man. After explaining to me the habits of practically every cow on the place, she turned to a discussion of the private land on this state farm. There are 300 families on the farm and each has 1¼ acres of land. Each family is entitled to have one milk cow and one calf, three sheep, and any number of chickens, geese, or other fowl. Of the total annual income of families on this state farm, one third comes from the private land.

I visited both state farms and collectives where the percentage of private income to total income was as high as 50 per cent. The private income of many farmers is 20 per cent or less of their total annual income in cash and kind. But the average, I believe, is around 33 per cent. Private farm income, in other words, is substantial in Russia; and private farm land plays an important role in the economy.

Moscow does not discourage this *private sector*. Rather, it encourages it. For example, there is no tax on the income from the private land. No matter how much those sales may amount to, the income is tax-free. That is true of the private land attached both to collectives and to state farms. There is in each instance a tax in lieu of the income tax. It is a tax on the land itself. It's not an onerous tax. It runs from about $8.00 to $100 a year per hectare (approximately 2½ acres), depending on the quality of the land, and is designed to be roughly equivalent to the income tax that workers pay on their salaries.

There is an elaborate tax system worked out to cover situations where the farmer cultivates more private land than his allotment or raises more livestock than his quota. There is a schedule of penalty taxes applicable to this situation. For example, if a farmer keeps two cows when the agreement allots him only one, he pays the state a penalty tax of 80 liters of milk a year or approximately 85 quarts. He may keep the extra cow or cultivate the extra land, provided he pays the penalty.

These private farming operations are not only very important to the Russian farmer; they are a substantial portion of the Soviet produce market. Of the fresh fruits and vegetables sold in the large urban centers of the Soviet Union, approximately 50 per cent are supplied from the *private sector*. In the case of meat, milk, cheese, and eggs the percentage is smaller but still substantial. The free market, however, does not carry all important food items. Bread, for example, which is the most important single item in the Soviet diet, is sold almost always through state stores.

The free market handles not only produce from the fields and gardens but some manufactured articles as well. The high crime in Russia is employment of labor by an individual. The law usually lays a heavy hand on the man who hires another to work for him. I have given some exceptions. Another is the employment of servants in the home. Labor within the family, however, is a pool for all sorts of ventures. Grandmother's knitting goes to market. So does the housewife's needlework, including lovely Turkmen and Bukharan rugs that are wall decorations in the hotels of Central Asia. So does a man's leather- or woodwork. All of these, like butter that a child may churn, find their way legally into the free market.

The central government encourages these private operations, not only by its tax system but in other ways as well. Very often the market places are improvised affairs, constructed by the farmers themselves. Sometimes the market is, indeed, nothing but a spot on the road, usually a shady one, where the man sits with his onions and potatoes or the lady with her eggs and chickens. Such are the private markets in Ashkhabad, capital of Turkmenistan. But in most places the cities have one or more market places laid out in orderly fashion with stalls, awnings, and running water. Some stalls even have refrigeration for the sellers of milk, butter, and meat. The cities own these stalls and rent them out. The rent is normally a nominal amount, either 1 ruble (8 cents) a day or at the most 2 rubles, depending on the facilities furnished. The Mayor of Novosibirsk explained it all to me, stating that the fees were designed to cover costs, including breakage and repairs, with a reserve for expansion of the market places.

These markets were for me the most colorful spots in mercantile Russia. The state grocery and meat stores are rather drab affairs and seem to be inefficiently run. The prices are set. There's no bargaining or haggling—no concessions for overripeness or inferior quality. Severe penalties are imposed on any clerk who deviates from the fixed price. In the state store, you take it or leave it.

Not so on the private markets. They are lively, interesting, and exciting. The price is whatever the seller can get; and if the buyer is a foreigner, the asking price is always higher. Bargaining and haggling go on from stall to stall. Russia's private markets are private enterprise in its simplest, most basic form. I found them most colorful in Central Asia. There the Uzbeks, Kazakhs,

Tadzhiks, Kirgiz, Turkmens gathered in their native costumes. They were happy, relaxed, and eager as they waited in their stalls. Tomatoes, peppers, paprika, grapes, melons, onions, honey, milk, meat, potatoes—all of the riches of the farms were there. There was a babble of voices; argument with customers; gesticulations and shouts; the shaking of heads; and finally the bargain. While I was in these markets of Soviet Central Asia, I felt as if I were back in Kabul, Baghdad, or Damascus. It was the same as when Marco Polo traversed the country. Then camels from the East were unloaded at caravansaries and spices, tea, and silks spread before the public. Now as then, the prices are what the traffic will bear.

In early morning the stalls are filled and competition is stiff. Prices level off. By noon some stalls are closed, and if the supply is not so great, prices rise. By late afternoon, some produce has wilted; and vendors of such perishable commodities as milk do not want to cart them back to the farms that night. So prices fall. Here on the private markets of Soviet Russia one gets not only color and romance; he also sees the actual operations of the law of supply and demand, more dramatic than any textbook can show it.

Bare figures do, however, tell an interesting story. I took the prices of the same commodity in state stores and in the free market. What I record is a sample only, but typical I think. The units of weight are pounds, except as otherwise indicated; and the ruble is taken at 8 cents, its approximate worth in Russia, as contrasted to its 25-cent value in foreign exchange.

	State Stores	Free Market
Pork	$ .72	$ .80
Beef	.48 – .60	.68 – .72
Mutton	.45	.98
Ducks (each)	2.25	2.40
Canned Fish (per can)	.48 – .80	.64 – .72
Coffee	.21	.28
Macaroni (box)	.16 – .24	.40
Milk (liter)	.20	.23
Potatoes	.03	.09
Onions	.17	.17
Carrots	.12	.17

These markets are strictly producers' markets, not the retail markets we know. There are few middlemen in the Soviet scheme of things who are not agencies of the state. The consumer co-operative is an exception. While the free markets operate successfully in and around towns and cities, many areas of rural Russia are far removed from markets. The farmers, therefore, cannot reach them. The consumer co-operative was introduced to serve that need. It is widespread in Russia, its members running somewhere between 30,000,000 and 40,000,000 people. These consumer co-operatives have nearly 300,000 retail outlets; and they employ in their stores over 1,000,000 people. At some places they compete with state stores. The consumer co-operatives purchase supplies both from collective farms and from farm workers. The parties agree on the purchase price and the resale price, the difference being designed to cover the operation costs of the consumer co-operative. The resale prices are not controlled by the state and in practice are somewhat lower than free market prices and higher than state store prices.

With these exceptions the private middleman or commission house is an outlaw under Soviet law. For a Soviet statute, enacted in 1932, makes "buying and reselling agricultural products and consumer goods by private persons with the motive of profit" a crime. It carries a penalty of five to ten years. It has been strictly applied by the courts to cover a host of articles from medicines to automobiles.

The Soviet press is filled with accounts of the trial and conviction of "profiteers" or "speculators" who bought goods from a state store and took them to another city to sell at a higher price. Thus, one man was recently convicted for attempting to resell 336 zippers and 36 tablecloths; another for reselling 200 silk scarves at a 400 per cent mark-up; another for trafficking in yeast. The cases are almost legion. For the opportunities are numerous and the temptations great. First, most consumer goods are in short supply. Second, one region may have been loaded up with felt shoes and rubber boots when it needed sandals and hosiery. A cumbersome bureaucracy often makes it impossible to get the right goods at the right place at the right time. The oversupply of one product and the shortage of another excites adventuresome people to turn a penny. How extensive these black-market operations are is difficult to say. They are, however, so common as to plague the officials.

The government has also been plagued in recent months by speculation in tickets to theaters and to sports events. Tickets are often hard to get. So the ticket speculators have moved in. One finds them in the dark corners of the street. They do an active business. And Soviet law has not yet decided whether a theater ticket is included within "consumer goods," as those words are used in the criminal code.

The Soviets have not changed human nature. The lure of profits and the attraction of the private market in Russia are a powerful magnet to the people. Moscow has no plans to abolish it or curtail it. There is, however, a drive on to broaden the law against speculators and to make guilty not only the speculators but also those who sell to speculators with knowledge of the scheme. Another proposal seeks to sweep into the act anyone who buys more goods than his family needs.

We Americans are accustomed to the government delivering the mail, operating the TVA, insuring banks, putting floors under farm prices, managing national parks, subsidizing airlines, and the like. We are acquainted with municipal ownership of streetcars and waterworks. Perhaps we could imagine the government owning the steel mills and coal mines. But no concept of socialism we have ever known went to the extent of sweeping practically everything into the *public sector* and making the government the employer of most of the citizens. When one suddenly steps into an environment where that system prevails, it's as if he were on Mars.

As of the end of 1955, there were fifty-three federal ministries in Russia. There is under their wings a great beehive of industrial and financial activity. They control most of the commercial and business transactions in the entire nation. Under their auspices steel mills negotiate with coal mines and iron mines for raw materials; coal mines and iron mines negotiate with machine factories for their equipment; machine equipment plants negotiate with steel mills for their inventory, etc. The prices are fixed by the ministries with a view to making a profit for the seller. When the contracting plants are under the same minister, he fixes the price. But whether they are under the same or under different ministries, there are negotiations over quantities, time and place of deliveries, qualities of products, etc. The flow of raw materials within the Soviet industrial plant and the Soviet agricultural economy is dependent on these contracts. The contracts are subject to much dispute, so much so that arbitration tribunals or courts have been created to deal with them. Every ministry has its own arbitration tribunal adjudicating disputes between organizations within that ministry. For disputes between organizations attached to different ministries, an arbitration court called *Gosarbitzrah* was created. The *Gosarbitzrah* can award money judgments; and it may also decree specific performance—e.g., that the work be done again, that defective materials be replaced with good materials, that the inventory withheld be delivered, etc. The extent of the controversies over these contracts between trusts or organizations under different ministries is shown by the fact that the *Gosarbitz-rah* handles some 400,000 complaints a year.

Municipal government in Russia is also involved in a vast bureaucracy. Each town has a mayor and a board of aldermen, all of whom are elected. A council is selected from the board of aldermen. That council plus the mayor are the active managers of city affairs. Whenever I met a mayor my first question was "How many people are on the city payroll?" The answers gave high figures, amounting on the average to at least half of the people in the larger towns and cities. Novosibirsk is a Siberian town of 800,000. It is being rebuilt into a lovely, beautiful city that someday soon will vie with Russia's best. It has a large steel plant, a shoe factory, a plant that makes electric bulbs, and other factories in light industry. I asked the Mayor what percentage of the 800,000 people worked for the city. His reply was 60 per cent.

In Russia, as in this country, municipal government offers health, police, educational, legal, and recreational services. But in Russia the municipality also runs the streetcars and buses, the electric lights, the telephones, the theaters. It furnishes the doctors, dentists, and hospitals. It employs the plumbers and electricians. It runs the retail stores (except the co-ops and the free markets I have mentioned). All manufacturing, mining, and transportation are run by the central government. The center runs the banks; it engages in the insurance business, writing most every type of insurance which we have in America except liability insurance. (There's no liability insurance in Russia.) As I said, these various activities are under a host of different ministries. The farms are under other ministries. A city in order to run its affairs must therefore deal with a large number of different ministries.

A municipality in order to get the inventory for its retail stores has to bargain with those ministries. First, it prepares a list of all the articles it will need for all its stores during the coming year. These are made out in detail—so many buttons of this size and that, so many women's slippers size 5½ and so many of the other sizes, so many needles, so many pounds of lard, so much milk and cheese, so many bottles of cognac, ad infinitum.

The lists of the various articles go to the respective ministries in charge of their distribution. I gathered that the city consistently overstates its requirements and that the ministry in question uniformly shaves down the requests. The ministry determines the quota of each item allotted to each city for the following year; and it ships the goods to the city at a price fixed by Moscow. I asked what happened when the entire stock of a particular commodity was sold—whether new orders would be filled. The answer was uniformly the same. "Sometimes new orders will be filled. Usually not." In other words, the city must forecast demand a year in advance and abide by the result—a condition that gives rise to scarcity in some places and surplus in others, attracting the speculator.

The price at which the city may resell is also fixed by Moscow. How great the margin is I could not learn. But the profit is a substantial one. That profit is the main income of the city. The city also receives the income of theaters and parks and the revenues of streetcar lines, buses, electric plants, and waterworks. But they are secondary in character. The profits of the city from retail stores constitute the main municipal income.

As I have said, this profit from the retail stores must pay the salaries of all the city officials and all employees of the city who work in the *public sector*. That includes, of course, the doctors and nurses and the actors in the local theater. Streetcar and bus fares are fixed so as to create a reserve for depreciation and obsolescence. But most of the city's improvements must be financed by the central government.

Capital expenditures are customarily financed in one of two ways. If there is a bridge to construct, a new factory to erect, a waterworks to install, the central government finances it either through outright grants or through loans from either the Industrial Bank or the Municipal Bank, two of the four investment banks created by Moscow for the making of long-term loans. But many of the capital expenditures in the city are made by the major industries located there. These industries are formed into trusts, all state owned. But they have a large degree of local autonomy. They are supposed to take care of the needs of the people who work in their factories. Thus a textile mill will build the entire settlement where its workers live. It will put up schools and hospitals, build homes and apartment buildings, make parks, and provide all the other community facilities its workers need, being financed at times by the Industrial Bank.

In Novosibirsk, the central government was financing a mile-long, modern bridge across the Ob River and a 400,000-kw. electric power plant upstream. But most of the new building in town was being done by the local factories. The importance of the latter activities is evidenced by the fact that Novosibirsk's city budget for 1955 was 300,000,000 rubles ($24,000,000). The local factories added 407,000,000 ($33,000,000) as their contribution.

There is no municipal borrowing in Russia. Not even a state (republic) can borrow money. Only the central government can do that.

The Kremlin is the stockholder of all the factories, airlines, railroads, ships, and state farms in the nation. The Kremlin is not only the stockholder; it is the board of directors also. It must determine prices, costs, labor policies, production quotas, and all the infinite details of the business. The task of the Kremlin is staggering. It must determine how much of everything there will be each year—

pins, buttons, nail files, collar buttons, corsets, etc. It must determine what factories can produce what commodities, what quotas will be fair, what the managerial capacity will be. Managers vary in ability. Some labor forces are more efficient than others. Some will have production problems others do not know. The Kremlin must be all-wise and omniscient.

The Kremlin needs severe controls over its managers. It has as one of its controls a system of cost accounting for every one of its producing units. As near as I could learn, this cost accounting system follows classical lines. It is designed as a control over the local managers. The denunciations which the Kremlin now and then makes of local managers are often based on the auditors' reports.

Since the Kremlin is both the stockholder and the directors and since the Kremlin also makes and unmakes the laws, it can with impunity dip into depreciation reserves for operating deficits; or it may declare itself huge dividends, even though the plant is in the red. The extent to which the Kremlin takes only profits from the enterprise is not known. But the importance of its position as stockholder is seen from the budget figures. The Kremlin's budget has three sources of income, of which earnings from industry are by far the largest:

Taxes .... 2 per cent
Loans .... 5 per cent
Earnings from industry .... 93 per cent

The income from taxes is low because most of the taxes go to the state governments. The republics collect the taxes and, with the approval of the Kremlin, keep as much as they need for their governmental purposes. Usually the states keep 80 per cent, remitting 20 per cent to Moscow.

The Kremlin's borrowing serves an important function. Since the Kremlin owns the major industries and all the banks, it need not borrow. But it does; and the purpose is to reduce the purchasing power of the people.

Those bonds, which run for twenty years, are mostly bought by the workers either with money in their savings bank accounts or from payroll deductions. Under Stalin, workers were required to contribute one month's pay to the purchase of the bonds. Under Malenkov, the requirement was relaxed, only two weeks' pay being demanded. In 1955 the one-month requirement was restored.

Soviet officials told me that these bonds carry interest of 4 per cent. They do—in a limited and queer sense. The bonds carry lottery rights. There is an annual lottery in which drawn numbers will receive the face amount of the bonds, plus prizes. Over a period of twenty years prizes will equal 4 per cent of the total value of the bond issue. But only 35 per cent of all the bonds will win prizes. The remaining 65 per cent will be redeemed without any interest. Thus the bonds are interest-free in the conventional sense.

The Kremlin has played fast and loose with its bondholders. Soviet bonds issued during World War II carried ordinary interest at 4 per cent. But the Kremlin ordered those bonds exchanged for 2 per cent bonds! It went even further and ordered an old bond of the face value of three rubles to be exchanged for one new bond of the face value of one ruble.

In the capitalist world, deflation and inflation take their toll. Under our legal system, insolvent debtors sometimes settle for a third of the debt. But we have never had a government that used confiscation as a weapon against the people.

CHAPTER 4

SOVIET AGRICULTURE

A farmer is healthy in spirit and body wherever one finds him. Living close to the soil produces a humble soul. It generates respect for the mysteries of life that give endless crops and species. The farmer knows that the time of the seed, the time of the flowering, the time of harvest, the time of rest are the symphony of nature. Man can produce new ideologies; but nature has her own scheme that man can only discover, not change.

I found the Russian farmer no exception. Of course he was often naïve and usually ignorant of our way of life. I would often be asked about "the peasants" of America, the way they lived, if they owned their own farms, and so on. The Russian farmer, like the factory worker, has learned of America only through highly colored news accounts and radio broadcasts. So he can be forgiven for his ignorance. But he needs no apology for his genuineness and straightforwardness. He is not a cowed, groveling person. He is robust and friendly. He has roots deep in Russia's soil. He is, therefore, devoted to his nation. He is not greatly concerned with dogma and ideology. He has pride in his fields, orchards, and livestock. But he does not have the chance to express that pride, to pour into the farm his enthusiasm and affection. The Russian farmer is hedged in by politics and red tape. He lacks the incentives for production. Not since Stalin collectivized the farm has he known the thrill of private initiative and freedom. A Russian farmer would feel very much at home on an American farm. And he would soon find it offered him greater opportunities than he had ever dreamed.

I came out of Russia convinced that there is no agrarian institution that is superior to the one-family farm, so firmly established in America. A man with his own garden, fields, and livestock has incentives for production and a personal interest in the enterprise that I have not found equaled. The lack of incentives and a lagging personal interest are indeed the great weaknesses in Russia's farm system.

Both the collective farms and the state farms are large units. The collectives farm from 2000 to 75,000 acres. The state farms on the average are larger, more of them being in the 50,000- to 75,000-acre bracket.

A state farm, like a Soviet factory, is under a manager responsible to a ministry. Below the manager is the labor force, all working on a salary. The state needs to set up controls around a collective in order to control its production and the prices at which it sells. The MTS (Machine Tractor Station) is one of those controls. But the state farm, like the U.S. Forest Service in our Department of Agriculture, is a governmental agency. There is no private ownership interest in it. The manager is named by the state, not elected by the workers. There is, therefore, no need for the MTS. Each state farm has its own machinery. The state need not buy the produce, for all of it is state-owned.

There is an intricate system of supervision and control over the collective farm. The committee in charge of the collective has authority to operate within the limits of the production plan laid down by the state. The committee has bookkeepers, accountants, and other controls of management. But it has other persons to reckon with. In the first place MTS has its men and women on the collective. They serve as a check on the management. The collective may have a loan from the Agricultural Bank, in which event there are more bureaucrats inspecting the place. The ministry in charge of receiving the annual quota of food and produce from the farm has its officials nosing around. The Minister of Agriculture has deputies and agronomists and secretaries with roving commissions to look into the affairs of the collectives.

All farms—whether state or collective—have another agency supervising them. There is a party cell—a small, well-organized, energetic unit of the Communist party—on every farm. It is all ears and all eyes, looking into books and accounts, the efficiency of members, the educational program in the schools, and all the myriad activities of the farm. It uncovers violations of rules and procedures. It reports whether tractor operators use too much gasoline or oil. It passes judgment on the breakdown of production, the storage of grain, the stacking of hay, the crossbreeding of pigs, the desirability of a comrade spending as much as four hours a day in his garden plot.

In Russia, the Communist party is given great authority and great responsibility too. Its officers are blamed for poor results even in the field of agriculture. The party organization on a farm is the general staff for that farm. It receives the whispered complaints and the indignant letters. It issues its orders and commands. It threatens, flatters, and cajoles. While the Communists on the farm spy on the farm officials, the other agencies I mentioned spy on the Communist officials. In Russia there is no belief that officials, operating on their own, can or will produce results. External controls are provided; and these controls proliferate until everyone is spying on everyone else. That is, of course, a slight exaggeration. But it is a prominent characteristic of agricultural Russia. I was amazed at the progress made in the face of this great loss of freedom and initiative.

Inefficiency or neglect in agricultural matters often leads to severe penalties. Shortly before I reached Kazakhstan, an agronomist, A. G. Skolenko, was tried for criminal neglect of her duties. She had 500 acres of corn sown with a seed drill intended for the sowing of wheat. Most of the seed was wasted and the entire field had to be resown. She was convicted of criminal negligence and sentenced to one year of "corrective labor." In addition she was fined 25 per cent of her year's wages. When I was in Kazakhstan, a director of a state farm was being prosecuted for falsely reporting that by May 10, 1955, his farm had sown 500 acres of corn, when in fact not one acre had been sown at that time. A combine operator was being prosecuted for cutting barley too high, resulting in many heads being lost. Another combine operator had just received a two-year suspended sentence for leaving his machine unguarded while he left the field. During his absence other farm employees stole some of the grain.

The state farm is presently favored by the Kremlin over the collective, as evidenced by the fact that the newly established farms are almost uniformly state-owned. I was told at the Kremlin that the state farm makes a more efficient use of manpower than the collective. I had independent evidence that this was the case.

An Iowa farmer with 160 acres of corn and hogs may operate his farm without outside help; or if help is needed, he may have but one assistant who is either a hired hand or a member of the family. In Russia, one sometimes finds one worker to forty acres of wheat or corn land, but more often one worker to twenty acres or less. Roughly speaking, agricultural Russia *averages* five times the number of people to the acre as America and often has ten times the number of workers per acre.

In America one man occasionally cares for 500 hogs or even more. In Russia it is common to find one woman caring for only 10 hogs. (On the average one person takes care of 100 pigs in Russia.)

The examples could be multiplied on end. As the American farm delegation that visited Russia in 1955 reported, Russian agriculture has many deficiencies when measured by American standards, the most conspicuous of which is the overstaffing of collective farms. The statistics are not available. But one has only to visit a few collectives to see the needlessly extravagant labor force they have.

A large labor force might be necessary if feudal farming techniques were still in use in Russia. But they are not. Russia has gone far towards scientific farming. Between 80 per cent and 90 per cent of the Soviet farms are mechanized. By our standards, some of that machinery is out of date. Much of it is at the stage of development of our own agricultural implements during the 1930s. But though much of the machinery is outdated, it does the daily job. Tractors, cultivators, corn ensilage cutters, wheat combines, cotton pickers—and most of the other agricultural implements that other nations have—work the Russian soil. Some are Russian inventions; many are copied from American machines bought by Russia in the 1930s or acquired under Lend-Lease. Some doubtless are offspring of the International Harvester plant confiscated by Russia in the '20s.

On the state farms, the machinery is owned and operated by the farm. On the collective, MTS not only supplies the machinery; it furnishes the operators of the machines as well. Those employees of MTS often live on the collective, giving it all their services.

The MTS for one district may service several collectives. At Alma Ata, capital of Kazakhstan, I visited Kaskelen MTS, under the management of forty-year-old M. A. Dacevich, a plump, happy, dynamic Russian. This MTS services five collective farms.

The Kaskelen MTS, like other stations, assigns operators to each collective on a permanent basis. It has 400 employees, 240 of whom operate the machines for the five collectives. They, in fact, live on those farms permanently and are a part of its life. In case of breakdowns the machines are brought to Kaskelen's central depot for repair. Eighteen men do nothing but repair tractors.

The administrative office of Kaskelen has a large bookkeeping staff. It also has a short-wave radio set that is in communication with each of its field brigades on each collective. Each brigade has a call number and can be reached at all times. When I was there we talked with brigade No. 7, cultivating at a remote point on one of the farms. We found out how many hectares had been cultivated that morning, how many remained to be done.

Kaskelen was a highly efficient business unit, as were the other MTS stations I saw. It had competent management, skilled mechanics and operators, and fairly modern machinery. It brought to five collective farms which not many years ago were old-fashioned, feudal agricultural units, modern methods of cultivation.

What Kaskelen does for five collectives, other MTS stations do all over Russia. There are in Russia 9000 MTS's serving about 90,000 collective farms. One has to see the MTS stations and the farming operations to appreciate the high degree of mechanization that Russian agriculture has achieved. The extent to which farm machinery is used is illustrated by figures I obtained from the Minister of Agriculture of Uzbekistan, a tall, thin, professional-looking Uzbek. Uzbekistan, whose capital, Tashkent, lies at about the same latitude as Akron, Ohio, has approximately 146,000 square miles, a territory just under Montana's. In Uzbekistan, there are 265 MTS stations that service all the collective farms in that republic. These MTS's in 1955 had the following equipment:

24,800	plowing tractors
30,000	cultivating tractors
1,375	wheat combines
15,000	cotton pickers
2,100	bulldozers
100,000	other farm machines

In Russia, mechanization in wheat, cotton, corn, and sugar beets is so complete that there is little need for manual labor. At most airports I saw small planes that dust or spray cotton, wheat, and potatoes, that spread fertilizers, and that sow grasses. Sprinkler irrigation is common for cotton and hay. Most cultivating, plowing, and seeding on all farms is by machinery. Of course, tomatoes, cucumbers, grapes, apples, and many other fruits and vegetables require much manual labor. And cows must still receive individual attention. (In Russia, the milkers are usually women.) But there is usually a machine where technology permits it; and most of the machines I saw are Russian-made.

The mechanization of Russian farms has, of course, vastly increased their production. But it has also displaced a great number of workers. The tractor alone takes the place of dozens or perhaps hundreds of people on a single farm. The MTS, by bringing onto the collective its own skilled operators, has created a further labor surplus.

Over half of these surplus laborers on the collective farm are women. The work they and the men do is sometimes practically useless.

They follow combines with rakes to gather the meager leavings.

Wagons pulled by horses follow machines cutting corn and haul silage back to ensilage cutters. The wagons are filled with women, many more than necessary for the job.

Other women follow the machines in the field, picking corn

that machines might as well pick and carrying it in their aprons to central depots.

Cotton plantations, wholly mechanized except for thinning and irrigating, commonly have hundreds of people who only spend part time at farming. Some tend gardens; others care for cows, pigs, and chickens. Most of them turn their energies to their own garden plots.

At a fanning mill where grain is cleaned, many women will be carrying the grain in baskets from piles on the ground to the hopper. The labor saving of the machine is lost by the absence of mechanical means to lift the grain from the ground to the hopper.

Great combines will cut and thresh the grain. But the straw will be stacked by hand.

Milking machines are used on most dairy farms. But the manner of getting feed to the cattle involves, by American standards, a lot of needless manual labor.

There are very few livestock fences in Soviet Russia. The number I saw on my long journey could be counted on one hand. Girls, boys, old men and women herd all the livestock, from sheep and cattle to ducks and geese. Simple fencing would save much Russian labor.

A state farm has no such problems. It can keep its labor force down by shipping excess workers to other areas. There are fewer workers per acre on the state farms. Wherever there is mechanization, the state farm shows smaller work hours per unit of production.

Wheat is highly mechanized, whether grown by the collective or by the state farm. State farms produce on the *average* 1 metric centner (220.46 pounds or 3.7 bushels) of wheat for 2½ hours of work. The best state farms produce 1 centner of wheat for 1½ hours of work. No collective has as good a record. On the *average* they produce 1 centner of wheat for 4 hours of work.

The extent of the oversupply of farm labor is indicated by the fact that in Russia about 40 per cent of the labor force is in agriculture, in America only 12 per cent.

From the over-all viewpoint, Russian agriculture is making progress and in another decade or two will probably equal ours. Certainly no one in Russia is starving; and there has been no rationing of food since 1947. Russia, like the United States, rarely suffers a complete crop failure since the territory is so vast that weather conditions tend to balance out.

Russia's agricultural economy is adequate in the sense that it provides enough food to avert famine or starvation. The agricultural economy is inadequate in that it does not produce the variety the Russians want and need. Bread is plentiful and cheap. Bread, grain, and potatoes constitute three fourths of the caloric content of the Russian diet. Meat and most other proteins are scarce and expensive. Meat comes close to 12 rubles or 96 cents per pound, though inferior grades may sell for 75 or 80 cents per pound. At the current wage rate, a pound of meat may cost 40 per cent of a day's pay. As a result, the average Russian has meat perhaps once a week.

The scarcity of proteins was one basic cause of the struggle for power between Malenkov and Khrushchev. Malenkov, in order to build up Russia's cattle, pigs, and sheep, proposed feeding them more grain. More grain was allotted to them; but the results were not pronounced. It takes time to build up herds and get meat products on the markets. The grain that was used for livestock was missed in the Russian homes. Malenkov's program was sound in the long run; but it meant temporary privations. Khrushchev with his ear to the ground decided that Malenkov's project would not be popular with the people. Khrushchev won in his bid for power, and Malenkov stepped down on February 8, 1955. Khrushchev thereupon began to push his vast, virgin land program vigorously. That program calls for the plowing and planting of 75,000,000 acres of virgin land by 1957. It lies for the most part in southwest Siberia and northern Kazakhstan. It had never before been tilled; it was land covered by sod never broken by the plow. Forty-three million acres were plowed and planted in 1954 and 1955; the rest will be under cultivation by 1957. And as I left Russia there was talk that new virgin lands farther east in Siberia would be turned over to wheat.

The main purpose of the plan is not to supply more cereals for human consumption but to release wheat lands, primarily in the Ukraine, for the production of corn. Wheat will be grown on the virgin lands. The new corn crops of the Ukraine will be used for cattle and pigs. Then Russia will at long last have the cheese, the steaks, and the chops for which her people are hungry.

I visited Siberia to see some of this land and spent a day at the Komsomolsky State Farm which is about an hour's drive out of Barnaul. This is a 47,500-acre farm in country that looks like the rolling land of northern Minnesota and southern Canada. The ravines are thick with a species of beech. There are long stretches of pine running like fingers into the prairie, pine that reminded me of the jack or black pine of our Far West. There are a few ponds and springs in this region, not many creeks or rivers. Most of the water must come from deep, driven wells. Though this region is mid-Russia, it lies between 53° and 55°—the latitude of Edmonton and Grande Prairie, Canada, respectively.

The summers are short; the winters are severe; and there is much snow. The rainfall is only between twelve and fourteen inches a year, too scanty, many thought, for extensive dry farming. But the Kremlin gave orders; and the scientists went to work. They learned that spring wheat will grow there.

When Khrushchev sent down the orders to convert this virgin land into wheat fields, there was a frenzy of activity. The Komsomol (the Young Communist League) moved into action and established many farms, one of them being the Komsomolsky farm at Barnaul. The director of the farm, L. J. Pyjikov, told me that all of the men and women who came there did so voluntarily. That may well be. But when I reached Moscow, I learned that labor was in effect often drafted for these new farms. For example, when the appeal was made to one government agency in Moscow for farm laborers, only thirty volunteered their services. The quota, however, was sixty. So thirty others were assigned by that agency to farm work. (I got my story from one of the latter group.)

However the labor may have been recruited, the farms sprang up like mushrooms. In two years, 450 new farms were established, numbering in size from 25,000 to 75,000 acres. The government assigned to those 450 farming units 76,000 tractors with skilled operators and mechanics to run and maintain them. Engineers moved in to make surveys, to lay out roads, to provide water supplies. Prefabricated houses were shipped in by the thousands. Clerks, chauffeurs, and other white-collar help, employed in the big cities, became farmers overnight.

Great inducements were offered to those who came to the virgin lands. For the first year, treble salaries were paid. (The regular salaries range from $65 a month for unskilled farm labor to $200 a month for tractor operators.) Moreover, those who came to Siberia for farm work were advanced 10,000 rubles (roughly $800) towards a house. Each person was also given 2000 rubles (approximately $160) as a fund to buy livestock for his private tract of land. With these inducements, several hundred people moved onto the site selected for Komsomolsky State Farm. They lived at first in tents, working feverishly to get their houses up before winter.

The first houses erected were frame buildings with a roof and an exterior of a composition board reminding me of our asbestos shingle. The houses built later on were made of brick in order to provide greater warmth. Each house has four rooms, a coal stove for heating, and an outhouse. No house has running water as yet. Each has electricity from a local diesel plant. Some houses have radios. Most get their news from a radio turned on full blast and fastened to a pole outside the administration building. Water is supplied from two 80-foot artesian wells; and women carry it in buckets at the end of long poles over their shoulders.

The residential part of the village sits on a low, flat ridge. Here are a kindergarten to care for children of working women, a seven-grade elementary school, a fifteen-bed hospital, a bakery, state retail grocery and clothing stores, and a makeshift administration building. Most of these buildings are of brick. A new administration building is going up that will have a theater and many recreation halls. But there is no church; and none will be built, for the Kremlin does not favor religion.

A half mile to the south across a shallow ravine is the industrial part of the state farm. There is a large crane for lifting tractors onto repair racks, numerous repair shops, a nest of fuel oil tanks, and a host of farm machinery, the most conspicuous of which are forty-two combines and fifty-six large tractors. On my September visit the shallow ravine between the industrial and residential parts of the state farm had acres and acres of cabbage growing on the farmers' private plots.

Mr. and Mrs. Pyjikov are near forty and parents of two attractive teen-age children and lovely twelve-year-old Vera who would bring joy to any home. Pyjikov is a dedicated man, a managerial product of Russia's system. He's able, energetic, imaginative; and he has tremendous drive. Komsomolsky is his life. He lives its problems; and every breath is taken in its cause. We sat at his dining-room table and talked while we ate. Mrs. Pyjikov, a bustling homemaker and an excellent cook, served piping hot cabbage soup, the best I ever ate. We had a kippered fish (carp, I believe) and fresh lamb on a skewer. As we ate, we covered many of the problems between Russia and America and all of the problems of Komsomolsky. The farm is isolated and remote, at least thirty miles out of Barnaul on miserable roads. I had seen no automobiles parked near any of the farmers' cottages and asked Pyjikov how

ASHKHABAD

Turkmen players at Ashkhabad held an audience spellbound with old Turkish songs.

A grape arbor on a collective farm near Ashkhabad is a social center.

There is much haggling at the private-farm markets of Ashkhabad.

Turkmen traders carry on a brisk business at the private farmers' market near Ashkhabad.

ASHKHABAD

The burro is still the main vehicle for country travel in Turkmenistan.

Camels are both transport and suppliers of milk and meat in Turkmenistan.

Uzbeks take a morning bre for melons at a collective farm near Tashkent.

An Uzbek feast on a collective farm near Tashke includes twenty-one course

the workers got back and forth. Some have bicycles for the long trek; most travel by a bus which the state furnishes. On a Saturday or Sunday the bus will load up and take off to town. Apart from those occasions the workers are pretty much isolated.

"We entertain ourselves," Pyjikov told me.

Komsomolsky has a soccer team. Musical and theatrical talent has been uncovered among the workers. They put on plays and musicales. Soon the teams and troupes of Komsomolsky will be on the road, entertaining in other villages and participating in competitions. Soon other teams and troupes will be visiting Komsomolsky.

I went on a tour of the farm, traveling over twenty miles to cross it. I saw corn, not much more than waist-high, raised for silage. I saw almost endless wheat fields (some nearly three miles long) being cut by huge Russian combines, flying the Red flag. This wheat land in 1954 produced twenty-four bushels to the acre. But in 1955 there was a drought, no rain falling after May. So the 1955 crop was skimpier, the average yield being twelve bushels to the acre. This record was better than that of the new virgin lands in northern Kazakhstan. Near Akmolinsk about sixteen bushels of wheat to the acre were raised in 1954; but in 1955 only five bushels.

I asked Pyjikov if the danger of drought did not imperil the virgin-land project. His dynamic response was the same I got later in Moscow when I talked to the ministries about the problem.

"We can meet costs here and afford to grow wheat if we get only 1.4 centners per hectare," he said. And 1.4 centners per hectare is only a shade more than two bushels per acre!

I went on to tell him of America's dust bowl problems. I said that we had put the plow to land that should have been kept in buffalo grass and that the consequences were dire. I explained how searing winds that blotted out the sun with dust had burned the crops.

Pyjikov knew almost as much about our dust bowl as I did. He admitted that this new Siberian land held that risk. But he had an answer. First, he planned to control some of the erosion by methods of plowing. Second, he would put up shelter belts. He mentioned particularly the beech trees I had seen and said that those trees were being planted in depth at regular intervals, so as to break the winds and catch the snows. He had read of Roosevelt's shelter belt across our Great Plains and set that as his example.

I left this friendly, dynamic man wondering how anyone could marshal for this bleak spot in Siberia the enthusiasm and affection he expressed. When I stepped outside his small frame residence to walk to the car, he and his wife and Vera joined me. The sun was getting low and there was a piercing chill in the air. It was only the first week of September but fall had come to Siberia. When we had toured the farm earlier, it had been clear and calm. Now a cold wind came down from the north. It came in gusts, as hearty as the Russian farmer himself. And with it came great billows of dust, so thick they blotted out a young Russian mother and her child who bent into it on their way along the unpaved street to their home. I knew then—and was to hear later in Moscow—that the potential dust bowl was, indeed, Khrushchev's big gamble in the virgin lands, that Malenkov was on much stronger ground with his livestock program.

Pyjikov followed me to the car, continuing to talk about Komsomolsky with the enthusiasm of a chamber of commerce representative. He must have noticed my concern about the swirling dust, for he told me another interesting fact about the farm. The Minister of Agriculture had assigned to it twenty-five graduates of agricultural colleges. They are experts in soil and wheat, giving full time to the problems of the farm. They are concerned with developing new species of wheat and corn, with meeting the threat of the dust bowl, with analyzing the chemistry of the Siberian soil. Some of the scientists believe that the soil is deficient for wheat and, over the years, will need much fertilizing.

"Soviet science will find the answer to all our problems," Pyjikov said just before we drove off in a cloud of dust.

Certainly it will, if Soviet science can match in ability the enthusiasm of the director of Komsomolsky.

Russia fairly crawls with agricultural experts or, as the Russians say, "specialists." These experts or specialists are mostly college graduates in agriculture. Russia is strong in agricultural education. About 1000 secondary schools offer agricultural education, and 97 agricultural academies offer graduate work. In addition, there are 1000 agricultural experiment stations in Russia. Qualified students enter the agricultural academies at the end of the tenth grade. The agricultural course is usually four years. On graduation the student is assigned by the Ministry of Agriculture to some farm, to an MTS, to a research laboratory, or to another governmental project. Some collective farms have their own agricultural experts. Most of the collectives, however, are serviced by experts assigned by the MTS. The 9000 MTS stations in Russia have 200,000 agricultural experts servicing 90,000 collective farms.

The Kaskelen MTS near Alma Ata, which I have mentioned, has thirty-two agricultural experts serving the five collective farms under it. These thirty-two men and women have various specialties—soil, wheat, beets, corn, cattle, sheep. They are furnished the collectives free of charge. Some are permanently attached to a collective; but more frequently they function as a pool of experts for all the collectives under the particular MTS.

State farms, such as Komsomolsky in Siberia, have their own experts. The 5000 state farms in the U.S.S.R. have 35,000 agricultural experts guiding their programs, advising on fertilizers, inspecting fields for disease, etc.

All told, Russia has 235,000 experts in agriculture, not including specialists without college degrees. And the agricultural colleges are turning out 25,000 graduates a year, as compared with our 8500. As I traveled Russia, I wondered how the farms could profitably use so many scientists, whether a lesser number at central points might not do as well or better. In Moscow I got an interesting reply. The Minister of State Farms, Ivan Benedictov, laughed when he said:

"We have so many farm specialists we do not know what to do with them."

Most Russian agricultural academies have pictures of Darwin, Burbank, and the famous Russian agriculturist, Michurin, on their walls. But the man who has dramatized Russian agricultural theory is T. D. Lysenko, the geneticist who believes that the heredity of a plant can be changed by environment, a theory that Julian Huxley explodes in *Heredity East and West*. American agriculture has been hitched to the Mendelian theory of stable inheritance factors carried in genes. Under the Mendelian school of thought, evolution consists in a change in the hereditary constitution brought about by natural selection in favor of the possessors of certain genes and certain mutations as against others. Thus, under the stimulus of environment or other factors, certain characteristics emerge and become predominant.

We select strains, inbreed to fix desirable characteristics, and then cross to produce hybrid seeds. Russians talk a lot about hybrids, especially in corn. But their hybrids are only straight crosses of open-pollinated varieties. Russia has no hybrid corn as we know it.

But this does not mean that Russian agricultural progress is nil or that its agricultural scientists are all a poor lot.

I had a good impression of the agricultural colleges and institutes. Agricultural education in Russia is on the whole of a high quality. That, I believe, was the judgment of Dean W. V. Lambert of the University of Nebraska, head of the American farm delegation, whom I met in Tashkent. Their equipment is often obsolete by our standards. Their curriculum emphasizes science, not the humanities. But in the main they are doing a good job in training agricultural scientists. These days Lysenko comes in for criticism and gets little praise.

In research the Russians are as busy as beavers. From 1953–54 they published nearly twice the number of technological pamphlets on agriculture as we did.

The Russian scientists have developed long staple cotton (irrigated) that has the same production per acre as our best.

Russian scientists have made considerable progress in wheat. The production figures for the republic of Kirgizia (that borders on Afghanistan) are the following for irrigated land:

       1913 – 12 to 14 metric centners* per hectare†
       1940 – 14 to 15   ··   ··   ··   ··
       1954 – 18 to 20   ··   ··   ··   ··

For non-irrigated land the Kirgizia figures are:

       1913 – 5 to 6 metric centners per hectare
       1940 – 9 to 10   ··   ··   ··   ··
       1954 – 9 to 10   ··   ··   ··   ··

At Tashkent I saw a research institute that has made important contributions to increased production in the last few years. It has increased potatoes from 11 tons per hectare to 14 tons (two crops a year); onions from 22 tons to 35 tons per hectare; tomatoes from 35 to 56 tons per hectare.

The Russians have done extensive research on grasses, seeking improved varieties for grazing. They have conducted extensive experiments designed to increase the weight of some sheep and the wool of others. Electric shears for sheepshearing are widely used. The Russians have introduced artificial insemination for sheep.

* 3.7 bushels per metric centner
† 2½ acres

They have inaugurated a greatly improved veterinary service. In Kazakhstan alone there are some 1300 veterinary and zootechnic stations with 5000 veterinary surgeons and assistants.

Some Russian farmers are off on tangents. Corn is planted in check rows; and all through Russia corn is cultivated twice or more each way. Four annual cultivations are deemed necessary because of the theory that capillary action in soil results in loss of moisture and that cultivation breaks up that capillary action. We abandoned that idea in the United States a quarter century ago and now cultivate largely to control weeds which absorb moisture and reduce fertility. Recently we substituted chemical treatment for at least one cultivation. Chemical treatment seems beyond the ken of the Russian scientists.

Night soil is still used as a fertilizer in Central Asia—to some extent on vegetables, mostly on sugar beets. In Siberia night soil is commonly used for wheat, never for vegetables.

Russia has the finest apples in Asia. But she has nothing to compare with the apples of Yakima, Washington. I felt her farmers had not yet learned the art of pruning that makes the strength of the tree go to fruit, not to wood.

Russian farmers are making great efforts to produce three ears of corn to the stalk, when they should be satisfied with one good ear.

Russia's scientists in animal husbandry are far behind ours. Russia has not specialized in beef cattle; and her beef is not first-class by our standards. Russian cattle are dual-purpose types. Her herds are a rather inferior lot; and they are about where they were in 1928, due in part to the great livestock losses suffered when Stalin forced collective farms on the people, and in part to World War II.

Russia has some extraordinary milk cows, such as the one I mentioned that produces 10,000 liters a year. But the Russian average is about 1000 liters. Russia's butter production is about where it was in 1913. And the degree to which Russia's milk problem is yet unsolved is indicated by the fact that 60 per cent of her milk cows are owned by individual farmers who are usually limited to one cow per family. Milk production for the urban masses is in its infancy.

There are many other inefficiencies in Russia's farming methods, apart from the overstaffed farms. Our farm delegation mentioned particularly:

—the need for more crop rotation, contour plowing, and terracing

—improved agricultural planning, as for example by planting grain sorghum in certain areas where corn is inefficiently grown

—the need to delay the harvesting of fodder crops so as to get greater tonnage.

By our standards Russia still has far to go in agriculture. By Asian standards she has already revolutionized it, increasing productivity and spreading the benefits to all the people. This revolution extends not only to agricultural production but to the agricultural community. One example concerns the sheepherders of Soviet Central Asia.

In the old days they moved with their cattle and sheep to the high Tien Shan Mountains in the late spring, following the green grass as high as it went and retreating to the plains with the first fall of snow. In central and northern Kazakhstan—the region of the great steppes—they followed the grass year around. Sometimes they had a sedentary unit of the family operating a farm. In that case they worked out of that base into the plains. Sometimes they were tied to no farm and no village. They and their families lived winter and summer on the vast steppes in rounded felt huts called *yurts*. From spring to fall most of these nomads were isolated from the towns and villages of the valley; some of them were isolated year around.

These nomads of Central Asia were rugged individualists who loved the freedom of the hills and prior to the Communists had never knuckled down to any authority. Today they do bow to authority. They are all organized into collective farms. All the livestock is collectively owned. The sheep and other animals are not owned by collectives dealing exclusively with livestock, but by those engaged in diversified farming. The herders receive their supplies by camel train brought from the collective farm in the valley to remote camps high in the mountains.

From 150 to 300 sheep and goats (or twenty camels) are assigned to one herder. Three men are always sent together, each working eight hours a day. Each takes his family. Some flocks have 3000 to 5000 sheep and goats. Hence the herders and their families make up a sizable unit, one that the government does not neglect.

High in the Tien Shan Mountains the government has erected permanent wooden villages for these people. They are at 10,000 feet or even higher. The *yurts* are still beyond them, close to the sheep. These villages, which are the main summer base for these people, have kindergartens for small children, schools through the seventh grade, and small hospital units. The government services them with mobile library units and an emergency air service. These villages have the ever-present radio blaring from the administration building. The government sends out theatrical troupes for the entertainment of the inhabitants.

The nomad still wears his great karakul hat or a conical one made of felt with trimmings of fur. His belt is still of felt, worked with silver. He usually has a dagger on his hip. His womenfolk still have long braided hair and flowing skirts. The female, like the male, can ride with the wind. She can do even more—she can give birth today and be off tomorrow to a higher camp in the hills. These nomads still sing the same songs and dance the same dances as their ancestors. They still warm their *yurts* with fires made of dung. But unlike their ancestors they are a part of a highly regimented society that keeps a rein on them even in the remote Tien Shan.

The revolution that has touched sheepherding in Russia is a part of the organized effort of government to keep close tab on everyone and make sure he does not become an ideological stray.

The intensity of the organization of community life is evident on every Soviet farm. The Stalin Collective Farm out of Stalinabad is fairly typical. It has 3000 families and 15,369 people. It has 26,-160 acres under cultivation and 40,000 acres of grazing land for cattle, sheep, and goats. This farm is in one sense a world unto itself. It has 4000 children in school and 126 school teachers. All the schools go through the seventh grade except two, which go through the tenth. There are no illiterates on the farm. One hundred and sixteen of the older students are off to college.

The farm has seven clubhouses where plays and lectures are put on and where movies are shown. It has five libraries and three tearooms and several retail stores. It has twenty-two day nurseries and four kindergartens to accommodate the women who work. There are twelve doctors assigned to the farm, and eighteen nurses. The farm has one hospital, one clinic, one maternity home, and three first-aid stations. Babies are delivered on the farm; and all operations, including the most difficult, are performed there. Individual radios are scarce at Stalin Collective Farm. But there are six communal radio centers where the radio is going full blast all day long and part of the night.

Both the collective farm and the state farm are highly organized social and educational units. They cater to all the community needs of the people, except religion. The collective farms, like the state farms, have no churches on them. Each one I visited has its own theatrical and musical troupe; and most of them have an athletic team. These teams and troupes compete with other collective farms. In several of the state capitals I saw quartets, orchestras, and musical ensembles from collective farms and state farms competing on a state-wide basis. The winner would go on to Moscow for the final competition.

Each collective and each state farm is strong on "culture." Speakers are always on tour, lecturing the people. The lectures cover Marxism of course. But they also touch scientific subjects. Plays are produced; dances are held; the local orchestra gives concerts. Children's choruses are trained. Dancers and singers are given local lessons or sent to Moscow for advanced training. The emphasis throughout is on the glory of Russia and the achievements of the regime.

Housing on Russia's farms has been hardly touched by any revolution. In Central Asia farmhouses are about as primitive as they were a century ago. The houses are flat-roofed, mud affairs with outside plumbing and no running water, but often with electricity. Meals are cooked in the courtyard either over an open fire or on a charcoal brazier. The courtyard almost always is the home of a cow, a sheep, or a goat kept for milk. On several occasions I shared these courtyards with a friendly family and their livestock, eating delicious lamb cooked on a skewer over charcoal as we sat long into the night discussing Russia, America, and the problems of Soviet farmers. The interiors of these homes are usually austere— skimpily furnished with only bare necessities. Yet they are adequate. The courtyard usually has a plane or pepper tree growing in it. Outside there is invariably a long trellis covered with grapes. Here the family sleeps on a platform covered with Bukharan rugs. This platform stands about three feet off the ground and has a short railing around it to keep the sleeper from rolling out. Except for the winter months, the life of the family is in the courtyard and under the trellis.

The farmhouses up north are more dismal affairs. The barns and silos are made of brick and concrete. But the houses of the farmers are made of cheap clapboards or logs. They are usually three- or four-room affairs, poorly furnished and dominated by the ancient Russian heating and cooking stove whose rounded sides reach into at least three rooms. These homes were mostly furnished in *Tobacco Road* style. Yet the hospitality of the Russian family made me forget their dinginess.

The farmer in Russia has perquisites the factory worker does not know. He has his own garden plot; he's a merchant in the private market; he works in the open and has some of the liberty every farmer loves. On the whole, he fares more poorly than the factory worker. His average annual income from all sources is probably not more than $560 (7000 rubles) a year. Many make much more than that. I met officials of collective farms whose total income in 1954 was $7200 (90,000 rubles). I met many who earned as much as $1600 (20,000 rubles). But at the bottom are miserable people who barely make a living. Their farms are often uneconomical units that operate at the subsistence level. Drought, pests, floods, laziness, ineptitude take their toll in Russia as elsewhere. The marginal farmers in Russia pull the average down.

But this average income *by Asian standards* is remarkably high. In Iran there is no individual farmer or tenant farmer who makes more than $500 a year. The median agricultural income in Iran is probably $300 a year. And there are thousands of Iranian farmers who make less than $50 a year. The figure of $50 a year is India's average national income—an amount which Ivan Benedictov, Russia's Minister of State Farms, who once was Soviet Ambassador to India, insisted in his talk with me was above the average income of India's farmers. He maintained that the average Indian farm family has only $30 income a year.

Whatever the true figure may be, it is clear that Russia's farm income per person is far above the rest of Asia's. By Asian standards Russia has made great progress in agriculture.

To the Asian, the amount of farm machinery on Soviet farms tells an impressive story. Russia's extensive use of farm machinery is in great contrast to Asia's farming methods. In most Asian areas, the wooden plough that turns two inches of soil is still common-place. One finds some machinery in Egypt, Lebanon, Iran, and the countries of the Middle East. India is turning to mechanization. But by and large the old, primitive methods still obtain. Certainly none has made the progress in agriculture that Russia has. Russia's farms bear the same comparison with Asia's as our streamlined trains do with horse-and-buggy transport.

American farmers, seeing Russia's agriculture, might not be too impressed. But Asians who see it are certain to be enthusiastic, for it is leagues ahead of theirs. It is not our reaction but the Asians' that is the important one. For the contest for the hearts and minds of men will be won or lost in Asia.

CHAPTER 5

SOVIET INDUSTRY

I visited many stores and markets on my Russian journey, sometimes to make purchases, usually to window-shop. The stores of the co-operative societies, which I have already mentioned, are commonly small specialty shops similar to those we see on America's side streets. They may sell a few varieties of women's wear, or kitchen utensils, or furniture. The state stores are usually department stores. GUM is Moscow's Macy's. It faces Lenin's tomb, constituting one side of Red Square; and it takes up a square block. It has everything from needles to hats to bicycles. It is owned and operated by the state. Its prices are the prices of every state store in the far-flung Russian empire.

In these Russian state stores one often stands in line. When he makes his purchase, he does not pay the clerk, take the package, and leave. Rather, the article he has purchased goes back on the shelf (or sometimes into a locked showcase), while he gets into another line leading to the cashier. He purchases from the cashier a ticket bearing the price of the article. With that ticket in hand he once more gets into the line leading to the counter where he made the purchase. If the article has not been sold by the time he returns, he gets it on presentation of the cashier's ticket. If he wants another article that is at a different counter, he repeats the performance. This is the routine in most Russian stores. If one shops in a speciality store or at a delicatessen, this routine is of course not followed. After the purchaser has made his selection, the addition is done not by machine but by the ancient abacus known throughout Asia.

In 1955, a few serve-yourself grocery stores were established, and one state-owned and state-managed mail-order house. But the revolution in Soviet merchandizing methods is yet to occur.

Russia has been under communism for forty years, and still the consumer demands have barely been touched. One reason is the emphasis of the Kremlin on armaments. Another was the need to rebuild vast stretches of Russia that were seared and razed by the Nazi forces.

Since 1940, consumer goods have increased 112 per cent. But even so the shelves of the retail stores are fairly skimpy with goods. One can find most of the essentials and some luxuries; but the supply is limited, the prices are high, and the quality is below the lowest grade advertised in our Sears, Roebuck & Company catalog.

Good blankets cost $35, good comforters $40. Ordinary cotton stockings cost from 60 cents to $1.50, while rayons run from $2.00 to $2.50. A man's dress suit costs $145, a gabardine topcoat $85. A pair of men's dress shoes costs $48, a pair of women's shoes $50. Ladies' millinery cost from $7.50 to $12.50. An alarm clock that costs $1.98 here costs $3.65 in Russia. Tea towels are 80 cents each and linen ones $1.84, men's handkerchiefs 57 cents, a child's dress $21.36, a child's sandals $2.80. These prices are kept high to discourage purchases; and, as I have said, the quality is low and the supply skimpy.

In staples, the prices are not as high. Macaroni per box is from 16 cents to 24 cents; sugar, 32 cents a pound; corn meal, 20 cents; coffee, 21 cents. Butter is 33 cents per quarter pound; margarine is 32 cents for a half pint; mayonnaise, 42 cents per half pint. Salt herring is from 35 cents to 80 cents per pound. These prices are computed with the ruble at 8 cents, its approximate purchasing power in Russia. The American visitor, however, pays 25 cents for the ruble, which trebles the prices I have quoted.

Consumer goods have greatly increased since World War II; there has been no rationing since 1947. But the increase in consumer goods has been considerably less than the increase in producer goods.

While consumer goods were increasing 112 per cent from 1940 to 1955, producer goods were increasing 277 per cent. Some of these producer goods were for use in light industry that manufactures shoes, suits, and refrigerators. But the great emphasis in Russia has been placed on other branches of the economy. Between 1929 and 1952 the funds invested in capital construction were 72,000,000 rubles in light industry, 193,000,000 rubles in transport, and 638,000,000 rubles in heavy industry.

Those figures are translated into more understandable terms when it is realized that a housewife has great difficulty in getting sewing machines, washing machines, toasters, vacuum cleaners, electric plates, and refrigerators. The smaller electric items are sometimes seen in the state stores. But they are of poor quality and the prices are high. A one-burner electric plate costs $20. A small electric flatiron costs $5.00, an ordinary table lamp $6.00, a vacuum cleaner from $42 to $54. Small, cheap radios can be had for $4.00 to $6.00. Better sets are difficult to obtain. Though Russian sewing machines and washing machines exist, they are difficult to find. One waits months or even years. Russia has electric refrigeration; but the refrigerators are scarce. Up to 1948 there were no electric refrigerators available to householders. In 1955, only 115,-

ooo electric refrigerators were manufactured for home use. This supply hardly made a dent on the demand. And the prices are high. An apartment, efficiency-size refrigerator costs $125; one with five cubic feet, $165. There are, moreover, no installment sales in Russia. It's cash on the line. And the average worker makes only $600 a year.

Air conditioning is known in Russia. But it's not available for homes or hotels. The only air conditioning I found on my journey was in a few factories. Electric fans are also occasionally found on the market. But they are very scarce. Throughout all of Central Asia, where the temperature in summer stays close to 100° in the daytime, I saw only two electric fans. One was a tiny one, no bigger than a saucer; and it sat on the desk of the short, swarthy Tadzhik mayor of Stalinabad, Ahmad Asrorov.

In India and Pakistan, there are usually overhead fans in hotel rooms and restaurants. In the country districts where electricity is not available there is the *punka*, a long, overhead beam with a deep cloth flounce pulled by a rope at a speed adequate to keep flies from a repast. There are no overhead fans or *punkas* in Russia. One battles the flies on his own.

Some of the large cities have television; and it is fast coming to all the others. Radio centers such as Baku on the Caspian and Tashkent, deep in the heart of Central Asia, are building television towers. But though there is television, there are precious few television sets. In 1955 only 170,000 sets were manufactured in all of Russia. These had mostly an eight-inch screen, though some were in the seventeen-inch class. Russia is even short on razor blades. In 1955, each man got on the average only five blades.

Of the three Russian cars, the Zim is the most aristocratic, the Pobeda is the most popular, and the Moskvitch is the cheapest. One can get a Zim on fairly short notice, perhaps a few weeks. But there are few people in Russia—except government officials —who can afford a Zim. For the Zim costs $3500. The highest-paid skilled laborer gets no more than $3000 a year and, as I said, the average only $600. There are some doctors who make as much as $9000 a year; but they are few in number. Even the popular Pobeda is not within the reach of many people. For it costs $1350. Moreover, the Pobeda takes two years to get. The Moskvitch, which costs $675, is much in demand and is closer to the budget of the Russian worker. But one waits from six months to a year for a Moskvitch. The result is that in the main the bureaucracy owns the cars; very few ordinary folk own any.

I could not get the official figures of car ownership. But it is safe to say that while in this country there is on the average one passenger car to about three persons, in Russia there is not even one car to 100. In 1955 Russia produced 445,000 motor vehicles, it being estimated that 115,000 were passenger cars and 330,000 were trucks. During the same year America produced nearly 8,000,000 passenger cars and 1,500,000 trucks. On my Russian journey I used simple checks to measure car ownership. I discovered that few people ever go to church or to the theater by car. I found hundreds at meetings and not a single car parked outside. Filling stations are few and far between. There are not many garages in Russia. A person to get a driver's license must be able to take the engine apart and reassemble it. For the driver is expected to make his own repairs.

All the bureaucracy, including those at the ministerial level, speak of the great hunger for cars and for other consumer goods. It's a political ground swell that cannot be ignored even in a dictatorship. The ground swell expresses much more than a desire for consumer goods. It extends to the whole standard of living.

The Russian has been brought up under a materialist regime. He has had dinned into his ears since childhood the importance of the material needs of man and the promise of the Soviet system to satisfy them. Progress has been made. But Russia has a long way to go to raise her standard of living to ours.

In Russia there are few main highways that are paved and in good condition. The roads are in the main yet to be built.

The large Russian cities have good airports. But in the country at large the terminals are shacks and the runways are grass and gravel.

All the streets of Moscow and Leningrad are paved. In most Russian cities only the main streets are paved (many with cobblestones or wooden blocks), while the bulk of the town is stuck in mud on wet days and swept by whirlwinds of dust on dry, windy days.

Hotel accommodations are few. Those that exist in Moscow and Leningrad are quite adequate. In the newly built towns such as Alma Ata, Tashkent, and Stalinabad, there are some new hotels that compare favorably with second- and third-class European hotels. But their rooms are very limited in number and overcrowded. Many rooms are, indeed, dormitories where eight or a dozen people sleep on cots crowded together and share a common washroom and toilet down the hall. In the old towns such as Petropavlovsk, Kazakhstan, hotel accommodations are almost nonexistent. That city has a population of 125,000 and one hotel with eight rooms and five beds in each room. I stayed in Petropavlovsk two nights—in a sleeping car parked on a railroad siding.

The absence of any hotel accommodations or the availability of only a few rooms in a town often leads Soviet officialdom to make the city out of bounds to a foreigner. My hosts at first barred me from visiting Petropavlovsk. Having been barred from other restricted areas such as Leninabad, a supersecret city of atomic energy, I at first imagined that Petropavlovsk also contained a secret which the Soviets desired to keep from me. But it turned out that I was wrong. The Russians did not want me to visit the place because they had no hotel room there for me. The Russian, as a host, is first and always a considerate one. The Russian also has great pride, as great as our own. Neither we nor the Russians like to route a foreign visitor to places of squalor.

The hotel situation in Russia is so acute that Russia of necessity must restrict foreign travel. She has such limited hotel space, even in places the size of Stalingrad, that only a few foreigners can visit the city at a time.

Most of Russia is still in the "Chic Sale" era. Moscow and Leningrad have inside plumbing. The new and beautiful city of Tashkent, being constructed under the plans of an energetic, able Uzbek architect by the name of Bukalov, has a modern sewage system. Eventually the entire town will be hooked up to it. Today the new, modern section of Tashkent has plumbing. The rest of the town—or 50 per cent of the people—live in the old, flat-roofed, mud huts of their ancestors, with outside toilets. Stalinabad, a modern city on the hot plains north of Afghanistan, and Alma Ata and Frunze, fairly new cities tucked away at the base of the Tien Shan Mountains in the southeast corner of Russia, are mostly connected to sewage plants. Ancient Samarkand, where Timur and his offspring built great shrines, is only partly converted to modern plumbing. Samarkand is mostly in the outhouse era. Bukhara, full of history and romance, is untouched by modern technology. So far as I could ascertain, it has no plumbing. Its only hotel is served by a large outhouse at the rear.

The few modern hotels I found in Siberia have plumbing. And the new public buildings that are going up in towns such as Novosibirsk are modern in every respect. But apart from them, the run of public buildings have no plumbing. When I was with the Mayor of Pavlovsky, not far from Barnaul, I asked for the washroom or as the Russian vernacular has it—"the gents." I found it a hundred feet away on the alley behind the wooden frame building. And at Petropavlovsk I found that the toilet of the Regional Court was on a miserable alley and was as dirty as any I had seen.

There are elevators in Russia; but they are few and far between and mostly obsolete.

Twenty years ago Russian railroads had locomotives fired by wood. Today there are many coal-burning engines on the vast network of rails that link the remotest points in Russia to Moscow by double-tracked lines. And on the Trans-Siberian railroad I saw more diesels than coal-burning engines. Russia's freight cars are quite modern. But the signal system is antiquated and the roadbed seems to suffer from lack of proper maintenance. The passenger cars are mostly obsolete by American standards. No trains have dining cars. Passenger trains stop at every station, where one can purchase black bread, cheese, bologna, and tinned fish. Outside each station is a hot-water pipe and faucet, where passengers can get water for their tea.

Russia has very few sleeping cars as we know them. The berths on the Trans-Siberian are bare wooden shelves. A deluxe train, comparing favorably with our own, runs from Moscow to Leningrad. Each car has compartments containing upper and lower berths. But the train has no dining room. One gets only hot tea from the porter.

In some respects Russia has made great progress in housing. In Moscow there are shiny, new apartments, some of them in great skyscrapers that Stalin promoted. In the larger cities of Central Asia the apartments usually are three stories high, all walkups, since Central Asia is in the earthquake belt. Only a few are made of reinforced concrete. Most of them are brick, with steel frames and floors of wood. They have antique plumbing with the toilet separate from the bath; and they are heated by steam. Though of shabby construction, they are adequate for sanitary living—and they carry a very low rental.

A two-room apartment costs at the most $3.00 a month; and three-room apartments from $3.00 to $5.00 a month, depending on location and view. The rate also varies with the salary of the lessee, the rental in case of the lowest-paid worker dropping to $1.00 a month. The policy is to fix the rate at from 3 per cent to 5 per cent of the family income. Electricity and water are extra. The electric rate is 3 cents per kw. no matter how many kw.'s are used. Water is 8 cents a month and not metered.

Some cities have new small houses of four and five rooms with garden plots attached. They are owned by the worker and financed by the government on loans. They cost from $300 to $800. I saw workers' homes at Tashkent in Central Asia and at Barnaul in Siberia that were newly built on government loans. They had four rooms and cost approximately $1250 each. These houses were being hooked up with the water and sewage systems. Most, however, are owned by the state and rented. The rent runs from $4.00 to $8.00 a month, depending on the number of rooms.

The new houses are laid out in neat additions, well designed so far as spacing, sidewalks, trees, and streets are concerned. But they cannot compare with any of the modern additions one sees in America. They have no flare, no mark of luxury. They are built at the austerity level.

I visited many of these homes and apartments and talked with the owners. The interiors varied, being as neat or as shabby as the housewife herself. None of these homes had any of the conveniences we have come to associate with our kitchens. I saw no refrigerators, electric toasters, electric mixers, garbage-disposal units attached to sinks, nor any of the other gadgets American housewives find so useful. So far as kitchen equipment is concerned, Russia is yet to have her revolution.

Though there are bright sides to Russia's housing, it is in general a problem of staggering proportions. Much of Moscow is in slums. Its shanties are dirty and dingy. In many areas of Moscow there are but one kitchen and one toilet for six families, a condition that has given rise to many disputes that reach the Soviet courts. Most of the smaller towns and villages of Central Asia still have their mud huts of last century. Baku is a modern city. Tashkent and Ashkhabad are half modern and half as squalid as any town in Asia. Bukhara is wholly ancient. Samarkand would probably be recognized by Timur were he to return today. The Siberian towns have vast slums built of logs, scrap wood, packing cases, and tin. There are ambitious plans to eliminate them. Novosibirsk, which occupies a lovely site on the Ob River and is inhabited by many Germans brought there by Catherine the Great, has a building program which the mayor told me would make it as beautiful a city as Leningrad. I was inclined to believe him. But if that building program proceeds on schedule, it will take twenty-five years to complete.

All over Russia there are tens of thousands of families restricted to one or two rooms. Four people to a room is common. Housing is Russia's number-one problem.

Outside Moscow and Leningrad even public buildings are dilapidated. Officialdom is mostly housed in buildings ready to be condemned. In Baku I climbed three flights of stairs to see the Minister of Communications—stairs with a handrail that wobbled at a touch.

I saw many courtrooms. But I never saw judges sitting in an adequate, let alone a splendid, courtroom. Outside Moscow, the courts are tucked away in renovated rooms of old residences or in the rear of worn-out office buildings.

Russia in a few respects is abreast of America. But in most respects she is where we were in 1890, in 1910, or in 1930.

At the time of the Revolution, Russia was primarily an agricultural nation. Today she is a great industrial power, the second in the world. In 1913, Russia produced 4,200,000 tons of pig iron; in 1955, she produced 33,000,000 tons. In 1913, Russia produced 29,100,000 tons of coal; in 1955, 390,000,000 tons. In 1931, Russia produced 4,200,000 tons of steel; in 1955, nearly 45,000,000 tons.

These statistics (which do not include the satellites) are a conservative measure of the growth of Russian industrial powers.

There are those who believe that those figures exaggerate the true picture because, they say, the Russians have no industrial genius. My journey to Russia dispelled those doubts. One has only to see Russia's jet planes to know that her airplane industry is close to our own in technology.

Russian scientists are planning to build a huge sun-power plant in Central Asia to harness solar energy.

The Soviets have undoubted excellence in the field of atomic energy. They have one 5,000-kw. atomic energy plant near Moscow that supplies electric power to the city. I did not see it. But I saw Russian movies of the project.

Russia is building atomic reactors in China, in various eastern European states, and has offered to build one in Egypt.

Many Russian machine tools compete with our own. The steel plant which Russia will erect in India will be as modern as any in this country. Her movies compare favorably, from a technical viewpoint, with Hollywood's.

I saw some of Russia's assembly lines and they seemed to me as efficient as Detroit's. The Stalin plant at Moscow turns out one truck every five minutes. Engineers might well find important defects. But the trucks, cars, and tractors they produce compare favorably with our own.

I saw the new 400,000-kw. hydroelectric dam under construction across the Ob River near Novosibirsk. It is not quite as large in terms of power potential as our Bonneville Dam. But they compare favorably. Once upon a time Russian engineers may not have known how to build dams. But they have mastered the art today. New dams on the Volga will generate 22,000,000,000 kw.'s a year. The new Kakhovka Dam on the Dnieper River, not far from the Black Sea, will eventually produce 1,400,000,000 kw.'s and impound water that will irrigate 2,400,000 acres of semiarid land.

In Siberia a new hydroelectric station is being built that will produce 3,000,000 kw.'s. In 1920 the ratio of our power production to Russia's was 59 to 1; today the margin has been narrowed to approximately 4 to 1. In fifteen years the Soviet engineers expect to be abreast of us on kilowatt hours.

When I came to Baku by boat from Persia, I saw dozens of oil wells in the bed of the Caspian. These offshore oil wells produce about one fourth of Baku's oil, which today amounts to 17,000,000 metric tons a year.

Russian rail transportation is far behind ours. But Russian engineers have great proficiency in providing up-to-date service when they are given the chance to take the lead. The fabulous Moscow subway (recently criticized by the Kremlin for being too ornate) is proof enough. It has forty-five miles of track and forty-five stations, serving a vast network of Moscow. Each station is separately designed, distinctively decorated, beautifully lighted, and meticulously clean. The trains, which average twenty-five miles an hour, run every one and a half minutes with clocklike precision; and a chart at the end of each platform shows by light how many minutes the incoming and departing trains are from the station.

Russia, of course, has learned much from the West. Russia has had the benefit of German scientific genius. And she has had great plants and factories in East Germany and Czechoslovakia to copy during her occupation. Russia also got machinery from us, from England, and from Germany in the 1930's. We sent large shipments of machines to her under Lend-Lease. Across Russia I saw duplicates of machines manufactured in Cincinnati, Detroit, Hamburg, and Birmingham. They are the product of Yankee, British, or German inventive genius, not the inventive genius of the Slav. Some think that if the West refuses to send more machines to Russia, she will have none to copy and will lack the genius to develop her new types. I do not know whether her technological laboratories match ours. But the delegation of American scientists that visited Russia in 1945 as guests of the Russian Academy had disquieting reports to make. Dr. I. M. Kolthoff of the University of Minnesota reported that our scientists were greatly impressed both with the quantity and quality of "pure" research which the Russians were doing. Another member of the American group, Dr. Irving Langmuir of General Electric, reported to Congress that the Russians honor even "the cultural value of pure science," that they have placed "a high priority" on pure and applied science, and that they "have already planned a far more extensive program in science than any contemplated by us." Russian engineers are preparing for a highly automated industrial era. Automation is, indeed, one of their most aggressive projects.

I saw enough to believe that where Russian science lags behind us today it will be abreast of us in a decade or so. I left Russia believing that there is no segment of science where Russians are not working like beavers, trying to catch up.

Russian factories are often dark and dingy, the floors greasy, the machines unguarded. They present hazards to labor that neither American management nor American unions would tolerate. On the other hand, some of her factories are spic and span and as strictly modern as any we know. Apart from auto and tractor plants already mentioned, I saw textile mills, agricultural implement factories, shoe factories, milling and planing plants that compare favorably with our best. The truth is, I think, that the Russian factory excels when the best talent is poured into it; it is inferior when it receives no priority in engineers or managers.

The great emphasis in Russia is on science and engineering. Even parents prefer to have their children enter those fields. Then they are out of politics and the turbulence of Communist activity. Practically every city of consequence has an institute that turns out some type of scientist or engineer. Students at the end of the tenth grade are given entrance examinations to these institutes.

If they qualify, they are paid $25 a month by the state, a stipend gradually increasing up to $50 in the senior year. There is no tuition or charge for books; and dormitory rent runs around $1.00 a month. Moreover, engineering students, like students in scientific research, students in medicine, and students in agriculture, get exemption from military service. They are not drafted but continue their studies without interference.

The engineering course is five years. On graduation, the state assigns the engineer to some project or some department of government. The courses are intense; and the teachers are talented. The students must learn English, for an important part of their education is found in English textbooks and in English technical magazines. I saw at these Russian engineering institutes all of the American technical magazines. As a result of the intensity of the engineering program in Russia, that country now graduates 45,000 engineers a year as compared with our 25,000. Nicholas DeWitt of the Russian Research Center at Harvard shows in his impressive book, *Soviet Professional Manpower,* that the Soviet engineering and scientific program is getting to be closely equivalent to our own.

Russia has many outstanding factory managers. I met some who would flourish in our competitive system. In Russia they operate at a great disadvantage. Management has little room for initiative or freedom.

In the first place, its production schedule must await approval on high. The plan is first formulated in the plant by the workers. Their recommendation goes to the manager. His recommendation goes to the ministry of the republic in charge of the particular industry. From that ministry the plan goes to Moscow. Moscow fits the plan into the mosaic designed for the nation as a whole. A particular plan may come back unchanged or drastically altered.

Second, any change in the design of a machine or in the layout of a factory or in the modification of an assembly line or in the creation of a new laboratory in the plant must go to Moscow for approval. The local manager can recommend. But he does not have power of initiation which is the very essence of factory administration.

Third, the manager can determine the number of workers he needs and send a requisition to his superiors for that number. But he cannot determine how many engineers or other technicians he needs. He may be woefully short of them or the plant may be crawling with them. The number in the plant depends on some bureaucrat's decision in Moscow. A manager cannot send an engineer or other technician out on a field trip without getting Moscow's approval.

Fourth, the Communist party cell in the factory is apparently as much a busybody as it is on the Soviet farms. It disciplines those who lag in their work. It keeps an eye on factory conditions with a view to improving the lot of the workers. It looks at the practices of the plant to determine whether they are consistent with the principles of the Communist party. It does educational work, trying to inculcate Marxist principles into the workers.

Fifth, the trade union in the plant is a group of which the manager is a member. Neither he nor the union has any say in fixing the wages or the hours of work. They are fixed in Moscow. Nor can they create a new position such as foreman, set the salary for the job, and promote a promising man or woman to it. That too must be done in Moscow.

Some of the most bitter controversies arise over the introduction of laborsaving devices. Whether or not a new machine shall be introduced is the ultimate decision of the minister in charge of the factory. But the trade union and the Communist party in the plant debate the issue and make their recommendations. If workers are laid off as the result of a new machine, those men must be offered comparable work at the same salary. And the union and the Communist cell in the plant police the readjustment.

The manager is only the titular head of the plant. He has little real power. And yet what a factory needs above everything else is a responsible, responsive head.

I concluded that efficiency experts from our factories would rate parts of the Soviet industrial plant as inefficient. Decentralization of authority is necessary for efficiency; and there is an effort being made by the Kremlin to bring it about.

The Soviet factories have functioned much better than we have imagined. Somehow the cumbersome wheels turn. In theory the machine should bog hopelessly down. But it does not. I suspect that in some manner informal lines of authority are established between the efficient plants and Moscow, perhaps through personal connections or influence. Or managerial ability of some individuals may tower above the bureaucratic machine and carry the day by sheer magnetism of personality.

The Russian factory system produces a vast supply of goods. Actual production figures are difficult to pin down. For the Russian usually speaks in terms of percentages—5 per cent increase over 1954, 100 per cent increase over 1928, and so on. Base figures on which the percentages are bottomed are seldom given. But one has only to see Russia's industrial plant to know that it has a great potential. To date it has been used primarily for war and to rebuild the areas devastated by the Nazis. If it can be turned primarily to works of peace, it can have a powerful impact both inside Russia and in neighboring countries and continents.

Today Russia's industrial plant is at once impressive and ominous. It is ready to complete the industrial revolution inside Russia and to carry that revolution to Asia and Africa.

Much of the industrial plant was doubtless built out of the hides of the people—by keeping wages low and by allowing a standard of living that held communities at a subsistence level. The history of the industrial plant has ugly chapters. How many slave laborers there are in Russia is a secret. I did not get to see any of the camps. There is one at Karaganda in central Kazakhstan, a city with vast, open-pit coal mines. These mines, operated on a small scale before the October Revolution, are now greatly developed. I had seen a Soviet brochure praising the industrial conditions in Karaganda and the homes, schools, and recreation halls of the workers. So I asked permission to visit there. It took a week to get final word from Moscow. Finally there was a message which, according to Nick, my interpreter, came "from the ministerial level," saying that Karaganda was closed to me. It has, indeed, long been restricted territory because of the notorious use of slave labor in the coal mines. Some Spanish republicans sought refuge in Russia after Franco's victory, got into trouble with the MVD, and were assigned to Karaganda. They worked in Karaganda's coal mines at least until recently. Other Spanish prisoners working in Karaganda's coal pits were members of the Blue Division that fought under the Germans in World War II. The pits have also been filled with Germans.

These slave labor camps are apparently scattered all over Russia. In Helsinki I learned from a Finn, who had had bitter experiences in them, that the camps vary in misery and comforts, depending on the individual in charge of the camps. And there seems to be general agreement that after Stalin's death the lot of prisoners in the slave camps improved. But the camps still exist; and they are a minor branch of Soviet industry.

The Kremlin considers all of the inmates (except the ordinary prisoners of war) as criminals. They are indeed criminals in a technical sense, for each has a record of conviction against him. The judgment of conviction usually was entered by a special administrative court which, until recently, the MVD—Russia's notorious police—maintained within its organization. The prisoner seldom appeared before the court. No counsel represented him.

He had no notice of the charge or even of the trial. He merely received notice that he had been convicted. The charges were often fancied or manufactured. The sentences usually ran for five years; and if at the end of that time the prisoner was still alive, another judgment would be entered—again *in absentia*—extending the sentence for another five years.

Those are the political prisoners we read about. There are other prisoners also in the slave labor category, who qualify as convicts in the usual sense of the word. They have been convicted of larceny, burglary, rape, murder, etc. They have been sentenced for various terms and spend their time working in Russia's industrial plant. In Moscow I got a look at some of them. I visited friends who live on the tenth floor of an apartment house. This apartment overlooks a large yard, nearly a block square. On one side is a three-story yellow building whose windows and doors, facing the street, are sealed. This is the barracks where the prisoners live. The other three sides of the yard are surrounded by a high fence with towers at each corner and guards in the towers. A concrete building-block industry is located in the yard. Trucks bring sand and cement from the outside; concrete is poured into molds; the blocks are piled for shipment. All of the laborers are women. Like thousands of other Soviet citizens, they are working out their prison terms in a state factory.

I learned from my talk with MVD officials that this use of prison labor is commonplace. Prisoners are sometimes paroled to factories but usually they are assigned under guard to particular workyards. One tall, tough MVD officer extolled the use of convict labor in Soviet industry.

"These people often have never done anything good or constructive all their lives," he said. "Now they are doing something for their country."

He went on to explain that they are all paid wages, after deductions for board and room, and that those wages are sent to their families or nearest relatives. I could not learn what the convict labor wage scale was. But from what I heard, I believe it is miserably low. Yet from what I saw and heard, I doubt if this kind of convict labor is abused or cruelly treated. From the reports I got, their food is adequate; they have medical care and attention; and they are kept in good physical condition for the allotted work.

Prison labor is in many respects like military labor. In Russia thousands upon thousands of GIs do construction work. In Central Asia I saw them building apartment houses, laying water pipes, working on sewage projects. In Siberia I saw Russian privates doing highway construction, digging drainage ditches, working on bridges. Russian soldiers are an important part of the Soviet labor supply. And their wages are so blushingly low that I found no Russian who would even discuss the matter.

Before my Russian journey I heard reports that all Russian industrial labor was in as lowly a state as convict labor. I had also read that Russian factory workers were, as some put it, mere "termites" working blindly in dark, dingy places that never see the light of day. These are not accurate descriptions. Soviet industrial labor is not made up of cowed and groveling people. The thousands of faces I saw in Russia's factories did not tell any story of suffering and oppression. Russian labor is, if anything, on a crusade to get a job done. In the main, it's a solid core of men and women, working with enthusiasm and drive. The enthusiasm may reflect no love of communism. It may mean no more than love of a job, of a community, of a nation. What loyalties inspire it is difficult for a stranger to divine. But there was enthusiasm in most every factory or plant I visited.

As I said, the Russians do not know the privileges of our workers. There is no right to strike; and there is no collective bargaining for wages, hours, and conditions of work.

The wages and hours for each factory are set by the government. Throughout Russia the workday is eight hours long; the work week, forty-six hours. The minimum age is sixteen years. There is time and a half for overtime. But not much overtime work is used. Factories usually have two shifts; many have three.

All workers get bonuses on a piecework basis for production above their quotas. I visited factories where 80 per cent of the employees had received bonuses in 1954 and 1955. These bonuses supply an important incentive in the Soviet system.

What is called collective bargaining in a Russian factory is the process of clearing grievances in an American plant. These grievances concern discharge or demotion of employees for inefficiency, the loss of seniority rights, loss of pay for tardiness, and like disputes and controversies that arise endlessly in any plant. If the grievance is not settled at the level of the foreman, it goes to the Rates and Conflicts Commission (RKK), composed of an equal number of workers and representatives of the management. If the controversy is not settled there, it may go on to the People's Court for adjudication. And in some instances, the laborer may sue in the People's Court in the first instance. There are also Comrade Courts in Russian factories—tribunals composed of workers and sitting in judgment on cases of petty crimes, insults, damage to factory machines, rowdy conduct not of the magnitude requiring criminal prosecution. Appeals lie from these courts to the People's Court.

In 1940 workers were "frozen," not being allowed to leave their employment without permission of the manager. That law apparently has not been repealed. But it does not seem to be uniformly enforced in Russia. There seems to be a high degree of mobility of labor—too great, according to the officials I interviewed. It is estimated that about one fifth of the total number of people employed in industry change their jobs every year. The number of people employed during a given year may even approximate the number of people leaving jobs in that industry. In 1954, 1,770,000 workers were employed and 1,450,000 left their jobs.

STALINABAD

The doctors at a city hospital in Stalinabad seemed like a dedicated group.

Three fourths of the labor force of the cotton textile mills at Stalinabad are women.

The cotton fields of Central Asia are highly mechanized.

The Tadzhik orchestra in the city park at Stalinabad had six pieces, including the tambourine.

Tadzhiks dance every night in the park at Stalinabad.

Tadzhik dancers at Stalinabad have a separate dance floor in the city park.

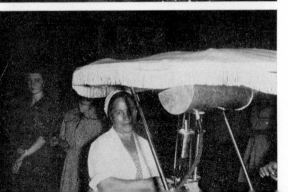

Street vendors who sell soft drinks on the streets of Stalinabad are usually members of a co-operative society.

Some localities, however, still require the manager's permission to quit a factory. That is the case, I discovered, in Novosibirsk. If a manager refuses a worker leave to quit, the worker can appeal to the RKK. If the RKK denies permission, he can appeal further to the People's Court. The legal basis for the decision is "the needs of the trade" in the locality which the worker seeks to leave.

Soviet industry treats women on the equality of men. They are treated so equally that the women often do pick-and-shovel work. I saw women digging ditches, loading freight cars with rocks, shoveling dirt at the hydroelectric dam on the Ob River, laying concrete, using welding torches, pouring molten metal, operating overhead cranes in Siberian factories, cleaning streets, driving trucks, operating streetcars, unloading baggage and express, serving as switchmen, flagmen, and porters on trains, and doing every conceivable kind of work in meat-packing plants. Women have equality of pay and equality of industrial opportunity. I visited textile mills where 75 per cent of the employees were women. And of the many factories I visited, there was not one where women numbered less than a third of the employees. Even on the mile-long bridge that was being built across the Ob River at Novosibirsk, a third of the labor force were women.

Men may retire at sixty; women at fifty-five. (In the Arctic areas, retirement age for men is fifty-five, for women, fifty.) One who retires gets a pension that is roughly equal to 25 per cent of his lifetime average salary—a pension which Kremlin officials admitted was very inadequate but which they hope to increase. If a worker continues to work after reaching the retirement age, as he may, he gets his full salary plus his pension. And when he dies, his pension continues for the benefit of his wife.

Each factory—like each state farm and each collective—is a community unto itself. The factory provides apartments and houses for its workers, renting them for nominal sums. The factory usually erects a Hall of Culture for the workers, a building that commonly has a movie auditorium, lecture rooms, library, gymnasium, and studios for those who want to pursue painting or sculpture. Small fees are usually charged for the movies; but the rest of the facilities are free. Some of these halls are amazingly well organized and equipped. At a planing and milling machine plant in Novosibirsk, I saw a lovely theater seating 800. That factory has a dramatics teacher whom I met, a man in his thirties. He has discovered theatrical talent in the factory, two so superior that they are being sent to Moscow for training. This factory produces four plays each winter. It has an orchestra and puts on musicales. Troupes from other factories and from collective farms perform here. This factory has a library containing 37,000 volumes. In its clubhouse for workers are special rooms for painters and sculptors.

The Russian factory is, in other words, a center of social activity. Some are even building great stadiums for athletic events. The factory lays out parks and playground equipment for children. It has nurseries and kindergartens where mothers may deposit their children in the morning before they go to work and pick them up at day's end. Schools, ranging through the tenth grade, are close by.

The union in the factory even arranges to send all children of workers between the ages of seven and fourteen to camps for twenty-seven days each summer, all expenses paid. The union also has rest camps where workers can spend their vacations. These rest camps are greatly used and overcrowded.

The Russian factory almost always has a lunchroom where a hot meal is served midway in each shift. I saw some that were quite attractive. The meals usually have three vegetables, bread, and tea—and sometimes stews. The price averages three rubles or twenty-four cents. Soft drinks and pastry are extra.

The factory also has at least one hospital, one clinic, one maternity ward, one first-aid station, and one dentist's office. They are staffed by doctors, nurses, and dentists assigned by the state and paid by the state.

The Russian factory is a community that is closely knit together by a myriad of activities and services. It's paternalistic in many of its activities—too much so to suit our tastes. But it's a lively center, serving most of the needs of the people except religion. It ties each worker and his family into an active group. He is not a forgotten man; he is catered to and cared for. And although he is at the same time regimented, he lives in an environment that gives him a degree of freedom and opportunity that the workers of Asia have never known.

The highest paid industrial workers are those who work in coal, petroleum, and the heavy industries. Some get as high as $240 a month, again taking the ruble at 8 cents. But they are not numerous. The highest paid worker in an auto plant makes $160 a month. The average wage in this category is from $80 to $120 a month.

The next highest wage group are railway workers and seamen. They average from $67 to $80 a month.

The third highest are in textiles, shoes, leather, food processing. These workers on the average earn from $40 to $52 a month.

These wages are not the true take-home pay. Income taxes must be paid; there is the assessment for government bonds; and there are dues to the union, which for a man making $80 a month equals 1 per cent of his annual salary. Even without these deductions the Russian wages are extremely low by our standards. The comparison is in some respects unfair to the Russian, because so many of the services for which we pay are furnished him free of charge or at a nominal rate. Rents for apartments and houses are nominal; charges for utility services are low, streetcar and bus fares usually amounting to 30 kopeks or about 3 cents; and all medicines and medical care are free.

Our standards are not the true criteria for evaluating Russia's industrial plant or industrial wage. Russia is to be compared not with America but with Asia. It is out of the Asian environment that her plant has evolved. Asia has been feudal from time out of mind. Her industry has been mostly handcrafts. The industries that were established were largely exploitive affairs, built on the pattern of sweat shops. In many parts of Asia unskilled labor today makes no more than $15 a month; only a few skilled workers earn more than $30 a month. Many of them have no medical care whatsoever. Infant mortality is high in Asia. From 50 per cent to 80 per cent of Asian babies die before they reach the age of one. There are few hospitals or maternity wards.

Russia's medical facilities, though not de luxe, are adequate. Medical care is within the reach of all the people, the facilities being widely distributed. The equipment is not as modern as ours; the buildings are not as well constructed; the rooms are dormitories containing several beds; and there are no private rooms except in psychiatric cases. But wherever one goes, there are antibiotics, doctors for surgery, and physicians for treatment. There is a nurse on every boat and one to meet every plane at the airport. In some respects Russia is further advanced in medicine than we are. There is one doctor for 666 people in Russia; in America, one doctor for 790. In Russia 60 per cent of the doctors are women; in America, 6 per cent. In 1956 Russia will graduate 20,000 new doctors, as compared with our 7,000. One measure of their competence is the fact that infant mortality in Russia is approximately the same as in America.

Many think that under Russia's scheme of socialized medicine the doctor loses his intimate relationship with patients. Some say that the patient is no longer an individual but a man in a waiting line with a number to be indexed and processed as quickly as possible to make room for the next person. Asia might well reject Russia's socialized medicine for our own, if she had the choice. But having only primitive medical care, she is likely to look to Russia's system with eagerness.

Russian housing is backward by American standards. But to Asians who live in hovels, as most of them do, the new apartments and homes of Russian workers may well seem to be paradise.

An American who sees Russia's industrial plant will be surprised that it works as well as it does under the cumbersome Soviet bureaucracy. He may not be impressed at Russian progress. But the Asian who sees the same industrial plant will likely be excited. From his starting point, Russia is far in advance. The workers' homes, the medical clinics, the recreation halls, the wage scale, the public schools and parks—these are merely in the blueprint stage in most of Asia. In Russia they are living achievements. The Asian is apt to be overwhelmed at that achievement, forgetting the means used to attain it.

This is why the impact of the Russian industrial plant on Asia is going to be penetrating and profound. This is why the Russian industrial plant is the most potent force in Asia today.

CHAPTER 6

THE POLICE, THE COURTS—
AND THE LAW

I learned on my Russian journey that the police—
the famous MVD—are always present.

I had heard many stories about the MVD before my Russian
journey. It was an open secret in Washington, D.C., months before
the story was printed, that the MVD had planted a resonator behind the Great Seal in the American Embassy in Moscow. Whatever the American Ambassador said was transmitted to the MVD.
The resonator was about the size of a matchbox. It was a metal
cup covered by a metallic diaphragm, with a tiny protruding an-
tenna. It had no batteries, no wires, and no connection with any
electric power. Its diaphragm was agitated by the human voice.
It was designed to receive and to echo a highly sensitive radio
beam. When the American Ambassador spoke, an electronic echo
broadcast his voice. Thus Stalin for a while sat in on the most confidential talks of our Embassy staff.

Before visiting Russia, I also knew of the small parabolic microphones which the MVD employ to pick up conversations at a distance of a hundred feet or more. I knew they used them to reach street-corner conversations and to record those talks.

I, therefore, knew before I went to Russia that no conversation indoors or outdoors was really safe.

I also had heard that the MVD was anxious to see the notebooks of travelers and that it was their custom to borrow them at night while the owner slept.

One night in Baku at the Intourist Hotel, I left the light in my living room on, closing the door to the bedroom. The light, which could only be turned on and off inside the room, was off in the morning. I followed the same routine the next night with the same result. Someone was entering my suite when I was asleep. So I decided to accommodate him by leaving my brief case and notebooks in the outer room.

One day in Alma Ata I interviewed the MVD. I met for nearly two hours with the Russian Deputy MVD Minister of Kazakhstan and five of his assistants—three Russians and two Kazakhs. It was a friendly but nevertheless tense meeting as I touched on all the sensitive points of MVD tactics—questioning of prisoners, secret trials, conditions in slave labor camps, and so on. That night before retiring I wrote up an extended account of my interview, put it in my coat pocket, hung the coat over the back of a chair in the living room, and placed it alongside my brief case and other bags. The door to the hall had two locks—an old-fashioned lock that almost any key would turn and a large hook that came across the door-jamb and fastened in a huge sturdy eye. I decided to use both locks. I turned the ancient key and then forced the hook into the tight-fitting eye.

"If anyone gets in tonight," I said to myself, "he has a flash of genius."

Someone had a flash of genius. For in the morning, though the door was still locked, the hook was hanging limp. Someone had managed to enter without disturbing me. And I'm sure that if I had awakened and apprehended the visitor, he would have been only the night watchman tracking down a trace of fire.

Perhaps I am unfair in suspecting the MVD. Certainly those who entered my room at night did not steal or destroy. All of my papers and possessions were left intact.

The police all over Russia were always polite and courteous. They, indeed, went out of their way to be nice to me. Once at Frunze I returned to my hotel room unexpectedly, unlocked the door, and entered. Inside was a Kirgiz man in his thirties. We could not speak each other's language. So I motioned him to follow me down the hall to Nick's room. Nick was greatly upset when he heard the story. The Kirgiz insisted that my door had been open and that he walked in looking for a friend who had occupied the room the day before. I told Nick that the Kirgiz may well have been right and asked Nick to drop the matter. Then I left. But by that time the manager of the hotel had heard about the episode. Unknown to me, he called the MVD. At breakfast the manager, full of apologies, told me that the MVD had arrested the Kirgiz and kept him all night. The manager submitted to me the MVD's report. It was a detailed document that included a blood test given the Kirgiz to determine whether he had been drinking. I was sure that the man was wholly innocent and that I unwittingly had caused him a long night of suffering. Though I thanked the MVD for being so attentive to my safety, I sent a note of apology to the Kirgiz. When I got to Moscow I told the story to an American seasoned in the ways of Soviet Russia. He smiled as I recounted the episode and when I finished said, "You may have missed the whole point. The Kirgiz you found in your room was probably MVD."

The MVD is a far-flung organization. It takes the place of local and federal police in other nations. It directs traffic, patrols streets and parks, investigates murders, and performs all the other tasks of our local police. It also performs all the tasks of our FBI in the enforcement of federal laws. The MVD performs other functions too.

The MVD maintains an overseas espionage ring, as Vladimir Petrov, former top agent of the Soviet in Australia, has vividly recounted in his recent revelations.

The MVD until recently patrolled the borders of Russia. Members of that branch wore dark green uniforms. I saw them often in the streets of the main cities of Central Asia. Since 1955 the border guard has been under the Ministry of Defense.

The MVD has charge of all the prisons in Russia—or did, at least, until recently—the slave labor camps as well as the more conventional prisons.

The MVD patrols all the highways of Russia and supervises their maintenance.

The MVD has charge of all the fire departments of Russia.

The MVD has infantry, tanks, and planes—a veritable army unto itself.

Until Stalin died and Beria was executed, the MVD had the Special Board of Review—which I have mentioned—the administrative court that condemned men and women to prison in secret trials at which the accused had no chance to defend and of which he often had no knowledge. The MVD in Stalin's time was responsible to him. Once Beria was executed, the MVD was placed under a career man who in turn was made responsible not to one man but to the entire Praesidium.

Above the MVD is the Russian prosecutor, who is comparable to the Attorney General in our federal system. Each republic has a prosecutor; so does each district (oblast) in each republic. These are all named by the Chief Prosecutor in Moscow and are responsible to him.

The Russian prosecutor has vast powers, greater than the ones our Attorney General enjoys. The prosecutor issues all warrants for the arrest of suspects (the MVD can of course arrest without a warrant if they see the crime being committed). The MVD may hold a man *incommunicado* for twenty-four hours after his arrest. At the end of that time the MVD must report the case to the prosecutor. But after making that report, the MVD may continue to hold the prisoner another two days. In sum the MVD can hold a person three days in all. At the end of the three days, the MVD must turn the prisoner over to the prosecutor. All judges and prosecutors told me that that rule was strictly enforced. I have independent evidence that it may be. When I was in Russia, an MVD official was prosecuted for violating the rule governing detention. In that case the MVD held a young student for a long period while they tried to exact a confession from him. He refused to confess and was acquitted. The MVD official, responsible for his arrest and detention, was sentenced to a year in prison.

The prosecutor has on his staff a large investigative unit. The investigators are usually, though not always, trained in the law. Many are women. Their average salary is $80 (1000 rubles) a month. When the prosecutor receives the prisoner from the MVD, the investigators take over. They have twenty days to make the investigation. If that time is not adequate, they can get a forty-day extension from the prosecutor—a total of two months.

In our federal system the police must take the arrested person before a commissioner or other committing magistrate "without unnecessary delay." If officers violate that command and hold the prisoner, exacting a confession from him, the confession is illegally obtained and is inadmissible at the trial. Not so in Russia. In Russia the prisoner need not be brought before a judge for sixty-three days. During that time he is under the exclusive jurisdiction of the police and the prosecutor. For sixty-three days he is definitely and completely *incommunicado*. But at the end of that period he must be brought to trial. Russian law imposes a penalty on prosecutors who neglect that duty. And judges are empowered to release a prisoner held longer than sixty-three days. All the judges with whom I talked in many different cities insisted that the prosecutors and the courts were meticulous in enforcing the sixty-three-day provision.

During the sixty-day period of detention by the investigator, the MVD has easy access to the prisoner. In petty crimes, e.g., picking pockets, the investigator often retains the MVD to complete the investigation. In the major crimes, the prosecutor's staff does its own investigating.

This long and close surveillance by the police and the easy use of confessions must produce a very high percentage of guilty pleas. In our federal courts there are pleas of guilty and *nolo contendere* in about 80 to 85 per cent of the cases. In Russia the pleas of guilty run much higher, though the exact percentage was not available to me.

The prosecutor—not the judge as in America—determines whether a search warrant will issue. The law is substantially the same as ours—that a search warrant will issue on a showing of probable cause. There is an exception to the requirement of a search warrant. The investigator may proceed without one if he is accompanied by two witnesses from the neighborhood when he knocks on the door or enters the room or building by force.

The prosecutor determines whether a charge shall be made against a prisoner. Russia has no grand jury system. The process of indictment is in the prosecutor's sole discretion. Russian law imposes both civil and criminal penalties against the prosecutor for false arrests and manufactured charges. Since Stalin's death and Beria's execution, many prosecutors have been criminally prosecuted for abuse of their powers under the old regime; and heavy sentences have been imposed.

The prosecutor, not the judge as in America, determines whether a prisoner will or will not receive bail pending his trial. Bail in the sense of a deposit of cash or securities to assure the return of the prisoner for the trial is never used. I found that Russian judges were quite unfamiliar with it. In one discussion at Baku, I noticed one Azerbaijani judge nudging another when I described that kind of bail. The nudge meant, "See, that's what I told you. In the capitalist country of America, the rich can buy their way out of jail." The bail that the Russians have is of a different variety. First is the written promise of the accused not to leave the city, oblast, or state pending trial. This is the type of bail used in 80 per cent of the cases. The second is the recognizance bond signed by two people of character known to the prosecutor. Except for murder cases and the political crimes which I will mention, bail before trial is readily available in Russia and widely used.

The accused has a right to a lawyer only at the trial. And no criminal trial is held without the accused's being represented by a lawyer. If he does not have one of his own choice or cannot afford to hire one, counsel is assigned by the court to defend him.

The Russians are so meticulous on this score that if the accused refuses to have a lawyer, the prosecutor is not allowed to participate in the trial. In that event the judges conduct the trial themselves.

The trial courts sit in panels of three judges. The presiding judge is a lawyer. The two side-judges or assessors are laymen, as they are today in most courts in Vermont. There is, however, no jury in Russia. In one sense the lay judges bring the jury to the bench. As one Russian jurist told me, the lay judges pull the court closer to the people and fulfill Lenin's dictum, "We must do the judging ourselves." Laymen bring to the bench not legal learning, but "their general experience." Law schools, however, offer special courses in law to the lay judges. The lay judges have equal standing with the presiding judge, with power to outvote him.

I saw many trials on my Russian journey and met dozens of judges. Some of the lay judges were housewives, some had been streetcar conductors and factory workers. They were drawn from the ranks of the unskilled as well as the skilled.

All of the judges of the People's Court (which is the main trial court and the lowest in the judicial hierarchy) are elected by the people. The judges in the higher courts of each republic or state are chosen by the soviet representing that political unit. The judges of the U.S.S.R. Supreme Court (seventy-five in number, sixteen of whom are women) are chosen by the Supreme Soviet. The judges of the People's Court are chosen for four years. Like all other judges, they must pass the scrutiny of the Communist party, either being members or persons in good standing.

The Russians seem very keen on their method of selecting judges. One day in Tashkent I visited with a number of Uzbek judges. They were much interested in learning how judges were selected in the United States. I explained that judges are elected by the people in about three fourths of our states but in the rest of the states and in the federal system they are appointed. There was a chorus of objections to the appointment of judges. "Judges should represent the people," the Uzbek spokesman said.

Russian judges do not wear gowns or robes. Many male judges sit in sport shirts with collars open. The female judges I saw were almost always dressed in cotton prints. There is no crier to announce the arrival of the judges. They walk in unannounced. There is only one formality—the audience rises as the judges enter and remains standing until they take their seats at the bench.

The prosecutor sits at a table on the right of the bench, the lawyer for the defense on the left. Closer to the bench on the left is the clerk who records in ink, not a stenographic account of the trial, but a summary of what transpires.

There is a preliminary session *in camera* where the court determines whether the indictment or charge is proper on its face. If the court approves the indictment, a public trial is had. A criminal trial in the *regular* (as distinguished from the *political*) court is always public. It opens with the presiding judge reading the substance of the charge of the investigator.

The charge in Russia, unlike the indictment in the United States, contains all the evidence against the accused. The prosecutor is required to disclose it at the very commencement of the proceeding. What the investigator puts in his report or charge is not evidence. Every element of the crime must be proved. There is a presumption of innocence. The burden rests on the prosecutor to prove the guilt of the accused. Russian law, however, has not yet formulated the concept "beyond a reasonable doubt."

After the presiding judge summarizes the report, the accused is asked to plead guilty or not guilty. After his plea is entered the witnesses are called. (Witnesses in criminal cases are paid their usual wages while in court. In civil cases, the party calling a witness pays as court costs the amount the witness would have earned had he not been called.) The witnesses are brought in as a group and, standing before the bench, are advised by the presiding judge of their duty to tell the truth. They then step to the clerk's desk and sign the following printed form:

We, the undersigned, witnesses in the case _____
_____

hereby certify that today, at the sitting of the People's Court, we were informed of our duty to testify everything known to us in this case, and we were warned about the consequences of refusing to testify or giving false testimony, in accordance with Articles 92 and 95 of the Criminal Code.

_____ *195___*

SIGNATURES:

Certificate was taken by the people's judge _____
district _____ *region.*

There is no oath administered to the witnesses, no "So help me God." Russia operates on the basis of the godless state.

In Russia the defendant is not sworn. He does not promise to tell the truth. He can commit no perjury. He is allowed to escape by fair methods or by foul. If a lie will save him, he may lie with impunity and be applauded for it.

Once the witnesses are sworn they leave the courtroom and wait to be called, one at a time. When one gives his testimony, he stands in a dock facing the judges. The lawyer who calls him theoretically examines him first. But at all the criminal trials I attended, the burden of the examination was carried by the presiding judge, with occasional questions from the side judges.

The judges assume an almost parental role towards the accused. It is their duty to protect him against the consequences of his ignorance, to advise him of his rights, to produce the witnesses he wants, to delay the trial, if necessary, when the accused asks for an additional witness, and to call a witness on his behalf when needed, whether or not he makes the request.

As I said, the judges take the lead in examining witnesses. After they have finished, the lawyers take turns in the questioning. When the judges, the prosecutor, and counsel for the defense have finished, the presiding judge invariably asks the defendant if he has any questions to ask the witness. Occasionally the defendant does. At one trial I attended the accused produced the most telling cross-examination of all. The charge was drunkenness and assault. The final witness was a lady who obviously had no personal knowledge of the episode. Her testimony was sheer gossip, hearsay of the rankest variety. The defendant took her to task for it.

"Why do you testify to things of which you have no knowledge? You say I threw a chair through a window. It turns out you had only heard that I did. How can you know it was not someone else?"

Many of our rules of evidence are not known in Russia. Others are familiar. For example, oral wills are not recognized. A will to be admitted to probate must be notarized. Bank accounts may be assigned by an instrument signed by the depositor but not notarized; and such an assignment is valid as a **testamentary** disposition. Testimony that there was an oral will or oral assignment is inadmissible.

Yet apart from such exceptions Russian courts have no hard and fast rules of evidence. Professor Shargorodskij of the University of Leningrad put the matter to me this way: "Your rules of evidence were designed to protect juries against unfair influence. Since we have no juries, we need no rules of evidence."

Hearsay is not excluded. It is freely admitted, the theory being that the judges will give it little weight if it's an unreliable account. Similarly Russian courts admit any confession which an accused has signed. They admit it as evidence, even though there is clear evidence that the confession has been obtained from the accused by force, coercion, torture, or other means which we would deem to be illegal. The accused may show that ugly methods were used by the MVD to obtain the confession. Those facts go only to the weight or credibility of the confession, not to its validity as evidence. Under Russian law an MVD officer who uses torture to obtain a confession can be held criminally responsible. I found no instance, however, where any such prosecution was instituted, though the MVD is apparently much more vulnerable to suit after Beria's death than before.

Wives may be compelled to testify against husbands and husbands against wives, both in civil and criminal cases. This rule of evidence, one judge proudly told me, springs from the Soviet theory that men and women are equal before the law. Certainly Soviet law applies the principle with a vengeance, creating no privilege in the courtroom that will protect the confidences of the marriage relationship.

In Russia, penalties for many crimes are more severe than in America. A Soviet court recently sentenced a man to ten years in prison for reckless driving while under the influence of liquor. A man who bought a radio-phonograph and resold it at a profit got eight years. A woman who bought 100 kilograms of sugar and resold it at twice the cost got five years. Her husband who helped her got two years. An accountant and manager of a co-operative who pilfered money from it were sentenced to twelve years and had all their property confiscated by the state. Another pilferer of state funds got ten years in prison and had all his property confiscated. A worker in a state store who appropriated $4136 (51,-700 rubles) of state funds got twenty years in a "corrective labor camp." Two drunks who interrupted a theatrical performance got four years and three years in prison, respectively. (Sentences up to five years are common in cases of disorderly conduct). Two men who stole a cow from a farmer and tried to sell it got ten years in a "corrective labor camp." A director of a plant who wasted materials and misappropriated funds, doing a total damage of $3200 (40,000 rubles) was sentenced to ten years and ordered to repay the amount of the loss.

Sentences of imprisonment are sometimes accompanied, as I have indicated, by a decree confiscating all of the defendant's property. The court may go further and disenfranchise him for a term of years following his prison term. Political and civil rights withdrawn include voting rights, the right to hold elective office in public organizations, the right to hold particular state offices, the right to wear honorary insignia, the right to a pension. Soviet courts, like the old czarist courts, also have the power "to banish" a man instead of fining or imprisoning him. I learned in Petropavlovsk that punishment by banishment is still commonly used. Now, as in the old days, the place of banishment is usually some region or town in Siberia.

Moreover, a Soviet court in a criminal case not only imposes fines and other sentences; it may also award damages, as some of the cases I have cited show. The embezzler can be imprisoned and ordered to pay back the depletions; the drunken driver is sent to jail and ordered to reimburse the injured passenger for his injuries, and so on. If state property is stolen, double damages may be imposed on the thief, as well as the usual sentence of fine and imprisonment.

In spite of these conspicuous differences, the Russian courtroom is a familiar place to the American lawyer. It is a place of quiet dignity. Professor Boris A. Konstantinovsky in his book, *Soviet Law in Action*, gives instances of the manipulation of courts and of tampering with judges by the Communist party. Soviet courts are, of course, main props to the entire Soviet regime. Lenin once said that "law is politics"; and the Soviets use law to promote and maintain the socialist *status quo*. But the judges I saw seemed to be a conscientious lot. I was, indeed, much impressed with the quality of the law-trained judges and of the members of the Bar.

I speak only of the *regular* courts, not the *political* courts. The Russian *political* court has been much publicized through the famous purge trials. They are of course an integral part of the Russian judicial system, being a department or branch of the Supreme Court, U.S.S.R. They are *ad hoc* courts—that is, tribunals called together for one trial only and then dissolved. Russia's regular judges have nothing to do with these courts. The court that tried Beria was composed of seven judges—one a military officer, two lawyers, and four laymen. It met, heard the evidence in a secret trial, imposed sentence, and then adjourned, never to meet again.

The procedure specified by law to govern that court disallows the accused what we would call due process of law. The trial is secret; the accused is not entitled to counsel for his defense; and he has no right to appeal. That court serves political ends, not the ends of justice. There have been four such special courts since the Revolution. There will be others in the days ahead. For these political courts are part of the catharsis of the Communist dictatorship.

The *political* courts also include military tribunals. They are under the general supervision of the Supreme Court and have jurisdiction not only over military personnel but over certain crimes committed by civilians, e.g., counterrevolutionary crimes.

Reforms are brewing in Russian law. Recommendations are being made by Committees of the Supreme Soviet, whose reports are expected to be before the Praesidium in 1956 or 1957.

There is a distinct movement to abolish some old offenses and to lighten penalties. Stealing rides on freight cars until recently carried a severe penalty. It is no longer a crime in Russia. Most penalties for crimes of lesser magnitude than murder are being reduced. For example, the spread of "subversive" propaganda carries a penalty of ten years; the recommendation is that it be reduced to five years.

There is agitation among lawyers and judges for a more explicit statement of the presumption of innocence of the accused.

There is a drive on to cut down the jurisdiction of military courts, enlarging the jurisdiction of the regular courts.

Sentiment is building up to make the investigator more and more independent of the prosecutor. Today, the prosecutor can direct an investigator to prepare a formal charge or presentment against an accused. The reformers want to give the investigator greater discretion in the matter. Today, only the prosecutor can grant bail. A proposed reform would give the investigator independent power to grant bail. Today, all investigators are under the prosecutor, as I said. The reformers want the investigators freed from control by the prosecutor. So they propose to transfer them to another ministry.

Today, an accused has a right to counsel only at the commencement of the trial, a rule substantially the same as that obtaining in our federal system. The Russian reformers want the right to counsel extended to the earlier period in the investigation, when it is decided that there is enough evidence to warrant a formal charge against the suspect.

In Russia, as in the United States, neither the victim of the crime nor any person representing him is a party to the criminal proceedings. The Russian reformists plan to make him a party, granting him power to call witnesses, to testify, to examine witnesses, and to assert all the rights of a party except the right to appeal.

Soviet criminal law has a fiercely unfair provision known as the doctrine of analogy which permits a person to be punished for an act which though not directly prohibited by law is analogous to crimes that are punished. This doctrine of analogy is at war with our principle that penal statutes must put the citizen fairly on notice of the crime, that vague penal laws fall for lack of due process. There is some sentiment in Russia to eliminate the doctrine of analogy.

Another proposed reform touches intimately the independence of the Bar. In Russia all lawyers must be members of the co-operative called the College of Advocates. The College has power to disbar its members for misconduct. All fees charged by lawyers must follow a schedule adopted by the College in 1939. If extra charges are to be made, the governing board of the College must approve. The lawyer is not paid by the client. His fee goes to the College, which retains from 10 per cent to 30 per cent, the amount varying in different regions. The balance of his fee is paid over to him on regular, monthly accounting dates. The amount retained by the College goes to pay its administration costs. It also is used to retain lawyers in cases where parties are too poor to retain one. The College is a sort of employment agency for the lawyers. Clients often go to it for a lawyer, not to the lawyer directly. Lawyers in Russia are, in other words, on quite a different footing than in the Western world. The difference is accentuated by the power of the Minister of Justice over them. The College of Advocates is under the Minister of Justice who may, after a hearing, disbar any lawyer in Russia for any cause he deems sufficient. That gives the Minister of Justice the power of life and death over the Bar. It is a potent political weapon to keep the Bar in line.

Lawyers in Russia resent this power. And there is a strong movement under way to take the power of disbarment away from the Minister of Justice.

As I have said, the Special Board of Review inside the MVD was abolished after Stalin's death and Beria's execution. Thousands of its sentences, however, are still in force. The injustices which that Special Board inflicted on the people are so enormous that the Chief Prosecutor has undertaken an investigation of its verdicts. That has led to the release of some prisoners and to the prosecution of some officials. How far he will go and how thorough his investigation will be are yet to be known. Moreover, the slave labor camps are being transferred to the Ministry of Justice. It is one of the steps taken since Stalin and Beria to diminish the power of the MVD. It may also mark the beginning of the end of the slave labor camps. There are some I met who felt that Russia's slave labor camps are so detrimental to Russian prestige and so uneconomic as producing units that they are in process of liquidation. The latter is speculative. But the dilution of the power of the MVD is definite.

These proposed reforms are not of course fundamental in the sense that they repudiate the Communist regime. They are not, in other words, seeds of revolution against the government like the complaint of James Otis against the British search warrants in our early days. But they are significant trends. They show genuine ferment in the Communist system and a growing sense of due process. What the final product of this contemporary reform movement will amount to, no one knows. But it's a healthy sign of evolution. It shows that even in Communist Russia a search for improved public administration is going on.

There is, however, no sign of the emergence in Russia of the writ of *habeas corpus*. The Great Writ is the citizen's key to the door of his prison, the one that enables him to obtain a judicial hearing on the legality of his confinement. It's a potent weapon for control of the police. It's the citizen's check on the despotism that puts him behind bars. When the Great Writ is available, man's liberty has a basic guarantee unknown in the lands of dictatorship. Russian laws penalize officials who hold men in prison beyond the allotted time. But they give the prisoner no relief against the unlawful arrest or the detention that flows from whim or caprice.

I discovered that many lawyers and judges in Russia never heard of *habeas corpus.* Of course, learned professors in Russian universities know the Great Writ and its long history. But as the lean, thin Minister of Justice of Kirgizia told me at Frunze one afternoon, "*Habeas corpus?* Yes, we know about *habeas corpus.* But it's what we in Russia call a part of the theoretical branch of the law." There is, indeed, no Communist regime that would tolerate the Great Writ.

The civil side of the administration of justice, as distinguished from the criminal, presents enormous problems. All of Russia is under a labyrinth of laws and regulations that reach every phase of the citizen's life. Bureaucracy is supreme; and the red tape that flows from the machine is beyond anything we of the West ever dreamed. There is no escape from this bureaucracy. But there is evolving some relief against its harsher aspects.

Today in Russia an "aggrieved" person may appeal for relief from an executive order. He must first go to the top of the ministry that issued the order, seeking his relief. Or as we say in this country, he must first exhaust his administrative remedies. Once he does that, he may then go into court to get his relief. Russian courts are free to run the whole gamut of relief—ordering vacation with pay, the reduction of rent, the reinstatement of a worker, the determination of his seniority rights, and so on.

The prosecutor has an even stronger sword. He can challenge a regulation *in limine* on the ground that it exceeds the authority of the ministry or encroaches on the rights of the citizens. The prosecutor does this by first exhausting all the administrative remedies that are available within the agency. If he loses there, he may go to court. This is a power not much used in Russia. But it seems to be emerging as a method of control over an ever-expanding bureaucracy.

At the same time, the Soviet law accommodates itself freely to the needs of the bureaucracy. For example, two organizations may have a contract relating, say, to the affairs of a collective farm or to labor matters. The local soviet can sue in the name of a member of one of the organizations without the member's consent for the construction of the contract. The local soviet has no immediate interest in the controversy except as a governmental busybody. But it marches into court under a law giving it power to protect the "interests of the state" in all private agreements. And the court is free to give any relief it chooses, even beyond that prayed for in the complaint.

I saw some civil trials and many criminal trials. Of these, two criminal trials stand out in retrospect from all the rest. One was in Tashkent. The defendant was a Russian. The charge was contempt of court for failure to obey an order of the court directing him to pay alimony to his two ex-wives and to support the teen-age child of his second marriage. The defendant was a Russian and two of the three judges were Russians, the third being an Uzbek. All three judges were women. The prosecutor was a woman. The lawyer assigned the accused by the College of Advocates was a woman. And the witnesses against him were his two ex-wives. I never saw a more benighted man. He was charged with an offense of which women would be apt to be most critical. And there was not a man in the courtroom to raise his voice and inject any touch of the male point of view.

To make matters worse, the defendant was a deaf mute. He spoke with sign language through an interpreter who translated into Russian. It appeared that the defendant's mother had broken up both marriages and was using up all of the man's income. He was an expert shoemaker, well thought of by the factory manager. And he made good wages. He did not drink or gamble and had a fine reputation for sobriety and hard work. His two ex-wives, however, had a different view. His two wives had many basic disagreements. But on one point they were agreed. They rated him as a low wastrel who had no streak of decency in him.

The prosecutor made an impassioned plea. She emphasized the great attention the state gives to the welfare of children. She stressed the importance of children to the nation. She described the defendant in vivid terms and made him out as a blackhearted character. She ended with a moving and eloquent plea to have this infamous character sent off to prison and made an example for all Russian husbands who fail to support their families.

The defense lawyer, like Portia, pleaded for mercy, saying her miserable client had learned his lesson.

The defendant then stood and asked the judges for another chance, promising to be good.

In thirty minutes the judges returned with their decision. The all-woman court did quite well by the deaf mute. Their judgment was tempered with mercy. "The defendant is convicted and sentenced to one year in prison. Sentence is suspended and defendant is put on probation so long as he makes the monthly alimony payments previously directed by the Court."

The last trial I attended was in Leningrad. The courtroom was on the ground floor of a decrepit office building and faced an alley. The high ceiling and white walls gave an impression of roominess. But the dirty windows on the alley let in little light. It was a dingy place without electricity. A picture of Stalin hung behind the bench. The judges sat in high-backed, stiff, wooden chairs, decorated at the top with the hammer and sickle.

The judges were Russians, the presiding judge being a distinguished-looking, forty-year-old jurist. The two side-judges were middle-aged women who looked as ordinary and as unsophisticated as any of those in Leningrad's private market selling their tomatoes and grapes. These lady judges sat in plain house dresses made of rather loud prints.

The accused was a Pole in his late twenties. He had no criminal record. He worked as an unskilled laborer in a factory where he had a good record. Until recently he had no blemish on his character. He met up with a girl who fascinated him. But he could not afford her the luxuries she wanted. One day in a department store he saw in a flash the answer to his problem. A lady had inadvertently left her handbag on a counter as she shopped. The Pole without premeditation seized the bag, put it under his coat, and made for the door. The lady saw him out of the corner of her eye and went in pursuit. When she reached the street she screamed, and the defendant broke into a dead run. The lady, about thirty years old and built like an athlete, took up the chase. She quickly gained on the Pole and he, to rid himself of the loot, tossed it into an ash can in the courtyard of a house. The owner stopped long enough to retrieve her bag and then took up the chase once more. The Pole was now a half block ahead. But she screamed again, attracting the attention of a policeman who nabbed the defendant.

That was the gist of the evidence given by five witnesses. The most effective witness was the young lady whose bag was stolen. She stood in the witness dock with dignity and gave her testimony with clarity and force. And as she testified her small, three-year-old child—a cute blond like his mother—tugged at her skirts and jumped up and down trying to get her to leave. The mother testified with the confidence that Russian women who were army officers in World War II had shown in their defense of Leningrad. This witness was defending her family and her property. Her testimony had a potent effect.

The defendant, who pleaded guilty, was a woebegone character

—stooped and pale, with eyes that fairly danced with nervousness. His plea and the plea of his lawyer were for mercy. They emphasized that this was his first offense and that the defendant had tuberculosis. The penalty for a first offense of this character is five years in prison. Even the prosecutor thought that was too stiff, for he asked for a lighter sentence. He was insistent, however, that a prison term be imposed. And the one that the court shortly agreed on was two years.

The most interesting phase of the case was the prosecutor's closing speech. He started with these words, "The Supreme Soviet has decreed the sacred nature of personal property. Property must be respected. This defendant did not respect it. All who do not work in harmony with the objectives of the state to make the right of property sacred and inviolate must be punished."

There is not much room in Russia for private enterprise. But the ideas of property have not died. They are lively ones. As Gsovski in *Soviet Civil Law* and Hazard in *Law and Social Change in the U.S.S.R.* show in detail, they protect the individual's home, his garden plot, his job, his interest in his collective farm, his share of profits in his co-operative society, his right to inherit property, his personal effects, and even his right to recover damages for tortious conduct that injures him. The Soviets have made a marked change by substituting the word "personal" for "private" throughout Soviet legal literature, as Berman in *Justice in Russia* relates. Socialist property—that is, goods and funds of the state—are protected by more severe sanctions than personal property. But even personal property has a deep taproot in Russian law.

CHAPTER 7

MUSIC AND THE THEATER

Every Russian city has at least one Park of Culture
and Rest. The culture is often no more than a ferris
wheel, a pool table, a weight-lifting machine, a tank for swimming, a basketball court, a soccer field, or a big pole that travels an
arc of 180° with the customer, for the price of a ruble, tied to one
end. There are parks for adults and parks for children. In some of
the children's parks there are miniature railroads with coal-burning engines pulling small day coaches along a track that runs in a
loop. Children operate the train and manage the enterprise. It's a
part of their training as Pioneers—the group from seven years to
fourteen years that the Communists organize and supervise in
preparation for membership in the Komsomol. I saw these railroads both in Baku and in Alma Ata.

In Central Asia the city parks are deep in shade, designed as a
haven from the dazzling heat that often touches 120° Fahrenheit
in the summertime. Some of these parks are rich in botanical spec-
imens. Frunze, one of the loveliest cities of Asia I have seen, has

100 different species of trees (including the locust and poplar) in her parks, species that have been collected all over Asia. As many or more could probably be counted in Samarkand and Tashkent.

In Central Asia it is common to find two dance floors in the parks—one for Russians, the other for natives. The segregation is not essentially a racial one. Rather, it provides the community with two different types of music. The Russian dance floor has European and American music; and it is by all odds the favorite one. The native dance floor has native music suited to the unique dances of that race. At Stalinabad, the Tadzhik dance floor in the park had a Tadzhik orchestra of six pieces—guitars, violin, drums, and a tambourine. A blind man played the violin. An old, old Turkmen with a peaked head and close-cropped gray hair played the tambourine. It was a cool night and the old man built a fire of old newspapers on the concrete dance floor over which he warmed the skin of the tambourine, hoping to give it a sharper tone.

The Russian parks commonly have lecture halls and movie theaters. They also have pavilions where orchestras or bands give recitals or concerts. At Baku, a brass band plays every afternoon and evening in one of the city parks. It is composed of men who have all the appearances of derelicts and who play slightly off key. But no one seems to mind, for the music is for children. Other bands I heard were more finished and polished. And the orchestras I came across in the parks were most competent. They gave recitals during the afternoons and evenings. The music was classical and attracted great crowds. The performances were free to all who paid the admission price into the park.

I remember particularly an all-Russian orchestra playing in a two-hundred-acre park at Alma Ata. This was a Sunday afternoon and at least a thousand people were gathered to hear the recital. It was a superb performance, worthy of any of our concert halls.

At Ashkhabad I attended a Turkmen "concert" given in a hall in Ashkhabad's largest park. Two men and a woman made up the troupe. One man played a fiddlelike instrument; the other two played guitars. The woman did all the singing. They were brightly dressed in Turkmen clothes and held an audience of fifty Turkmens spellbound with old Turkish songs.

These Russian parks are municipal projects, operated by an official responsible to the mayor. The entrance fee is usually a ruble, though children get free admission. The young, energetic director of the two-hundred-acre city park in Alma Ata explained the business end of the enterprise to me. The city makes a profit from all the items sold in the park. There are pushcarts selling ice cream, beer, soft drinks, cigarettes, tobacco, cough medicines, and contraceptives. The carts are, in substance, branches of the local retail stores owned by the city. There are fees for the ferris wheel and all the other attractions, including the movies. The park must pay Moscow for the movie films; and its admission charge (usually one ruble) is designed to recoup the cost and make a profit. Moscow also charges the city for orchestras that perform in the park. The Russian orchestra I heard in the park at Alma Ata cost the park 1200 rubles ($96) a day. There is no way to charge for open-air concerts. So the park must pay for the orchestra out of its profits.

These orchestras—both big and small—travel all over Russia. Many other theatrical troupes do likewise, all of them being constantly on the move by car, by train, by plane, visiting city after city, entertaining in theaters, in parks, on farms, and in factories.

All musicians, dancers, singers, actors, stagehands, directors, designers of costumes and scenery—the whole entourage of the theater—are on the payroll of the state. Entertainment is in the *public sector*. There are no private theatrical companies in Russia. Every comedian, every trumpet player, every ballet dancer gets a monthly check from the Ministry of Culture.

The average actor or musician gets a salary that ranges from 800 rubles ($64) a month to 1300 rubles ($124) a month. The great stars get much, much more. Galina Ulanova, the famous ballerina, draws 7000 rubles ($560) a month. And she, of course, has much more independence than the average actor or musician. The average artist does his daily stint. He works eleven months a year and gets a month's vacation with full pay. When he travels, he gets his expenses from the state. The state supplies the costumes, the scenery, and the musical instruments. More accurately, the state gives each troupe an annual allowance for these items—an allowance the troupe can spend as it chooses. These allowances are generous. The Russian artist, like the Russian worker or farm hand, can retire when old age comes, at one quarter of his average lifetime salary. The Russian people dress poorly; and their diet, though nutritious, does not have much variety. But nothing of splendor or luxury, either in quantity or quality, is spared in the Russian theater. When it comes to the opera and ballet, all of Russia goes on a splurge.

I do not have the figure of the number of people employed in the theater and on the stage in Russia. But from what I saw I believe it would be a staggering one. For the Soviets have gone into entertainment on a vast scale. Part of it is for propaganda purposes. But the true reason strikes deeper. Russians love music and the theater. The opera and the ballet are almost as important to them as bread. That, at least, was my impression, an impression that has supporting evidence. For example, during World War II when the Germans were invading, the Russians moved many of their factories to Siberia. Novosibirsk, a city of 80,000, grew in a few years to 800,000. Factories were moved there, including a large planing and milling plant which I visited. With the factories came a host of war workers. One of the first demands was for housing. Another was for an opera house. And so in the midst of a war that almost severed Russia in two, the Soviets put up in Novosibirsk a magnificent opera house that seats 3000 people.

Many of the truly great heroes of the Russians are theatrical stars. Galina Ulanova, the ballerina who dances so lightly she seems to float, is loved and adored. So are Emil Gilels, the great pianist, and David Oistrakh, the outstanding violinist, heard by American audiences in 1955. These people are almost gods, being above the storms and stresses of life. They represent great spiritual values—the values of beauty, rhythm, and harmony. The Russian gives these values perhaps the highest place in his scheme of things.

The theater has experienced a tremendous renaissance under the Soviets. Young, promising actors, musicians, or dancers are taken from farms and factories and sent off to Moscow for training. New talent is being constantly searched out. Musical troupes coming to the big cities from collective farms and factories are carefully screened. The departments of entertainment in Russia are on the lookout for promising youngsters, much as the American baseball industry combs the sand-lots looking for major-league talent.

Once the youngsters are trained in Moscow, they are assigned to some troupe or company; and their careers start.

The Soviets truly blanket the nation with traveling musical troupes and theatrical companies. I saw professional Russian singers and dancers from Moscow performing at special dinners tendered by collective farms in Central Asia. I saw Russian movies that show traveling theatrical troupes going into remote areas to entertain the country folk. Some go high into the mountains to reach sheepherders and their families. Others travel rutted roads to faraway collective farms. All over Russia dancers, singers, and comedians go on circuit, so to speak. So do the lovely ensembles that every republic has. The Azerbaijan Ensemble of sixty men and women travels much of the year. It has a flute, an accordian, drum, tambourine, guitar, and violin for its orchestra. The music is excellent, the costumes exquisite, the singing and dancing good. The Ensemble gives a whole evening of entertainment with a dozen or more acts. I heard them in an open-air theater at Baku on a warm summer night. The stage, set at one edge of a large courtyard, had a rounded ceiling that produced excellent acoustics. The setting and effect reminded me very much of the Watergate in Washington, D.C.

This Ensemble not only moves throughout Azerbaijan. For a month or so each year it travels to Moscow and to the capitals of the other republics as well. Azerbaijan's Ensemble builds its program mostly around folklore, Azerbaijan history, Azerbaijan music. One of its famous productions is *The Girl's Tower*—a Romeo and Juliet type of drama. The Girl's Tower still stands in Baku. It's an ancient stone affair, rather nondescript in the setting of modern Baku. It is now surrounded by land. In olden days it sat on the edge of the sea and served as a lighthouse. It got its name from a girl who committed suicide by leaping from it into a raging sea. She was in love with a Prince Charming whom she was barred from marrying. Her family forced her to marry a count who, unlike her true love, had prestige and fortune. But she resolved never to give herself to the count. After the wedding festivities, she fled the palace and sought refuge in the Tower. The count went in pursuit. The lover followed. He and the count met in a duel of knives on the ground floor of the Tower. The lover killed the count and raced up the wide stone stairs to claim his sweetheart. She stood on the parapet filled with fear and panic. She heard the footsteps rushing up the stairs and thought the count had finally cornered her. She would never give herself to the count. She would be ever true to her lover. So she cast herself from the parapet into the sea, not realizing that it was her lover who had come to claim her.

Azerbaijan also has a philharmonic orchestra dedicated to classical music. Azerbaijan has in addition an opera and ballet. These too travel all over Azerbaijan and make national tours as well.

Each republic has an ensemble, philharmonic orchestra, and an opera and ballet. Many large towns also have their own opera and

BUKHARA

The old wall
of the ancient city
of Bukhara still stands.

Bukhara was long a center
of Moslem fanaticism.

A mullah calls the faithful
to prayer at a mosque
in Bukhara.

The walls of the Registan
at Samarkand are being
fully restored.

BUKHARA

Left: The Registan at Samarkand is one of the great architectural glories of the world.

Bottom left: The Tower of Death at Bukhara is an ancient place of execution.

Below: The Bug Pit at Bukhara has been converted into a popular museum.

TASHKENT

A middle-aged Uzbek woman is head of a textile co-op at Tashkent.

At Tashkent an old residence has been converted into a courthouse.

The Baptist minister at Tashkent asked me to deliver the sermon.

A worker and his family own a new four-room house at Tashkent.

TASHKENT

Thinning cotton blooms is one of the few kinds of manual labor that remains on Russia's cotton farms.

Children have dancing classes at a Pioneer camp near Tashkent.

The farmers' markets at Tashkent are large and well organized.

Some farmers sell their farm produce from the shady side of a road near Tashkent.

ballet companies. Novosibirsk has one that plays all the cities as far east as Vladivostok. Many of the larger cities also have their own circuses. Novosibirsk has one as a part of its theater. This circus goes on a long tour each year. I did not see a Russian circus. But I did see quite a number of theatrical companies or troupes before I reached Moscow. None quite compared with those of Moscow and Leningrad. But they were, nonetheless, composed of distinguished artists who were well trained and talented.

There are traveling theatrical companies out of Moscow and other large cities entertaining crowds all across Russia. In Bukhara I saw the Samarkand players—an accomplished lot—put on a play called *Ivan Rybakov* that concerns the dissolute son of a prominent revolutionary hero. The son had forsaken the Communist path and had no interest in the serious affairs of state. He had given himself up to vodka, women, and song. The ending shows his conversion—his realization that he was wasting his life; his desire to lead the disciplined life of the party worker.

In Central Asia as in other parts of the nation, the Russians have used the theater to further the Communist cause. One of the literary lights of Central Asia whom they have extolled is Alishir Nevayi, a distinguished Persian poet of the fifteenth century. Nevayi is chosen because his life can be used to portray the evils of the old khans and the ancient feudal system under which the people lived in czarist days. Moreover, Nevayi has export value. He was a Persian and his home was at Herat in Afghanistan. The choice of Nevayi is, therefore, a studied one. He is being built up as a spiritual tie with Afghanistan and Iran against the day when Communist governments control those countries.

The Russians, of course, use the native arts to promote the Communist cause. Even the lovely ensembles are turned to propaganda. The Tatar Ensemble in Tashkent opens with songs praising Lenin and the Soviet cause. The Azerbaijan Ensemble has a finale with dancers dressed in the costumes of the people of each Soviet republic. Each group in turn does a dance typical of the republic it represents. Near the end, a group of four, dressed in red and representing Russia, enters, whirling and stomping in a wild Russian dance. Then they form the hub of a great wheel with some sixty dancers forming the spokes. As the wheel turns, Miss Russia is raised in the center. She represents the role of the Russian in uniting divers racial, ethnic, and religious groups. She symbolizes the dominant role of the Great Russian in the affairs of all the affiliated people.

The Krai Ensemble at Barnaul has thirty excellent voices. One of the baritones is a close image of Justice Holmes at eighty—mustache and all. Most of the songs they sang were Czech and Hungarian. One Russian song told how bleak Siberia was before the Revolution. "Not till then did even the fresh wind blow," sang the talented choir in great seriousness.

In the park at Stalinabad I visited the Tadzhik dance floor twice. The first night only men were dancing—each putting on a solo performance. The next night the music attracted both men and women, each of whom did his own individual dance. Sometimes two dancers would come together for a few movements; but they quickly separated, never touching. The dancing was beautifully done; and the crowd that lined the edges of the floor was an enthusiastic, happy one. The dancing lasted for at least two hours. It was about eleven o'clock when I suggested to an attractive Tadzhik couple that they sing us some Tadzhik songs. A group of a dozen or more young people in their teens quickly assembled and burst forth with a rousing song. The music was unmistakably Persian. But the theme was Russian. It called for co-operation of all Tadzhiks with Russia and ended with a great burst—"Hail to Russia and to the great Stalin."

Russia's nationalism is hitched to communism; and it is communism that is the measure of patriotism. Where American songs help teach patriotism to American children, Russian songs teach

patriotism to Russia. And the theme of that patriotism is socialism. Socialism, though a Russian phenomenon, has manifestations
in many other countries. The Revolution which Lenin proclaimed
runs throughout the world. Therefore, the Russian song writer or
singing teacher does more than develop the theme of Russian socialism.

The point was well illustrated at a Pioneer camp which I visited
at Tashkent. This camp had 265 children between the ages of
seven and fourteen, most of them Russian and supervised by a
dozen teachers. They remained in camp for twenty-seven days,
at the end of which another group reported. Three groups in all
are taken each summer.

The camp was a pleasant, shaded place of generous acreage.
There was a large dining room; separate dormitories for girls and
boys; a library; basketball, volleyball, and tennis courts; a swimming pool; table tennis; and a small outdoor theater. Children are
read Communist literature; they participate in Communist discussion groups; they learn Russian dances and Russian music; and
they sing Russian and Communist songs.

The singing and dancing groups put on a special performance
for me on a wooden platform out under the trees. The music was
an accordion played by a teacher. Couples danced; there were individual performances; there were dances reminding me of our
polkas; there were four teams of four children each doing complicated steps. In between dances there were many folk songs,
some Ukrainian, some Russian, and a few Uzbek. There was one
Uzbek song that had an especially distinctive rhythm:

> *I have a chicken*
> *It will soon be a hen*
> *The hen will have chickens*
> *Then I'll have lots of chickens*
> *I'll take good care of them.*

At the end of the program the entire student group assembled as a choir and sang the famous "Dock Worker's Song":

The dock workers of France will not fight the dock workers of Russia; the dock workers of France will not fight the dock workers of other lands.

Not all of the Russian theater is prostituted for propaganda purposes. Foreign literature that does not clash with the Communist ideology or that shows the seamy side of "capitalism" is often dramatized. When I was in Alma Ata the Moscow Players were in town for a week. They were presenting Dickens's *Our Mutual Friend* at Alma Ata's beautiful opera house that holds a thousand people. They played there a week. The matinees were for children; and they packed the theater. It was also packed at night for a non-political, hilarious comedy involving two lovelorn young men and several lovelorn young women.

At Frunze I saw *Moon Beauty* performed in a lovely theater that holds a thousand people. *Moon Beauty* is an opera based on an ancient Kirgiz ballad that has passed down by word of mouth. The producer, whom I met, is a Kirgiz who traveled all of Kirgizia to get the various versions of the story. On his long journey he also did research on Kirgiz music and Kirgiz dancing. He came back rich with ideas and suggestions. What he worked out and finally produced is a superb performance.

There is an orchestra of forty instruments led by a talented Kirgiz and very strong in the strings.

Kizibayeva played the heroine, I Churek. She has a powerful voice of great range. The male voices, though not outstanding, were good. The men were dressed in high-crowned hats with turned-up brims, having a distinct Spanish touch. The Kirgiz old men wore either a droopy mustache or a long goatee, often on the thin side. The male dancers had high leather boots; and they were most adept at leaping and springing. Some of the men's robes were like the silk ones presented to Bob and me at a collective farm near Frunze—mid-calf length, multicolored stripes with green, red, blue, and white predominating, and tied with a brilliant, red silk sash. The Kirgiz women, unlike most Central Asian actresses, wore dresses, not pantaloons. These women were small and graceful; and they danced exquisitely, taking fine advantage of their delicate hands. The Kirgiz came to Kirgizia about a century after Genghis Khan roared through the region. They came down from the north to escape oppression. Though Mongol in antecedents they have long been Moslem in tradition. That is why some of the Kirgiz actresses have a suggestion of a veil in their headdress. Others of them wear a huge white turban with a six-inch band of gold cloth. The stage has great depth and height; and the acoustics are perfect. The stage settings are elaborate and beautiful, being done in good taste and without skimping.

I Churek is in love with Cementai, played by Chodraigov. Cementai already has a wife. But that is no deterrent in Kirgizia, for it is a Moslem country. There is, however, one serious obstacle. I Churek's father is in great danger. A rival prince has a superior army made up of savage characters.

> *Their scalps are heavier than big kettles.*
> *Their eyebrows are like lying dogs.*
> *Their mustaches are like poleaxes.*
> *Their eyes are as deep as the depths of lakes.*
> *And deadly for all are their terrible looks.*

So sang one actor, as these savage troops closed in on the father of I Churek. There is one easy solution of the difficulty. The rival prince will recall his hordes if I Churek promises to marry him. The marriage must take place in forty days—or else.

I Churek reluctantly agrees. Then the ugly warriors leave with the rival prince and I Churek sings:

> *How unfortunate am I,*
> *Why am I not a daughter of a slave?*
> *Why am I not a daughter of the moon?*
> *Why am I not a daughter of a wave?*
> *Then I would sleep on the bare ground,*
> *The moon would shine upon me,*
> *I would fly as a moon's ray,*
> *Lighting the roaring spring.*
> *I would run as a wave*
> *Over the broad homeland.*

At the end of the forty-day period she turns herself into a swan and flies away to Cementai's country. There she meets Cementai's wife, quarrels with her, and marries Cementai. Then starts a long bitter fight between Cementai and the rival. The rival races across the stage on a horse to battle Cementai who is also mounted. The rule is that the contest goes to the one who can pull the other from his horse and carry him away. Cementai performs the feat and takes the rival off stage. Then he reappears with two horses and rides off in glory with his new bride.

It was a packed theater. The Kirgiz audience was enthusiastic and there was curtain call after curtain call in response to the applause. The actors were worthy of acclaim, because their performance was a moving one. I told them as much when I met them backstage for color pictures after the final curtain. I think it was that opera and the backstage meeting that made me first appreciate the high professional character of the Russian theater.

I liked this Kirgiz troupe so well I attended the Frunze theater the next night also. That time I saw the Kirgiz ballet, *Cholpon.* The leading ballerina was Djamanova, the leading man Nurdin—both Kirgiz. It was almost as lovely as the ballets which I later saw at the Bolshoi Theater in Moscow. It was indeed superbly done. Djamanova is on her way to becoming another Ulanova.

This is the ballet where the hero is beset by three women. Djamanova is the wholesome country girl in love with Nurdin. One of her competitors is a beautiful but evil witch, dressed in black and carrying a huge, white silk scarf. With one wave of the scarf she easily interests the hero. The other competitor is a sophisticated damsel in white. She too has great beauty; she is the incomparable siren. Djamanova discovers the secret of the witch. Her power is in her white silk scarf. Without the scarf the witch will die. She who possesses the scarf can work her own magic. And so Djamanova resolves to get the scarf. Here occurs, in a funereal scene, one of the most beautiful ballet dance scenes I have witnessed. Both Djamanova and the witch are superb. Djamanova seizes the scarf; the witch whirls in frenzy. She slowly dissolves into a writhing mass on the floor. Soon she is dead. Then comes the triumphal scene of the victory of Djamanova over the siren. This scene is more relaxed. The finale comes unexpectedly. Djamanova at the end of one slow movement holds the scarf for a moment in front of the siren who has just curtsied, lifts the scarf, and the siren has dissolved into thin air. Nurdin and Djamanova then unite to do a stirring dance; and the final curtain falls.

I went backstage and met Nurdin and the lovely Djamanova. Peter Tutlis, the Kirgiz deputy of the Mayor of Frunze and a most gracious host, was with me. He had told me in the theater that Djamanova excelled even Ulanova. I had not seen Ulanova at that time. But I told Djamanova of Mr. Tutlis's praise and she fairly beamed. I told her that while I could not compare her with Ulanova, I knew she was as accomplished as any ballerina who ever appeared on an American stage. She is, indeed, one of the great artists of the world.

While Russia has exploited Kirgizia, she also has done much for that country. Prior to the October Revolution the Kirgiz had no written literature, no drama, no written music, let alone a ballet. Russia brought them all to Kirgizia and discovered great talent among the people. Djamanova is one of those discoveries.

The Uzbek theater has also undergone a great development under the Soviets. One of those responsible is Bukalov, the energetic
Uzbek architect of Tashkent. Bukalov, a short, slight man about
fifty and graying, is an artist with a real love for his Uzbek people
and their heritage. He showed me the Uzbek Opera and Drama
Theater in Tashkent for which he was primarily responsible. It is
spaciously built, seating fifteen hundred people. The stage is massive, the acoustics perfect. A huge glass chandelier hangs in the
middle of the theater and this chandelier carries out the motif
of the small Uzbek hat one sees everywhere in Tashkent. There
are three floors to the theater, each floor having two separate halls.
Each of the six halls represents a school of Uzbek art. Fergana is
there. So are Bukhara and Samarkand. Each of these halls has
friezes and panels delicately carved. The most delicate of all is
Fergana's. The most distinctive is Bukhara's, for the latter has glass
behind the delicate rock and plaster carvings. The lobbies and
entrance hall have murals showing Uzbek historic events. They are
delicate in the Persian sense of the word and are brightly painted.
Bukalov took me by the arm when we reached these paintings
and gave me a lecture "for the benefit of the West," as he put it.

"You Westerners think that Islam did not foster the arts, that it
outlawed paintings. That was not true in Central Asia. Here in
Uzbekistan great artists flourished under Moslem rule."

Bukalov's special pride was the tall, delicate columns and the
high, graceful arches marking both the exterior and the interior.
One sees duplicates of them in the Uzbek pavilion at the Agricultural Fair in Moscow. They have fine lines, delicate and majestic.
I admired them greatly and said as much to Bukalov. I started
to compare them to the Ionic and Doric columns in Greece. He
quickly interrupted to say there were no borrowings from the
Greeks in Uzbek architecture.

"Even though Alexander the Great got to Samarkand, he left no architectural heritage behind."

Whether that is true I do not know. But the Uzbek columns and arches that adorn the Opera and Drama Theater in Tashkent are the loveliest I have seen anywhere in the world.

I saw one drama in this beautiful theater. The play was *Farhad and Shirin,* one of Nevayi's most famous productions. Farhad is an Asian prince who traveled to Greece. There he was presented with a sealed box that contained his future. He was warned that he should not open the box in Greece but wait until he had returned to Uzbekistan. If he opened the box prematurely, evil results might follow. Farhad, however, could not wait. He opened the box in Greece to see in a mirror the vision of a beautiful Uzbek girl. He hastened home, searched for the girl, and found her. Her name was Shirin and the two fell madly in love. Difficulties, however, quickly developed. The prime minister of the realm had his eyes on Shirin and planned to marry her. He laid a plot against Farhad. There was heavy fighting and Farhad was killed. Shirin to escape the prime minister took poison and died.

This drama was beautifully enacted by an Uzbek cast. There must have been over 100 actors and actresses on the stage. The scenery was exquisite. An Uzbek orchestra under an accomplished director gave an outstanding performance. This dramatic company would rate high on any stage in the world, and I told them so when I visited backstage after the final curtain.

The development of the theater in Kazakhstan has been a vital part of the Soviet program. The Soviets have developed all aspects of the Kazakh theater. They have discovered local talent, sent the young ones off to Moscow for training, and organized them into troupes on their return. They have resurrected old Kazakh dances, scoured the hills for Kazakh ballads, sent their scouts into the farthest reaches of vast Kazakhstan to find ancient stories and legends out of which they could build plays and musicales. The ballet now flourishes in Kazakhstan. Operas, plays, musicales, and ballet are indeed big business in Kazakhstan. The Soviets have so developed the theater in Kazakhstan that in 1955 there were twenty-five established theaters serviced by eight concert, dramatic and ballet troupes. These groups have several troupes each. They give all told about 20,000 performances a year. Alma Ata, its capital and a modern city of 400,000, produced thirty different operas in the winter of 1954–55. Some of these were Russian. Many were German and Italian. The list included all the classics with which we are familiar in America.

I saw Kazakh artists perform. One of their musical instruments looks like a banjo. Another looks like a zither, only three times as large. Another is something like a xylophone and played with two hammers. It has eight flat steel bands about an inch across that are tuned at various pitches.

The Kazakh songs reminded me very much of the cowboy songs of our West. In one I could almost hear the shuffle of the feet of sheep; in another the pounding of the hoofs of cattle; in some the sound of wind; in others the loneliness of the cowboy. Kazakhstan is, indeed, great sheep and cattle country. Alma Ata sits at the base of the Tien Shan Mountains of Sinkiang. Great snow peaks rise behind the city to the southwest. To the north stretch vast rolling plains—the great steppes—that reminded me very much of the country north of Denver. This is country to ride to the wind horseback. Here are probably the finest grazing lands in all of Asia. It would be natural to hear hoofs of livestock, the whine of the wind, and the loneliness of the rolling steppes in the music of the people who live there. I also saw other signs of the cowboy environment in the Kazakh dances. Some of them might well have been done to a "hoe down" with "The Turkey in the Straw." One dance is an excellent imitation of our square dance—the Texas Star. The Kazakhs, however, have five couples rather than four in that dance. But the essential movements of the two are the same.

Kazakh women dancers wear pantaloons and sleeveless jackets (usually blue) over a white dress that has full and flowing sleeves. The women use scarves in their dancing so as to leave a suggestion of a veil.

The male dancers wear boots and full pants. Their typical hat is karakul—round and low-crowned. Another hat has a very narrow brim and an eight-inch dome made of alternate strips of white and dark pieces of leather or cloth.

The dances are strenuous affairs with much whirling and stomping.

I did not see the Alma Ata opera, for the troupe was on vacation. Three of their stars, however, tendered Bob and me a dinner at a small resort hotel about eight miles outside of Alma Ata, as I related earlier. The hosts were the soprano, Nina K. Kuklina, the alto, Jamal Omarova, and the baritone, Ermek Serkebaev. They sang both Kazakh songs and Russian songs. Then they sang from European operas. Serkebaev sang some selections from *The Barber of Seville* and Kuklina sang some from *Faust*. These artists were all trained in Moscow. They all have received various awards for their professional achievement. Serkebaev won the Bucharest contest in 1954. Each is a powerful singer with a great range. Each has strength of character that comes through with every song.

"We love our work," Kuklina told me in broken English. And it was obvious that they did.

It is the custom in Russia for the guest to contribute to the entertainment as well as to enjoy it. After the hosts have performed, he is called upon—at least in the country districts. Once at a Pioneer camp I had to do a Russian dance with a twelve-year-old girl. Once I had to do a thumping Cossack polka with a Russian teacher. This night in Alma Ata after the operatic stars had performed, Bob and I were called upon to sing. We selected from our short repertoire Yale's "Whiffenpoof Song" (which like Kazakh songs has black sheep in it) and received hearty applause. Then two of the operatic stars responded. Kuklina sang a Kazakh song entitled "Come Again," and the great baritone sang "The Return of the Traveler."

Later in Moscow and Leningrad I was to see great operas and brilliant ballets. What stands out are the opera, *Ivan Susanin,* which I saw in Leningrad and two well-known ballets performed at the Bolshoi Theater in Moscow. They were *Swan Lake,* in which the famous Golovkina danced the lead, and *The Fountain of Bakhchisarai,* in which Ulanova was the star. Both nights the Bolshoi was packed, even the seven gold and red balconies that rise on each side of the theater. One night two thirds of the entire audience was Chinese or Malay. The second night Asians also outnumbered Russians and other Europeans. Both nights the theater was filled with a conglomerate of people of many races and tongues all drawn together by the common love of the theater. The crowd loved the director of the symphony almost as much as it loved Ulanova. Every time the director took his post he received a deafening applause. At the end, Ulanova took nearly two dozen curtain calls, the audience standing in the aisles refusing to leave. As I stood in the midst of this phenomenal demonstration, I remembered Kuklina and Serkebaev in far-off Alma Ata, and Djamanova in remote Frunze. I also remembered some of our own great—Vladimir Horowitz, Arturo Toscanini, Artur Rubinstein, Eugene Ormandy, Yehudi Menuhin, and Marian Anderson. The love of music and beauty that moved the audience in the Bolshoi also moves us.

There are many differences between people—differences of race, religion, politics. But music bridges all these differences. The musician speaks the universal tongue. He draws all men together into one fraternity. The great musician is the symbol of the world's artistic unity.

This night Ulanova had full command over the multiracial audience assembled at the Bolshoi. Emil Gilels, the Russian pianist who makes the piano sing, and David Oistrakh, the famous Russian violinist, evoke the same response. So do our great American musicians and artists. Our artists will take to Russia the knowledge that we too speak the universal language.

CHAPTER 8

FREEDOM OF EXPRESSION

There is no freedom of expression in Russia as we of the West know it. That is true whatever the medium. In the West, art is not required to have an ulterior purpose. It is not an instrument of political parties or of economic or social groups. True, it is sometimes used for political ends, e.g., as part of a reformer's project. A play, a painting, a novel may be used to expose, ridicule, or condemn with a view of getting a law passed, a slum cleared, an institution such as slavery or child labor abolished. But the play, the painting, the novel need not have any value but an aesthetic one. It may express no more than a mood or the artist's conception of the infinite.

In the Soviet world, most art and literature have served a different end. Under Stalin art had to be class art that advanced the class struggle. All creative effort had to serve that end. It had to glorify the achievements of communism, depict the depravities of "capitalism," challenge the workers to new tasks, or in some other way advance the Communist cause. As the *New World* wrote in

1949, Soviet literature is "an active ideologico-artistic weapon in the struggle for happiness of all mankind."

Regimentation of art and literature is, of course, not new. Nor is it peculiarly an invention of the Soviets. The Renaissance did service in freeing art from strictly moral and religious ends. It took great revolutions in England, France, and America to get rid of thought control, prior restraints on publication, and other forms of regimentation over the press.

The Soviets have maintained a strict system of regimentation. The purges of authors and artists in modern Russia, especially under Stalin, have been numerous.

Since Stalin's death there has been a change. Literature and art previously banned have had their legitimacy restored. Authors and painters once on the black list are now respectable. Foreign authors, previously outlawed, are now legal.

Dostoevski, who had been condemned as "reactionary," especially for his early works *The Double* and *The Possessed,* has been recently acclaimed. A new collection of his works is now being prepared in Moscow.

The *New York Times, New York Herald Tribune, Chicago Tribune,* and several other American newspapers, and the *U.S. News & World Report, Business Week, Nation,* and several other American magazines are now to be found in a few of the institutes or colleges, though none of them can be purchased in the kiosks on the streets. The ordinary Soviet citizen is free to subscribe only to foreign papers or magazines that are published in an eastern Europe Communist country, Red China, North Korea, North Vietnam, or Outer Mongolia.

More and more scientific treatises and magazines from America and England are made available in libraries. An increasing number of American books and newspapers will be going to Russia (and Russian publications coming here) under a new exchange program worked out by the Library of Congress and some American universities.

A new Soviet periodical called *Foreign Literature* has appeared, which will publish the works of modern writers of foreign lands. Hemingway, who had been outlawed by the Soviets for his book *For Whom the Bell Tolls,* has some of his standing restored. His classic, *The Old Man and the Sea,* will now be published. So will works of Longfellow, Steinbeck, Caldwell, and Sinclair Lewis. *The Crucible* by Arthur Miller is being produced for the Leningrad theater.

There has been a substantial lessening in censorship of the foreign press and an opening to the press and to the photographers of many areas of Russia, formerly forbidden.

A few years ago the Communist party condemned much French art and left the Soviet's collection in storage. The collection includes Picasso, Manet, Matisse, Renoir, Gauguin, and Cézanne. Today they are no longer "decadent." Today the ban is lifted and this fabulous collection is on exhibition with a brochure explaining that some of the impressionist paintings "reflect modern bourgeois realities." And the *New World* that had previously condemned the French impressionists now says that they represent a school that should be studied as a phase in art history and that the Soviet artists can learn much from these impressionists in the use of color and technique.

Porgy and Bess has now played in Moscow, and other American plays such as Thornton Wilder's *Our Town* and Eugene O'Neill's *Desire Under the Elms* will follow.

These are samples of the new literary and artistic mood prevalent in Russia today. The list is long.

I met no one on my Russian journey who felt that the change was basic. Some thought it showed a trend toward liberalism. It may turn out to be a radical and important development. For wherever books penetrate, wherever people go, ideas travel too.

And ideas, especially ideas from the West, can be dangerous ones, since they reflect freedom and a way of life that have more eternal values than the Soviets yet realize.

But I left Russia feeling that this growing tolerance of foreign art, literature, and people did not reflect any fundamental change. The dictatorship is still as complete and powerful as ever. The tolerance of today can be transmuted to arrogant antagonism tomorrow. The new tolerance will be permanent only so long as it serves Soviet ends.

Under Stalin, Soviet art and literature became crude as well as servile. He wanted flattery and praise. Literature, plays, and art were judged by that standard. That attitude is changing. The new regime thinks the Soviet cause can be more skillfully served if it has greater freedom. It now regards great artistry as an asset. It now gives an author or painter greater range of choice.

The new trend dates back to the Second All-Union Congress of Soviet Writers held in December 1954. At those meetings some artists pleaded for more freedom; others defended the use of art and literature to extol the Communist cause. As I read the proceedings, they seemed to end with an over-all agreement that Soviet literature should serve a dual role.

First, Soviet literature must follow the Party line: "In our literature truth does not diverge from the Party spirit but is closely bound up with it. We know that great art will always be tendentious. The writer is not an observer of life, he is its creator."

Second, Soviet books should "portray not extremes but the wide world, books which show the thoughts and emotions of millions of Soviet people."

Or as another speaker stated, the Soviet writer should, *first,* devote his literary talent to "the cause of man's victory over the dark forces of evil," and, *second,* he should live up to the standard set for the dramatist by Aristophanes: "For truthful speech, for good advice, and for the fact that he makes his compatriots wiser and better."

The message of the Central Committee to the Congress emphasized the same dual role of Soviet literature in the years ahead.

Today an author need not deal with a political issue. He need not prostitute his skill to promote a propaganda drive of the Kremlin. He is of course applauded if he puts a lazy, inefficient bureaucrat identified with Stalin and Beria against one who is eager and efficient by the standards of the new regime, as Korneichuk does in *The Wings*. But these days, if he wants to avoid all contemporary problems and write of people and their emotions, he may do so. I have not seen the book in English, but I was told that Vera Panova, previously attacked by the government, has now produced a classic in *Serezhka*, the story of the loneliness of a boy.

Ideas can be glorified provided they are consistent with the Communist theme. They will indeed be tolerated if they are not inconsistent with that creed. But the state does not yet have the attitude of tolerance which permits the free-for-all to which we are accustomed. There can be no flowering of letters and art under this new regime, though more creative genius is being unleashed than was ever dreamed possible under Stalin.

The new trend reflects, I think, confidence in the Soviet system. Stalin, suspicious, scheming, and evil beyond words, has gone. The present rulers grew up under Stalin. They were, indeed, his number-two men. There can be no doubt that they are greatly relieved at his passing. The Kremlin is now more relaxed. The new rulers see the nation firmly regimented to socialism. They are in full control. As I have said, there are no signs of rebellion. Moreover, there is no one in Russia under forty years old who has not spent practically his entire life under the Soviet regime. There is no one under fifty who has not spent the life he clearly remembers under the Communists. Forty or fifty years of indoctrination, education, propaganda, political organization, regimentation has produced a highly integrated society. There are dissidents; but they are not dangerous. The Soviet leaders who now allow unorthodox ideas to creep into books, plays, art galleries, and libraries are confident that their system is strong enough not to be perverted. The war against the Nazis united the country in a great common endeavor. The devastation that followed in the wake of the war called for heroic action. The peoples of Russia united in projects of great dimensions and found a new solidarity in their joint endeavors. The system today has its inefficiencies and inadequacies. But it works. And given a period of peaceful coexistence, Soviet Russia can reach a new standard of living of which Asia never dreamed.

I discussed the matter of freedom of expression with many university people on my Russian journey. I had one talk at the University of Tashkent that lasted two and a half hours. The Rector of the University, the Vice-Chancellor, and eight faculty members were present. They were an alert, learned group; and one of them, Bondarcosky, who is the head of the Department of Oriental History, speaks excellent English. (There are 200 students and twenty-two faculty members in that Department, all of whom speak English. And in the Department of Political Science about 50 per cent speak English.) As a result of Bondarcosky's fluency in English I covered much ground in this long session.

We talked at length about academic freedom at the University of Tashkent and at other universities and institutes in Russia. The entire group instantly responded when I said that Russian educational institutions did not have the academic freedom which we enjoy at my college, Whitman, at Harvard, or at Columbia. They challenged my statement vigorously. They referred to Article 125 of the Soviet Constitution which at first blush seems to be a charter of liberty:

> "In conformity with the interests of the working people, and in order to strengthen the socialist system, the citizens of the U.S.S.R. are guaranteed by law:

"a) freedom of speech;

"b) freedom of the press;

"c) freedom of assembly, including the holding of mass meetings;

"d) freedom of street processions and demonstrations.

"These civil rights are ensured by placing at the disposal of the working people and their organizations printing presses, stocks of paper, public buildings, the streets, communication facilities and other material requisites for the exercise of these rights."

The faculty group denounced the point of view I had expressed. They pointed out that the University of Tashkent has many magazines published in the United States on foreign affairs, economics, and political science.

"We are hungry for more," said Bondarcosky. "We need to know the world; we need to study all societies, past and present."

"But you extol only communism in the classroom," I replied.

"Communism is our ideology and we are proud of it," Bondarcosky answered. "But we encourage exposure to the ideas of other systems."

"Only to denounce them, not to study them objectively," I said.

"More objectively than some of you look at communism," he replied.

"You would be discharged if you criticized communism in the classroom," I suggested.

At that, the room was in an uproar. Bondarcosky politely but emphatically denied my suggestion. He went on to point out that the Soviet papers and periodicals are filled with criticisms of the Communist party. Only recently, he said, Bulganin had criticized Soviet achievements in industry and Khrushchev had denounced Soviet agriculture.

"The press is full of the shortcomings of our government," he shouted.

Then it was that I first realized what the Soviets mean by "freedom of speech" and "freedom of the press."

"You mean," I said to Bondarcosky, "that there is complete freedom of expression in Russia, provided it is within the discipline of the Communist party."

"Exactly," he answered, as his fist hit the table.

"Within the discipline of the Communist party." That's what Article 125 means. There is freedom of expression, provided it is "in conformity with the interests of the working people" and strengthens "the socialist system." Those words by qualifying the right define the area of free discourse. One can denounce a Russian for being an inefficient, ineffective Communist. One can excoriate the party for failure to fulfill a plan. One can denounce deviationists for bringing discredit on the Communist creed. But one may not denounce the presence of the party in the classroom.

Those who have this freedom are not government officials alone. The press may also operate freely "within the discipline of the party." The press is, indeed, filled with critical accounts. One almost thinks at times that the age of the muckrakers has come to Russia. The press pokes and peers into conditions in factories, on farms, and in bureaus. Dozens of critical articles appear. The following is a sample from the August 16, 1955, issue of *Izvestia*, printed when I was in Central Asia. A roving reporter had discovered a sad state of affairs on collective farms and state farms in southern Kazakhstan:

"A large number of animals died in 1954 because of a fodder shortage. Productivity was much lower than the planned figure. Unfortunately, this lesson did not teach local officials anything. Haying has been in progress in the Chu Valley for ninety days now, yet the assignment for fodder procurement has not even been met 50 per cent.

"How do Comrade Itkin, chairman of the Kurdai District Executive Committee, and Comrade Dzholamanov, chairman of the Chu District Executive Committee, explain this adverse situation in fodder preparation?

"In unison they claim:

"'We do not have enough harvesting equipment.'

"But how is available equipment used?

"The Uspenka Machine and Tractor Station in Kurdai District has 12 power- and 33 tractor-drawn hay mowers. If this equipment were used properly, the mowing could be completed in 35 to 40 working days. But the MTS machine operators are not meeting output norms. They are mowing 300 to 320 hectares per day instead of 700. An unrepaired silage-harvesting combine stands on the grounds of the station. Hay-harvesting machines and ensilage cutters are idle on collective farms in this MTS zone. Large gaps have developed between the mowing, raking, and stacking of hay.

"Instead of organizing work in the preparation of hay and ensiling fodder, officials of Soviet and agricultural agencies in these provinces are flooding republic organizations with petitions to reduce the number of livestock. They are submitting inflated requests for additional equipment although the existing harvesting equipment is not utilized adequately. Parasitic attitudes are particularly strong in Dzhambul Province.

"Officials in the republic Ministry of Agriculture show only a superficial interest in fodder preparation."

The Soviet press is filled with the agitation stirred up by the press and by the party over poor housing, inadequately trained labor, wasteful industry, lagging agriculture, antiquated mining methods, miscarriages of justice, inefficient courts, and even "feather-bedding" of labor.

Self-criticism—within the discipline of the party—has always been a Communist habit. It is, indeed, encouraged to improve administration and to put the bureaucrats on their toes. Even hotels and restaurants have complaint books where aggrieved persons can record their grievances.

I was told that when the party cell meets for discussion of a problem on a farm or in a factory, the discussion is a free-for-all. The discussion has no limits or restraints, provided the permanency and inviolability of the Communist regime is taken for granted. Once the discussion is ended and a vote taken, democratic centralism binds the minority to the majority in an indissoluble bond. Then the cell moves into political action as a united front, a strategy that gives the Communists greater power than any other political group.

That practice has not changed. Party discipline is as strict after Stalin as before. Anyone who thought differently was corrected by the Molotov episode. Molotov in a public paper had referred to the Soviet Union as a place "where the foundations of a socialist society have already been built." Months later Molotov was required by the Praesidium to disapprove that statement. He did so, saying his prior statement was "theoretically mistaken and politically harmful," since it "brings confusion into ideological questions and contradicts the decisions of the party on questions of building a socialist society" in Russia. "It throws doubt," he said, "on the presence of a socialist society which has already been built in the main in our country."

Deviation from the Communist creed is serious enough. Criticism that strikes deep is suspect talk, dangerous discourse carrying severe penalties. Nowhere in Russia—in a park, on a platform, or in a lecture hall—can one with impunity make a speech and say, "We're off on the wrong track. Private enterprise in farming would be better than what we have. Let's bring back the *kulaks*."

On the surface there is great unanimity of opinion in Russia on the major issues. But human nature being what it is, there must be great differences and cleavages under the surface. There must be millions who would prefer more rather than less private enterprise, millions who desire greater freedom of expression. It is clear that there is no dissident group organized to get greater liberty. How deep the differences and cleavages are is difficult for the foreigner to know. I think I came close to it one day when I was talking to a young English-speaking Russian lady thirty years old who told me about her early life. She had been brought up through the nursery and kindergarten and well indoctrinated with the Communist creed. In the summer she had gone to the Pioneer camps until she was fourteen years old. Then she was qualified to join the Komsomol or Young Communist League. I asked her if she had joined it. She said she had not. I asked her why. Her reply was revealing:

"Only those who truly believe in the principles of Lenin and Stalin join the Komsomol," she said. And then she added quickly, so as to cover her thoughts, "Of course we all believe in those principles. But some believe more than others."

I visited numerous libraries in Russia. In fact some of my most interesting talks were with librarians. A good librarian, like a good farmer, is a universal type. He has a love of books and learning that comes before his politics. I felt I met a few of that stripe in Russia. In Tashkent I visited with the librarian and his deputy. They were both tall, thin, and aesthetic-looking. The deputy hovered over books as a mother over children. He handled them tenderly and plainly treasured them above everything else. He had studied under Professor V. Barthold, the famous Russian authority on Central Asia. Barthold taught at Leningrad and at Tashkent until his death in 1930; and it was plain that he had infected this librarian with an interest in all Central Asian affairs. The deputy dug out for me dozens of ancient tomes and handled them as though they were priceless art treasures.

At Stalinabad, I talked with two ladies who were assistant librarians. They too were highly professional and very efficient. They too love books for the sake of literature.

At Alma Ata, I met another dedicated woman in charge of the city library.

I learned in each of these libraries that the favorite American authors are those called "progressive." The librarians included in this category Theodore Dreiser, Howard Fast, Jack London, Harriet Beecher Stowe, Mark Twain, and O. Henry. Very little other American literature is available. The only books I could find on American history, economics, and law were Fowler's *History of the United States,* published about the time of the Civil War, and Sterne's *United States Constitutional History* published in the '80s. There doubtless is a better collection in some of the university libraries. But this was the meager American collection touching on our political and governmental organization that I could find in Central Asia.

"No wonder," I told the librarian at Alma Ata, "that the Russians misunderstand America so thoroughly."

I knew that Moscow had banned many books, including those of "capitalist" Henry Ford. I was anxious to discover if any library had his writings. At Alma Ata I was rewarded. *Today and Tomorrow* and *My Life and Work*—both in Russian—were at last found in a dusty section of the stacks. They were obviously only museum pieces, not works that were circulated or readily available. But I discovered that most of these libraries have the European classics—Dante, Aristotle, Milton, Shakespeare.

All foreign books must be requested from Moscow. No librarian has foreign exchange which he can spend as he chooses on foreign books. Moscow alone has control over their import. The local librarians do have some foreign exchange which they may use for scientific magazines and journals. It is, indeed, the foreign technical magazine, not the foreign magazine that touches government and the humanities, that is prominent in Russian libraries.

The library is a great institution in Russia. There are city libraries in every town of consequence. Each university or institute has its library. The city library has mobile units that service the mills and the city parks. Each district in a state has a district library. These district libraries also have mobile units that go out to collective farms and into the high mountains where the sheep camps are. Libraries cover Russia as thoroughly as the MVD. There are for example 200 districts in Kazakhstan. Each has at least one library. In all of Kazakhstan, where only 6 per cent of the people were literate under the czar, there are 2500 libraries.

These libraries are very popular for reading and study. They are stocked primarily with products of the government printing press. That printing press is built on staggering proportions. There is at least one branch in every republic. The branch at Baku turns out 150 different publications. Some are magazines that receive all or part of their formats from Moscow. Some are newspapers with a wire service out of Moscow. These Baku newspapers are printed in Russian, Azerbaijani, Georgian, and Armenian. Paper-covered books carrying the Communist message are printed in various languages. So are scientific books and the Russian classics. So are books that show the seamy and vulgar side of life in a capitalist country—*The People of the Abyss,* in which Jack London portrayed the evils of London's East End, as of 1902, and *The Financier* in which Theodore Dreiser portrays one Frank Cowperwood as the archetype of the American money king.

Each republic pours out tons of the selfsame literature in many languages. The millions of books, pamphlets, and papers go to the corner kiosks for sale, to the libraries for deposit, and to the thousands of mobile units that reach every factory, farm, and sheep camp in the land. On the street corners, glass-enclosed bulletin boards contain the daily paper that is spread out so all the pages can be read.

The state is the one and only printer in the land. There is no private press, no source of indignant pamphlets or books to criticize the state's perversion of the free press. This state monopoly makes it easy for the censor to operate. And the censor does operate thoroughly and pervasively. I ran across some samples in Central Asia.

The Soviets have been quick to condemn any literacy trend that might feed nationalist flames or forge a dangerous link with foreign people. In Turkmenistan a movement got under way about twenty years ago to adopt Anatolian Turkish as the literary language of the republic. This move was roundly denounced by the Communist hierarchy as "anti-Marxist" and "anti-Leninist." A literary tie with weak Afghanistan and Iran is permissible. But a linguistic tie with strong, modern Turkey might fan too strongly the hidden flames of nationalism in Ashkhabad.

The list of literary purges in Central Asia is long and unending. I made inquiry of them as I visited the libraries along the way. "Do you have native poets and authors?" "Who are they?"—those were my questions to the librarians. The answers were what I expected. The "great" writers were always men like the late Jambul, the Kazakh, who turned his talents to the promotion of the Soviet cause. Contemporary Kazakh writers who are much praised by the Russians for their "progressive" viewpoint are Avezon, Mukanov, Mustafin, and Musrepov. These men have done high service for the Kremlin. But the nationalist poets—the Kazakh, Maghjan, and the Uzbek, Cholpan—are forgotten. I always asked whether the works of these nationalist poets were in the library. A search would be put on and almost always the answer was in the negative. Once I was rewarded. I found Cholpan and Maghjan in their native languages in the Rare Book Department of the Tashkent Library. They have been barred by Moscow from general circulation.

Public school attendance is compulsory in Russia; and the Soviet Constitution guarantees seven years of education. In the cities, ten grades are offered. In the rural areas there are usually only seven. But that is changing. I saw villages of a few hundred people that already had the complete secondary school system. By 1960 all Russian villages and cities will have, it is expected, the full ten grades.

There are various trade schools for metal workers, miners, and other skilled laborers with courses from six months to two years, called labor reserve schools. There are specialized secondary schools for nurses, auto mechanics, librarians, locomotive engineers, accountants, *et al.*, with courses from three to five years. Above the secondary schools are the universities, institutes, and academies that are in every sizable city in the whole nation. This school system is under the complete command of the state. There are no private schools or academies.

The great emphasis which Russia places on her educational system is indicated by the fact that it accounts for about one eighth of her annual national budget.

State monopoly of the printing press gives the Communist educators complete command of all textbooks. There is no chance in Russia for "deviationist" books to reach the classroom. As near as I could tell, the three Rs in Russian schools are efficiently handled. The teachers that I met seemed to be well trained and professionally competent. Every classroom has some course on Marxism and Leninism. The content of every course is decided in Moscow. Even when one reaches the college level, Moscow has complete control over the curriculum. Each course in the lower schools and in the higher ones is laid out according to a plan prepared by the Minister of Education of the republic. That minister is appointed by the Supreme Soviet of the republic, but he is directly responsible to Moscow. If the Minister of Education says to teach Shakespeare, the course is given. If he says to include one work of Thomas More but no others, only the one work is studied. If he says to drop a course, it is dropped. There is no conception in Russia of the faculty as we of the West know it. The faculty does what it's told. It does not sit to tailor and design curricula to fit its tastes or its ideas of what is needed or desirable. It has no real voice in the adoption of a teaching program. For example, at the Foreign Language Institute at Alma Ata, the Chinese language was taught for several years, then dropped. No one on the faculty knows to this day why that course was discontinued.

Sometimes the Minister of Education plans with a view of opening wide vistas. For example, I found the course in pedagogy to include Rousseau, John Locke, Thomas More, Diderot, Dewey, and Thorndike. Some history textbooks are downright misleading. They teach that Russia had the Nazis beaten before we landed in Normandy and that it was Soviet Russia that caused Japan to acknowledge defeat. Moreover, from Soviet courses in political science and government a student has no chance of being set afire by any ideas of liberty that swept the West.

If by chance any of those ideas crept into a classroom, the Communist party would be instantly alerted. For each school and every college has a Communist party organization in it. The Komsomol is in most of the grade schools of Russia. I learned that every public school in Kazakhstan has a Komsomol organization. In Central Asia the Communist party organization within the school is aware of the old Soviet dictum that "nationalism" is a dangerous survival and wholly alien to Communist ideology. The campus Communists in Central Asia are organized to fight "nationalistic deviations." Textbook writers for schools are still being drilled to play up Soviet patriotism, friendship with Russia, and proletarian internationalism, and to play down "nationalism." And the campus Communists are there to see that the textbooks are truly "orthodox."

All over Russia the campus Communists are organized to promote the Communist cause. They exercise few social functions. They are there, as the Rector of the University of Kirgizia told me, "to see to it that the ideals of the party are understood and put into practice." The Rector of the University of Alma Ata also emphasized to me the disciplinary role served by the campus Communists. They not only help students who are "backward" in their ideology; they also police corridors and dormitories for hooliganism and delinquencies. He found the campus Communists helpful in maintaining order and in promoting industry. The campus Communists are indeed the all-seeing eye, present in every classroom, every locker room, every dormitory. They are alert to report any deviation from the orthodox, either by professors or by students. They go further and spread tales about the United States. They say for example that our students are afraid that they will be charged with "subversion" merely for knowing how to speak Russian.

In 1955 some hundred Russian school textbooks were being revised. These were being rewritten to eliminate praise of Stalin who is fast being forgotten in Russia. There is also new stress on the "literary values" of writings and less on their "ideological content." But this does not mean that many new windows on knowledge are being opened for the student. The Minister of Education tailors the curriculum from the nursery to the university so as to reduce the risk that "counterrevolutionary" ideas will start working in the minds of the students. That, at least, was my strong impression. It is wrong, very wrong, to think that there is a renaissance in Russia. Over the years ideas will penetrate and make profound changes. But that is the long view. Today the Soviet censor is still active and persistent, even when it comes to rather innocuous news stories filed in Moscow for transmission abroad.

I heard in Russia a story that the Soviet press delegation told in Washington, D.C., on their visit here in the fall of 1955. It's a classic story on freedom of expression that touches off the Russian's keen sense of humor.

A British soldier and a Russian soldier met in Berlin and got into an argument about freedom of expression. The Britisher boasted to the Russian that he could climb on a soapbox in Trafalgar Square and criticize the British Government all he liked.

"You can't do that in Russia," the Britisher said.

"Oh yes I could," the Russian replied. "I could climb on a soapbox in Red Square and repeat exactly what you said."

I saw the other side of the same coin at Frunze, capital of Kirgizia. I had a lively visit at Frunze's university with the Rector and a half-dozen faculty members. A young Russian with reddish hair, by the name of Kaspov, who speaks English fluently, led the conversation. The discussion turned to debating. I explained the institution of debating in America, how teams from various schools and colleges debated on political topics. The topic may be "The United Nations should be abolished" or "Red China should be admitted to the United Nations" or "The minimum wage should be raised to $1.50."

I was told that there were no such debates in Russia. In physics and mathematics? Yes, sometimes there would be debates in those fields. But never public debates on political, economic, or governmental matters.

"All debates of that character take place in meetings of the Communist party. Once the party speaks on matters of policy there is conformity down to the smallest group," Kaspov replied.

"But why?" I asked. "There's room for differences of opinion on most public questions."

Kaspov took a second to answer, and when he spoke he tried to conceal the exasperation he felt.

"We are all socialists now and there is nothing to debate," he said.

CHAPTER 9

CHURCH AND STATE

"We do not believe in religion. Religion is for backward people only." The speaker was Kaspov, the
young Russian professor of the university in Frunze, whom I mentioned. He faced me across the table in the office of the Rector,
Dr. Unusaliev. Russian and Kirgiz faculty members filled the room
where we sat. When Kaspov announced that religion is for "backward people only," I raised my right hand and said, "Then I'm a
backward person." Kaspov instantly replied, "No insult was intended. I merely state our socialist point of view."

I had opened the subject by asking if there were any religious
groups on the campus of the university, explaining that, in America, college students often organized those societies for spiritual,
educational, and social ends. I was given to understand that in
Kirgizia's universities all religious groups were superfluous. I asked
why.

"First, because the Communist party on the campus does all
the necessary educational work," the Rector replied. "And, second,

PETROPAVLOVSK

*The streets of
Petropavlovsk are unpaved.*

*Women load rocks
at Petropavlovsk.*

*Factories, not housing,
receive priorities
in Kazakhstan.*

*The homes at Petropavlovsk
remain unchanged since
the czarist days.*

The author and his Leica visit a Pioneer camp near Tashkent.

I saw more diesel engines on the Trans-Siberian railroad than I did coal burners.

L. J. Pyjikov and his family of the Komsomolsky state farm near Barnaul tendered a delicious luncheon.

Peterhof near Leningrad is more beautiful than Versailles.

there are enough activities to keep the students busy without re-
sorting to religion."

I asked whether students would be disciplined if they formed a
religious society on a university campus. I was assured that though
religious societies were not welcome, students who joined them
would not be penalized. "Church and state are separate in Russia,"
I was told. I asked whether a faculty member would be penalized
for joining a church or being active in church affairs. The Rector
assured me he would not. It was at that point that Kaspov broke
in to say that "religion is for backward people only." When I
pressed for a definition of "backward people," I was told that they
are "the old people"—those too old to throw off their "bourgeois"
or "capitalistic" philosophy.

Article 124 of the Russian Constitution does indeed provide for
separation of church and state:

> In order to ensure to citizens freedom of conscience, the
> church in the U.S.S.R. is separated from the state, and the
> school from the church. Freedom of religious worship and
> freedom of anti-religious propaganda is recognized for all
> citizens.

Only in a limited sense are church and state separate in Russia.
The state does not interfere with baptisms, burial services, prayers,
singing, or any of the other rituals of the church. One may go to
church without being fined or imprisoned; and the police do not
break up church services. But in other respects the state applies
powerful sanctions against the church.

—The Soviets confiscated all church property, taking title to all
land and buildings. The churches occupy the property merely at
the sufferance of the government.

—The church is not a juridical person in Soviet law. That is to
say, the church cannot defend its property rights in the courts nor

receive bequests under wills. (Soviet courts have winked at that prohibition by recognizing bequests made to ministers or priests.)

—The church is subject to the income tax, paying 13 per cent of all its revenues to the state.

—The youth of Russia are taught that religion is evil, that atheism is the true faith. These teachings are dinned into their ears, beginning with the nursery.

—The state has destroyed the pulpit, as we of the West know it. Today no priest, no minister would dare preach social justice from his pulpit, except and unless the social justice he championed fit precisely the Communist pattern.

—No person who belongs to a church can qualify for membership in the Communist party. No candidate for office, whether or not a party member, will be endorsed by the party, if he belongs to a church or is active in religious affairs. And a candidate without party backing has no chance of being elected. The churchman or churchgoer is, in other words, disqualified from every public post, whether it be alderman, mayor, or governor. (This is the rule and the general practice, though there are, I learned, some Communist members who are believers.)

These restraints are placed on all churches, whatever their creed.

There is another which hits the Jews harshly. There is no possibility of staying away from work on the Jewish Sabbath, unless by chance the work week makes the holiday fall at that time. And there are two restraints of which the Moslems alone are victims. First, there is Ramadan, the month of fasting, when from sunrise to sunset the Moslems neither eat, drink, nor smoke. Ramadan is an exacting fast, one that can be successfully completed only if one slows down and receives some accommodation from his employer. There is no employer in Central Asia who will relax the party's strict demands. And so Ramadan as an institution has withered away.

Second, every Moslem desires to make at least one journey to Mecca during his lifetime. Once he makes the trip he is worthy to be called a *hajji*. The trip from Central Asia to Saudi Arabia is a long and arduous one for the average man. There are mountains to traverse and deserts to cross; and the trails are bitter cold in winter and blistering hot in summer. Nevertheless the faithful all through the centuries made their long treks to Mecca from the heart of Central Asia, hundreds of them going each year. When the Communists came to power and seized Central Asia as part of the Russian empire, they sealed the southern border. It is sealed to this day. No Moslem headed for Mecca can cross the border without a permit. Over the years the Soviets have granted very few.

During my visit to Soviet Central Asia, I talked with many of the Moslem clergy about these pilgrimages. The Soviet travel restrictions have, indeed, hit hard at them. There is no layman who has made the trip to Mecca since 1917. Only a few of the clergy have been granted the dispensation by the Soviets. Many of the mullahs have never seen Mecca.

One day in Alma Ata, I talked with a group of mullahs about this problem. I had visited a mosque without an appointment. It was Friday, the Moslem Sunday; so the bulk of the congregation was present—perhaps a hundred people, all of whom were fifty years old or more and a third of whom were women. This mosque is not ornate like those one sees in Iran. It's an ordinary wooden building painted blue. Its distinctive feature is a graceful crescent high on the steeple. The churchyard is enclosed by a drab mud wall. The grounds were untidy, without grass, flowers, or shrubs. The interior of the church was as dreary as the yard. No artist had enlivened it. The walls and ceiling were as monotonous as the worn-out rugs where the faithful prayed.

I introduced myself to the head mullah. His brown eyes sparkled and his whole face lightened as I mentioned Mecca. This

195

man of fifty-five years has been to Mecca once and that was in 1953. He told me how the Soviet Government in recent years has relaxed its restrictions—and worked out a quota system for pilgrims. The republic of Kazakhstan sends its quota every fourth year. During the intervening two years, the other four Central Asian republics send their quotas. I inquired how the quotas were determined. It appears that one pilgrimage plane a year is allowed to go from Baku to Teheran. The mullahs must, of course, pay for the plane. The length of their purses and the seating capacity of the plane determine the size of the quota. There were eighteen who went from Kazakhstan in 1953. It would be Kazakhstan's turn again in 1956.

The mullah, who related these facts to me, expressed gratitude to the Soviet Government for making the pilgrimages possible. This priest, like every clergyman I met in Russia, was docile in his attitude toward the state. Among the clergy I met, none ever gave any telltale evidence of dissatisfaction with the Soviet Government. Forty years under a Communist regime have taught them that the way to survive is to remain silent on controversial issues and never to speak in disparaging terms about the government.

Under Stalin the clergy was often insulted and persecuted. In 1954, after Stalin's death, Khrushchev issued a decree on behalf of the Central Committee which, while urging renewed efforts to spread "scientific-atheist propaganda" against religion, spoke out against "insulting" attacks on the clergy and the churchgoers. It is, he said, "stupid and harmful to cast political doubt on Soviet citizens because of their religious convictions."

In 1954, Malenkov assured Alexei, Patriarch of Russia, that any "administrative measures or rudeness to believers and the clergy are incompatible with the party line." Khrushchev said in the fall of 1955, "I do not see anywhere any anti-Soviet actions from the priests." Nor did I on my long journey. In the early days of bolshevism many priests did speak out against communism; some raised their voices in defense of the small farmers and the nomads during the bitter years when the Soviets forced collective farms on the people. Those priests were liquidated or imprisoned.

One day in Tashkent, capital of Uzbekistan, I unexpectedly met the Grand Mufti of the Moslem church in Central Asia. I arrived at Tashkent's main mosque about two o'clock in the afternoon. It was a bright, hot day. High on the roof a mullah was calling the faithful to pray. Shortly some two-hundred Uzbeks and Tadzhiks came into the churchyard from various gates that open into narrow, winding streets of the old city. The worshipers were all middle-aged or old men; and they kneeled in rows in the mosque, facing Mecca.

When the service started, I stood in the churchyard under a locust tree, visiting with Babahanov, the chief mullah of the mosque. He is the forty-five-year-old son of the Grand Mufti. He explained to me that the mosque, the largest in Tashkent and serving five hundred people, was one of sixteen in that community; that the Grand Mufti is not only in charge of all the mosques in Tashkent but the spiritual head of all Moslems in the five Central Asian republics.

"He wants to meet you," Babahanov said. We went into a small courtyard of a private home where jasmine grows against a white wall. The Grand Mufti, dressed in a striped silk robe and a tightly wound white turban, shortly appeared. Though ninety-six years old, he stands erect. He carries his years with grace and dignity; and he is agile, for unassisted he climbed steep stairs to a second-story dining room.

The luncheon he tendered had twenty-one courses. Fish and cold meat came first. In the middle, the famous shishkebab was served; at the end, sweet melons and grapes. It was oppressively hot under the low ceiling; and the small electric fan at the far end of the room made no ripple at the table. The Grand Mufti proposed a few toasts in wine; and I responded. But in the main the conversation was desultory. Finally, when hot green tea was served, it was time for serious conversation.

I asked if many priests had been liquidated by the Soviets. The Grand Mufti replied:

"No mullah was ever harmed for his religious work."

"Were any priests tried in court?" I asked.

"A few were arrested for political activities," he answered. "But they were held in prison only a few years and then released."

"Were any executed?"

"No."

The liquidation of priests or their assignment to Russian concentration camps was so notorious that I repeated my questions. The same answers came back, this time from the son. It was obvious that I was getting stereotyped answers.

"Is there not a conflict between the teachings of communism and the teachings of Islam?" I asked.

"Islam does not concern itself with communism but teaches only the Islamic faith," the Grand Mufti replied.

I had noticed an absence of young people in the mosques I had visited. I mentioned that fact and asked for an explanation.

The son of the Mufti gave an answer which, by avoiding the question, impliedly conceded that the younger generation had deserted Islam. All that he said was, "The state does not prohibit the young people from attending mosques. They are free to come if they want to."

I pressed my inquiry concerning the interference by the state with church affairs. And once more I got only the stock answer, "The state is completely separate from the church and in no way interferes."

Finally, when the questioning was ended, the Grand Mufti presented me with a lovely gift—a gaily colored Uzbek hat shaped like a skullcap and a full-length flowing robe. This robe—one of my prized possessions—is made of heavy satin with two-inch-wide longitudinal stripes of red, blue, white, and gold. The robe is lined with a paisley print. Every time I wear it I think of the doughty Grand Mufti who, though his tongue is tied, carries his head high in an atheistic land.

The clergy in Soviet Russia give only stock answers to questions concerning religious freedom. Any clergyman's plea for greater religious freedom or his complaint against oppression might lead to a charge of subversion "with counterrevolutionary intent"—an offense which carries the death penalty if specific intent is proved.

Clergymen to serve their people must bow to the laws governing their society. The clergymen of Russia have done that and even more. In 1952 the heads of all the churches in Russia assembled at Zagorsk pursuant to Stalin's call and did his bidding. They defended Russia's foreign policy, denounced American "imperialism," condemned American "bacteriological warfare" in Korea and the American atomic bomb, and in other respects consistently took the Soviet view on international questions. Those speeches can be partly explained by the spirit of nationalism which possesses every people and which tends to make them identify their interests with their own government and own people. They can partly be explained by the compulsion of citizens in a Communist state to obey a command. And in part they reflect a climate of opinion created by a press that year in and year out blankets a nation with one point of view, until in the end the citizen is unable to distinguish propaganda from fact.

The church has suffered since the Communists took over Russia. Church membership has declined, church prestige has suffered, religious education has been greatly neglected. Forty years of Communist indoctrination has set the faces of millions towards atheism. The trend is noticeable everywhere.

Churches built for large congregations often have meager attendance. I attended mass in an Armenian church in Baku where there were seven priests conducting the service and only four old women and one old man in the audience. In Bukhara, once a great center of Islamic learning, there is only one active mosque and it is in a state of disrepair. At one important service I saw less than twenty worshipers—and they were all old men. Bukhara once had many religious schools serving all of Central Asia. Today, as I said earlier, it has but one seminary with only 100 students in attendance. That is, indeed, the one and only Moslem training school in all of Central Asia.

There are over three million Jews in Russia and about two-hundred congregations. There are synagogues in most of the cities I visited. These congregations are active. But not many of the younger generation are being taught the precepts of Judaism. And the rabbis complain of the difficulty in getting cantors.

Everywhere in Russia one finds some old churches in ruins and others that have been turned into cinemas, warehouses, and museums. A magnificent mosque in Ashkhabad, capital of Turkmenistan, was partly demolished on October 6, 1948 by an earthquake that nearly destroyed the town. That mosque today stands in ruins, unrestored. Most of the mosques in Central Asia are in disrepair. Leningrad, which suffered heavily under German artillery, has rebuilt all her magnificent buildings—all except some of the churches that still carry the wounds of war.

All over Russia more and more churches are being turned into museums. The old churches of the czars within the walls of the Kremlin are now only famous show places. Like the throne of Ivan the Terrible, they are merely symbols of royalist days.

The famous Cathedral of the Virgin of Kazan in Leningrad has been converted into a museum dedicated to "The Evolution of Religion and Atheism." As one walks in he sees a picture of peasants carrying a golden cross, on top of which is a fat man with a cigar in his mouth and a whip in his hand. Christ is walking ahead in a golden robe.

Another picture shows a peasant woman carrying the cross and a child on her back.

A picture of Christ has the inscription, "A Jewish Fortune Teller."

Another painting shows Christ in the center with four men on horses trampling down the people of the world.

A large fresco shows Christ as a Roman governor and the Apostles as Roman nobles.

One picture shows Christ and ancient Greek gods, each with three heads.

Over the walls are quotations from Marx, such as "Christianity glorified the position of slave owners."

St. Christopher is shown with the head of a horse.

There is a model of the Inquisition together with tools of torture, said to be the originals.

The walls have pictures of drunken monks and nuns.

A picture of the Pope, when looked at sideways, reveals the head of a mule.

In an alcove is a replica of a church with windows in the shape of bullets. On them are written "Bethlehem Steel Co.," "Morgan & Co.," "Krupp & Co."

In all of Russia the campaign against religion is incessant. It starts in the nursery and kindergarten that are found in every town and factory and on every farm.

They open at 7 A.M. and close either at 7 P.M. or 8 P.M. They are dependable, efficient, and free. They not only make it possible for mother to work; they also put the child in the hands of the state during his early years. He stays in a kindergarten until he enters public school at the age of seven. During these first seven years the nurses tune the ear of the child to atheism, not to God.

A Jesuit maxim says, "Give me a child for the first seven years, and you may do what you like with him afterwards." Lenin in 1923 rephrased that maxim to read: "Give us a child for eight years and it will be a Bolshevist forever." The nurseries and kindergartens of Soviet Russia are dedicated to Lenin's creed.

The atheistic influence does not end there. A child from the time he is seven until he reaches fourteen usually has a chance to go to a Pioneer camp during the summer months. That again is free to the children. The ones I saw are healthful places in the physical sense, being located in the mountains, on lakes or rivers, or in the country. At these camps there are games and sports, music and dancing, and other group activities. But there are also classes in reading and storytelling. The library is filled only with Communist literature. I saw and heard enough to know that all libraries and discussion groups open to children are barren of any religious influence and interest the mind only in material things.

The anti-religious campaign extends to the adults as well as to the children. That campaign is no longer a police action. As Khrushchev said in the fall of 1955, "Our anti-religious campaigns are done by the written word or through discussion and argument." The campaign goes on even though the severest critics of the church concede that today there is no "class basis" of religion in Russia.

Literature available either at sidewalk bookstalls or at libraries is non-religious and often outright anti-religious. If there are great religious classics in Russia, they are buried deep in rare-book collections of the libraries. The slant of the Soviet press is anti-religious. And if the press is lax, some party member speaks up to remind the government to liquidate all "religious survivals." In a myriad of ways the state has done its best to liquidate them. As I said, when witnesses are sworn in court, "So help me God" is not included in the oath.

But there is a survival of religion in Russia; and it worries the Communists. Several excuses are given for its persistence. Some, like the professor at Frunze, say that it will pass with the old people who got indoctrinated when they were young. Other Russians attribute it to the influence of capitalistic encirclement. Some say that floods and crop failures make people believe in the supernatural, and until Russia masters the forces of nature so as to guarantee safety and security against the elements, people will still pray. Some say that the poorer the people, the more persistent the religious influence, and that the way to eliminate "religious survivals" in Russia is to make everyone prosperous. Finally, the most adamant Communist maintains that if the press and radio do their business, people can in the long run be "educated" away from religion.

On my Russian journey I was at first depressed at the great erosion which the church had suffered. The first churches I saw were at Baku. The meager number who came to worship, the run-down condition of the church properties, the look of poverty that marked even the robes of the clergy filled me with despair. I recall particularly the Armenian mass, already mentioned. That morning religion seemed to me to be on its way out in Russia. As I watched the handful of poor people kiss the Bible held by the priest, memories of my Father and Mother came back to me. Father had given his life to the Presbyterian Church. Mother was his faithful co-worker. All of their ideals seemed to be forgotten in this Communist land. The God of my Father and Mother seemed alien to Russia. A pagan one had taken His place. And so at the end of the service I bought two candles from an aged, shawled lady dressed in black and lighted them with a prayer for my parents. That morning the power of religion in Russia seemed to me no stronger than the flicker of those two lonely candles.

But as the days passed and I saw more churches, my opinion changed. I became convinced that religion in Russia will last as long as the Russian people; that it is as sturdy and enduring as the shawled women and booted men who kneel before the Cross.

Though the churches have suffered a great setback under the

Communists, they are still strong. In the larger cities such as Moscow and Leningrad, the people turn out by the hundreds for services. On holy days, such as Easter, the crowds that pack the cathedrals run into the thousands. At Alma Ata, 3000 people attended the various masses at the Russian Orthodox church on the Sunday in August 1955 when I visited there.

The Catholic service is the same in Moscow as in America. The Russian Orthodox church too has a rich ritual; and it puts great stress on miracles and the life hereafter. The Protestant pulpit, though not designed for Henry Ward Beecher, is still active. The sermons are partly theological essays (usually of the fundamentalist type) and partly dissertations on the life of Christ, His teachings, and the inspiration of His example.

Though the church does not have the hold on people that it once had, the nexus is not broken. I saw young people bringing their babies to church for baptism in the Catholic church of St. Louis in Moscow and in the Russian Orthodox churches all the way across Russia. I mentioned earlier that the synagogues were not indoctrinating the youth in the principles of Judaism as they did before. But the old rituals continue; and the ceremony of the confirmation (bar mitzvah) is still a vital one. For example, at the Choral Synagogue in Moscow, which has a congregation of perhaps ten thousand Jews, about twenty boys receive their confirmation every month.

Every church is still popular for marriages.

The church also remains a favorite place for burial services. The state does not provide many undertakers; and there are few funeral parlors. Private enterprise in that field is not allowed. And so one must provide his own hearse. The funeral service in Russia is, therefore, marked by the coffin carried on a pickup truck.

Birth, marriage, and death—these are the great milestones of life. They are events to commemorate with solemnity and dignity. No matter what the party may say, it cannot compete with the church on these occasions. The church has a ritual steeped in symbolism. No party can rob it of its charm. The church, as a mother institution, will be there long after the party has changed its spots.

Once there were czars in the Kremlin who oppressed the people. The people withstood the oppression and continued to worship Christ the King. There are new dictators in the Kremlin. But Christ continues to live on in the hearts of the people. The spirit of Christ will live on after the names of the dictators are forgotten. I left Russia with new confidence that religion is the most durable of man's creations. It does indeed satisfy the deepest urge of all— the need of man to establish his relations with his fellow man and with the universe.

The indestructibility of religion in Russia was brought home to me vividly in Tashkent at a Sunday evening service in the Baptist church. The Baptist church was established in Russia about two hundred years ago. The Tashkent church was founded in 1905. By the end of World War II it had only sixty-five members. By 1950 its membership had grown to seven hundred. The present pastor took over in 1951. Since then the membership has increased to two thousand.

This night some six hundred were present. A majority were women, but there were many men and many young people in the audience. The wooden frame building, which on the outside looks more like a factory than a church, was packed. The seats were benches without backs. They were filled and people were standing in the rear. There was no organ or piano. But on the platform was a choir of forty male voices led by a man in shirt sleeves. There were no stained-glass windows. A banner over the pulpit read "God is Love." Apart from it, there was no decoration for the barren hall.

When my party entered the church, the pastor knew at once that foreigners had arrived. He stopped the service and came to the rear of the church to greet us. When he learned I was an American, he insisted that I share the pulpit with him.

I never heard such singing as I heard that night. In Russia the choir, not the congregation, does the singing. This was a well-trained choir, beautifully balanced. Many of the songs were new; some were familiar. One did not need to know the words to appreciate that these songs were stirring declarations of man's faith in the infinite. I knew when I heard those hymns that no concentration camp, no firing squad, no secret police could ever subdue the religious spirit of the Russian people.

The prayers also deeply moved me. They were interspersed with the announcements. For example, one announcement was to the effect that an elderly man who belonged to the congregation was ill. He asked the members to pray for him. The whole congregation prayed out loud. Each prayed in his own words, in his own way, but all in a loud whisper. They prayed for their brother as they later prayed for President Eisenhower when he was stricken: "Save him, O God, save him." The prayers ended at different times, trailing off until only a few were unfinished. Finally all had ended and the church was silent. Another like announcement was made and more prayers were said. Over and again it happened, the voices of the common people of Russia beseeching God for the comfort, aid, and assistance of their friends and neighbors. I knew in those moments of prayer that the Russian people belonged to a common fraternity among all men.

When the announcements and prayers were finished, the pastor asked me if I would deliver the sermon. The request was a surprise. I had come wholly unprepared. I hesitated a second and then told him I would. He promptly introduced me, and I found myself in the pulpit with my Intourist interpreter by my side, looking into a sea of faces. The women were unadorned—no powder, no lipstick, no hairdress. They almost invariably wore shawls over their heads and long, plain dresses. Many of the men were in their shirt sleeves. A few wore coats; none wore ties. The congregation was plainly a collection of common folk—most of them farmers, some of them factory workers. They were as plain as the church where they gathered. Their faces—intent and serious—were dimly lit by a few electric bulbs.

I took as my text the words printed on the streamer over the pulpit: "God is Love," I John 4:16. I told these Russian peasants and workers that we in America worshiped the same God they worshiped. I described church services in America and compared them with this one. Some of our services, I said, were different in form from Russian services. Some of our churches were more ornate; some of our services had more rituals. But the source of our faith was the same. The words of Christ were our common inspiration. We worshiped through Him the same God.

God, I said, was the common bond between men of all races. We are all equal in His sight. God has no preference in language or race. Christ taught that all men are brothers. The gospel according to John is "That he who loveth God love his brother also." That truth is not exclusively American nor exclusively Russian. It is the common heritage of all people.

I went on to say that the world has developed great schisms. I said that it is the responsibility of people everywhere to find common ground in the search for peace. Americans want peace as much as any people. The press that pictures America as the imperialistic power or the aggressor is false. America has no designs on any nation. The heart of America is warm; the American capacity for friendship is great. America does not desire to interfere in the domestic affairs of Russians. America in turn wants Russians to abstain from meddling in her internal affairs. Charity of people to each other is the key to peace. When the Apostle Paul spoke of faith, hope, and charity, he finished by saying, "But the greatest of these is charity." Charity is, today, the solvent of the ills of the world. Where there is charity, there is no conspiracy by some people against other people.

This was my sermon in the Russian pulpit. I finished by saying that I brought greetings to the Baptists of Tashkent from all the church people of America. I no sooner said it than the whole audience rose and replied in a chorus, "Greetings."

The pastor then prayed, thanking God for directing my footsteps to this remote church in Central Asia and asking Him to keep the feet of the American and Russian people on the path to peace.

When the service ended there were so many hands to shake I had difficulty leaving the church. When I got outside I was surrounded by a huge crowd that filled the street and stopped all traffic. There was a great overflowing of emotions on this Sabbath evening. Tears filled the eyes of many people as they pressed close to shake my hand. As an official I was wholly unknown to these Russian people. But as a symbol I was important. For I who spoke of God, of charity, and of brotherhood was a citizen of the nation they had been taught to suspect. Now they had found common ground with America. They were overjoyed to know that Americans were not the evil lot which the Soviet press had depicted. The discovery was for them, I think, an overwhelming emotional experience.

CHAPTER **10**

RUSSIA'S COLONIAL EMPIRE

Russia has within her own borders a brand of colonialism similar to the kind the French have practiced in Morocco.

In Soviet Central Asia there are segregated schools, special courts for the trial of Russians, concentration of political control in the hands of the Russians, discrimination against the native people, and a ruthless suppression of all nationalist sentiments.

Central Asia, which stretches from China on the east to the Caspian Sea on the west, has long been populated by non-Russians: Turkmens who, as their name suggests, are tied to Turkey by language, race, and customs; Tadzhiks who are Persians and Afghans; Uzbeks, Kirgiz, and Kazakhs, who, like Timur the Lame, have Mongol antecedents and speak a Turkish tongue. All five were bound together by a common way of life and by the Moslem religion. Their republics, part of the Soviet Union, are Turkmenistan, Tadzhikistan, Uzbekistan, Kirgizia and Kazakhstan. The total population of these republics is over sixteen million.

These people are as different from Russians as the Filipinos are from us. They have a lively sense of nationalism and of race. The barrier between them and the Russians is being broken down. But it still exists. I remember a talk with a highly talented and well-educated Uzbek in Tashkent. As we were discussing this problem, he recited to me Kipling's verse:

> *East is East and West is West*
> *And never the twain shall meet.*

I said, "Do you believe that?" He replied, "The two met in Tashkent." Then after a pause he added, "We Uzbeks are the East. Russia lies to the west."

Czarist Russia conquered these peoples in a series of military campaigns that ended near the close of last century. The conquest was a part of Russian expansion designed, *first,* to check England in India and Afghanistan, and, *second,* to make Russia independent of America for cotton.

By material standards, Russia has done quite well by Central Asia. Towns such as Tashkent, Stalinabad, Ashkhabad, Frunze, and Alma Ata are fast becoming modern cities with good water supplies, sewage systems, broad streets, attractive parks, hospitals, and all other modern facilities. Though parts of these towns are still in squalor, they will be wholly modern in a decade or two. Even today they are show places for Asians who are accustomed to filth and poverty.

The same wage is applicable to Central Asia as to Moscow. Central Asia has the same school system as other parts of Russia. True, Moscow's schools go through the tenth grade, while in Central Asia most schools end with the seventh. But that is not a discriminatory practice, for Central Asia will soon have a ten-year school system. Central Asia, like the other parts of Russia, has a highly developed medical program. Each republic has at least one medical school, Kazakhstan having three. There are hospitals for everyone; doctors for everyone; medicines for everyone. And they are all free. Villages that never in history had as much as a first-aid center now have doctors and hospitals. There are hospitals and maternity wards and dental offices on almost every farm. Every factory has its hospital, maternity ward, dental office, and first-aid center. Kazakhstan has sixteen ambulance airplane stations equipped to fly to the remotest village or sheep camp to bring back sick or injured persons.

Central Asia is highly industrialized with textile mills, agricultural implement factories, meat-packing plants, light-metal industries, steel mills, coal and chromium mines, hydroelectric projects, and a vast network of rail and water transportation. Great irrigation projects are under way. Once upon a time the Amu Darya (Oxus) River flowed not north to the Aral Sea as today, but west to the Caspian. Under Stalin a project was started to build the Turkmen Canal, diverting the river once more to the Caspian. Today that project has no high priority; but work on it continues. And there are dozens of projects to build additional dams and canals and to bring new lands under cultivation in Central Asia.

The truth is that Central Asia has already undergone the industrial revolution that most of Asia is yet to experience. The people of Central Asia already have many of the good things of life that to the average Asian are still as remote as the millennium. The average income in Central Asia is about the same as it is across Russia. By Asian standards, Central Asia has fared exceedingly well, if material standards alone are considered. In other respects the natives of Central Asia have been treated like colonial people.

The introduction of the collective farms in the late '20s and early '30s was one of the bloodiest chapters of Central Asian history. On my Russian journey I tried to reconstruct those years and learn what happened. Some of the people I questioned were cowed by the party member, present in most of the conferences.

Some did not know what had happened. The statistics are buried in court files and in the files of the secret police—the MVD. The Chief Justice of Kirgizia, a quiet, spectacled, professorial type of man told me (truthfully, I think) that it would take two weeks of hard work to collate the statistics of the judicial trials of *kulaks* and others who resisted the program of collectivization in Stalinabad alone. Even judges were hesitant to talk about the matter. They, too, feared the consequences. The Chief Justice of Uzbekistan, a middle-aged, round-faced, rangy type of man, told me in Tashkent that he knew of no such trials. "Perhaps a *kulak* or two was tried. But we were all young then and do not remember."

He looked me straight in the eye as he gave this answer, even though he had come to the bench near the end of the period of the collectivization and had been in the prosecutor's office during all of that time. That night I went back to the Chief Justice through another interpreter, delicately suggesting that I knew he had not told me the truth. The Chief Justice remained true to party discipline and disclosed no facts. His answer, however, was revealing:

"I will not give the Justice the figures for fear they will be published."

The statistics of the judicial trials of the *kulaks* of Central Asia will never be seen by Western eyes. For the total liquidation during the five-year period beginning in 1929 was enormous. The charge was resisting the law "with counterrevolutionary intent." The accused were the landowners—small ones as well as big ones, for in Russia one who owned only ten acres was a *kulak*. The accused were also the mullahs who favored private ownership and the *status quo*, and nationalist leaders who, though Communist or Communist-inclined, favored self-determination by these Asian people rather than remote control from Moscow.

There were murders at the hands of the MVD. Men who resisted party organizers sent out from Moscow were shot. Others were seized, sentenced to prison, and sent off to labor camps or farmed out to industrial plants. The statistics on these various categories will never be public property. But I found enough evidence to know that the number is legion.

Some of my informants told me that, of course, a nomad or *kulak*, big or small, who opposed the collective farms was shot or exiled. "Those people defied the law, and that is a crime in Russia." Others were more evasive, saying that it was the nomads and *kulaks* who attacked government officials and that the police had to restore order. One afternoon through an English-speaking Kirgiz, I got a long account. This man was an eyewitness. His sympathies were with the nomads—simple Kirgiz people with no revolutionary thoughts in their heads, simple folk who loved their flocks and their land. They resisted almost to the man and were bayoneted, shot, and exiled. "It was a dreadful time for Kirgizia," he said. "And the resistance was so strong it took the Soviets five years to force the collectives on us."

The Soviets served multiple purposes by these terroristic tactics. First, they broke the resistance to the collective farms. Second, they seized on this program of collectivization as an opportunity to force excess farm labor into industry. And third, they used the reign of terror to eliminate leaders who were more nationalist than Communist.

Kirgizia and Kazakhstan suffered most. These were countries of the nomads, who were tough minded, individualistic, and who long knew adversity and flourished on it. They, rather than the sedentary farmers, formed the greatest opposition to the Soviets in Central Asia. The nomads were, in turn, the chief victims.

The livestock figures for Kirgizia and for Kazakhstan tell part of the grim story.

In Kirgizia there were 5,906,000 sheep and goats in 1929. By 1937 that number had dropped to 1,886,000. Kirgizia had 1,084,-000 cattle in 1928, while in 1937 it had only 486,000.

Kazakhstan had 18,000,000 sheep and goats in 1916 and only 8,000,000 in 1940. In 1916 it had 5,000,000 cattle and by 1940 only 3,300,000. In 1916, Kazakhstan had 4,000,000 horses and only 900,-000 by 1940.

Bloody episodes lay behind that great loss of livestock.

When the nomads were shot or sent off to labor camps, their flocks perished for lack of attention. And many slaughtered their animals rather than turn them over to the Soviets. But that is only part of the story. The resistance of the nomads continued even after the program of collectivization had been imposed on them. In Kazakhstan alone, nearly three fourths of all the collective farms which were formed beginning in 1929 had disintegrated by 1932. The nomads, who had been forced into these farms, deserted them, slaughtering the livestock before they left. Order was restored only when Moscow decreed in September 1932 that each nomad in a collective farm could privately own 10 cows, 100 sheep and goats, 10 horses, and 5 camels.

I explored these telltale figures of livestock losses with most of the officials I met on my journey through Central Asia. No one would admit he was sufficiently familiar with the topic to comment. Some did not believe the figures, even though I had obtained them from the Ministries of Agriculture.

I moved on to the population figures, pointing out that there had been a great decline in the Kazakh population of Russia between 1926 and 1939. Caroe in *Soviet Empire* estimates the decline at one third. Some Russians had seen that figure. But all denied its accuracy. The denial was especially emphatic when I talked with a group of university professors at Tashkent. In Alma Ata the figure was dismissed as fantastic. In Petropavlovsk the room burst with laughter at the idea of such a figure.

At that point in the interview I always produced the Soviet census figures showing a great decline in the Kazakh population between 1926 and 1939. According to the Soviet census, there were 3,968,289 Kazakhs *in all of Russia* in 1926 and only 3,098,764 in 1939. That loss is nearly 1,000,000 people; and 1,000,000 people do not disappear without someone knowing about it. In any nation it would be a notorious event. But not even that startling figure produced any response. Each time my announcement of it was followed by complete silence. But in Alma Ata I thought the professor at the end of the table who was a party member would burst a blood vessel. His eyes fairly danced with anger; and he was so excited at my statement he had to leave the room. The Russians would usually close my inquiry very politely with the statement, "We are not acquainted with the census." Down in Tadzhikistan one judge had a constructive suggestion to make. "One million of Kazakhs must have gone to China," he said.

Some did in fact flee to China, for in 1951 I myself had run into a few hundred of them on my trek across the Himalayas. But the idea of a million Kazakh refugees fleeing to China was not credible. Certainly they would have been accounted for by Communist China before 1955.

The account as I pieced it together was a cruel one. It showed that twenty years ago hundreds of thousands of Kazakhs and Kirgiz either were liquidated by the Soviets or starved to death as a result of Communist oppression.

Russia in her foreign policy supports the liberation movements of subject peoples. Late in 1955 Khrushchev, in speaking of the Moors under the French in North Africa, said, "The position of the Soviet people is the position of moral support and sympathy for the aspirations of the national liberation movement of the peoples." Russia has quite a different policy when it comes to national aspirations of subject races within her borders.

A prominent aspect of Soviet colonialism is, indeed, the relentless suppression by the Russians of all nationalist sentiments in these Central Asian republics.

In 1927 the Communist party of Kazakhstan gave Kazakhs priority to the agricultural lands of that republic. Moscow reversed that decision, denouncing the discrimination against the Russians. And the Kazakhs who backed that policy were purged.

Russia under the czars tried to make Central Asia dependent on Russia for food by encouraging the production of cotton instead of cereals. Cotton was King in Central Asia, pretty much as it was once King in our own South. To some extent the Soviets have followed the old czarist policy to this day. But the desire of many Communist nationalists was to make these republics self-sufficient and not dependent on Russia. The proponents of that program were purged or liquidated in 1937 and 1938. These included Abdurakhmanov, the Kirgiz, who opposed the export of grain from his republic, and Khodzhayev and Ilkramow, the Uzbeks (tried with Bukharin), who opposed Moscow's cotton policy for Uzbekistan. These heroes are today remembered in Central Asia but seldom mentioned.

In Tadzhikistan, Communists who showed pronounced nationalist tendencies were also purged in the 1940s. Some wanted Russians excluded from the country; some were not wholeheartedly behind the collectivization program; some could not work themselves into a rage over the *kulaks*. The names of the purged leaders are Maksum, Khodzhebayev, Rakhimbayev, and Shotamor, men never known to the world but still remembered by Tadzhiks. During the same period, there were liquidations of prominent Communists in Turkmenistan who wanted greater autonomy for their republic. The leader in that movement was Aitakov. No colonial power was ever more sedulous in ferreting out the nationalists in its midst than was Russia in Central Asia.

Russia has consistently promoted what all the nationalists of Central Asia, including Communists, have most feared—a Russianization of these countries. This is partly a natural result of the Russian conquest and partly a studied effort.

Central Asia is rich in natural resources. Uzbekistan has great uranium deposits. The Tien Shan Mountains have good iron ore. Kazakhstan is probably first in the world for its chromium. It has a third of the Soviet Union's iron reserves and a third of its manganese. It produces 50 per cent or more of all of Russia's copper, lead, and zinc. Soviet Central Asia also has much tungsten, nickel, cobalt, chromite, molybdenum, and uranium. These minerals require mines, plants, and factories for their development. It was Russia, not the Central Asian republics, that had the engineering genius for the task. And so the Russians moved in; and they are there today in increasing numbers.

The Russians have done an amazing job in industrializing Central Asia, as good a job if not better than the French did in bringing an industrial plant to North Africa. Before the October Revolution, Central Asia was a vast feudal domain with few industries. Today it is a veritable arsenal of Soviet power—atomic energy, coal mines, copper smelters, oil wells, textile mills of all varieties, and a miscellaneous group of factories manufacturing anything from agricultural implements to machine tools.

The industrial plant is a Russian creation; and the Russians dominate it. They occupied the strategic positions in practically every factory I visited. Most of the labor staff is drawn, of course, from the local people. Some of the natives have moved up the ladder to skilled posts, to administrative positions, to supervisory roles. There are Kazakh engineers, Uzbek foremen, Kirgiz supervisors, Turkmen mechanics, and Tadzhik managers. But I noticed that in every factory where the natives outnumber the Russians in supervisory or managerial posts, the Russians occupy the command posts.

The Russians are encouraged by Moscow to emigrate to this hinterland in Central Asia. Moscow does not use exhortation alone. It promises tangible, financial rewards. Every Russian who goes to Central Asia to work—whether as doctor, teacher, engineer, or manager—gets 30 per cent more salary than the same job pays the Asian. The Soviets have adopted for Central Asia the same preferential salary scale as the French adopted in North Africa. The Russian, like the Frenchman, who goes to his country's colonial frontier to work is paid more for his services than the native of the same training and skills who does the same work.

The Russians have poured into Central Asia in such great quantities that the subject is a touchy one. Everywhere I went I asked, "What percentage of the town is Russian?" The answer was almost invariably, "Twenty or 25 per cent." Yet it was obvious that in the capitals of the five Central Asian republics the population was at least 50 per cent Russian. One has only to walk the streets, visit the shops, or go to the Parks of Culture and Rest at night to know that the Russians are close to being a majority in these Central Asian capitals and an overwhelming majority in places like Alma Ata.

The Asians are, of course, in titular control of their governments. In each of these republics the city officials are mostly natives. So are the Ministers of the Republic. So are the judges. And a majority of the state legislators are also Asians. Moreover, it is the policy of the Russians to recruit the civil service locally. But these statistics tell only a part of the story. The Central Asians share their state parliaments or soviets with the Russians. The approximate figures showing the percentage of seats held by the natives are as follows: Kazakhstan, 50 per cent; Kirgizia, 63 per cent; Tadzhikistan, 83 per cent; Uzbekistan, 74 per cent; and Turkmenistan, 78 per cent. The Russians are scattered through the secondary posts in the local government, so as to sit astride most of the channels controlling the important decisions, just as they were in Yugoslavia when that nation broke with Russia. The deputy to the Kazakh mayor will be a Russian. The deputy to the Uzbek Minister of Education will be a Russian. And so on. Moreover, the head of the local MVD and a majority of the top officers in that organization are Russians. In Kazakhstan there was a dramatic shift of political power from Asians to Russians in the summer of 1955. There were purges of key Kazakhs in the Communist hierarchy of Kazakhstan in 1954 and 1955. Zhumabai Shayakhmetov had long been the strongest single political figure among the Kazakhs. When I was in Central Asia, the Soviets demoted Shayakhmetov and his Kazakh assistant and cast them into political oblivion. They were replaced by two Russians—Leonid I. Brezhnev and Ivan D. Yakovlev—as first and second secretaries of the Kazakhstan Communist party. Even the façade of Kazakh control over Kazakhstan in these key positions has now been removed.

The direct and indirect control which Russians exercise in Central Asia over Central Asian affairs, important as it is, is overshadowed by the central control that Moscow has over the basic affairs of the republics. Under the Soviet Constitution thirty-two federal ministries in Moscow have *direct control* over local affairs. These include communications, city building, electric power, coal, labor reserves, machine tools, etc. There are twenty-one federal ministries in Moscow that *supervise* state ministries in the same field. These include MVD, education, public health, agriculture, finance, judicial administration, etc. In other words, the political power is in the center, located at Moscow. The Asians can man all the local posts and yet have no real voice in vital affairs. There is some effort to decentralize authority. But a decision to build a new schoolhouse in Frunze must still be made in Moscow. The apex of authority in Moscow is the Praesidium. But it has no members from Central Asia.

The Asian in these republics leads a busy life voting. The Kazakh votes for his representatives in the federal parliament—the Soviet of the Union (comparable to our House of Representatives) and the Soviet of Nationalities (roughly comparable to our Senate). He votes for his representatives in the Kazakh Supreme Soviet and for his representative in the Alma Ata City Soviet. If he is on a collective farm he votes for the committee that governs the farm. If he works in a factory or on a railroad he votes for his trade union committee.

But all the ballots on which he casts his vote must first be approved by the Communist party. There is no other party. Write-in ballots are permissible. But no write-in candidate has ever won even a substantial vote in the controlled balloting in Russia. The Communist party is a powerful force, more powerful than the government itself. At the top Bulganin represents the government, Khrushchev the party. The party parallels the government at every level. There is a party organization in every Supreme Soviet of every republic. There is a party nucleus in every city government. The party is organized everywhere—in labor unions, in universities, on collective farms, in every precinct. The party is the all-seeing eye, alert to pass on to Moscow every deviation from the orthodox course, every dangerous innovation. The most dangerous innovations of all are the principles of nationalism and the right of self-determination of peoples. Those heretical principles have no chance of success in Moscow. For the Central Committee of the Communist party, which is 133 strong, has on it only thirteen natives from the five Central Asian republics.

In short, the Soviet political system is aligned against these subject people. They have in fact no more real independence than the Moors of French North Africa had before the return of the Sultan.

The discrimination against the native extends to most phases of life. There are new apartment buildings springing up in every republic of Central Asia. There is no law segregating these new quarters for the Russians. But in practice the Russians usually get the new flats and houses, while the natives are relegated to the mud huts of the old city.

In Central Asia there are separate schools for the natives and separate schools for the Russians. The native schools are taught mostly by native teachers. The teachers in the Russian schools are almost always Russian. Instruction in the native schools is in the native language. There are native-language courses given in the Russian schools that the Russian students may or may not take, as they choose. In the native schools there are courses in Russian which the native children must take. The pressure, in other words, is on the side of Russianization.

Some Uzbek teachers in Tashkent and some Kazakhs who were in the Alma Ata city government defended segregation, pointing with pride to the provisions in their state constitutions that the native people are guaranteed the right to receive public school education "in the native language." And so they are. But the natives are still at a loss to justify the practice of putting the Russians in separate schools.

Moreover, the right to be educated "in the native language" has been twisted to the Soviets' own end. The purpose was plainly to keep alive in oncoming generations the spirit of national consciousness. Some of these people have a literary tradition. The Tadzhiks and Uzbeks have glorious ones. If the youngsters could be taught their native tongue, they would have access to those ancient literary treasures. But the Russians saw great danger in much of that literature, for it teems with nationalistic and racial sentiments. The Russians, therefore, impaired the constitutional guarantee by introducing the Cyrillic alphabet in all the native schools. The youngsters are now taught the Russian script, not the Persian or Turkish. Therefore the youngsters can read only those classics that are printed in the Russian alphabet. Since the Soviets have complete command of the printing presses, they stand between the Uzbek youngster and the glorious deeds of his ancestors. The natives of Central Asia are, therefore, barred from their literary treasures, except and unless the Soviet censor grants permission. The result is twofold. First, the literature of the native schools is heavily saturated with Soviet doctrine and the Russian viewpoint. Second, unless the native gets a new education and learns his native script in some graduate school, the literature of his ancestors, including the Koran, will never be known to him. There are language courses in Arabic, Persian, and Turkish. But they are for the select graduate students in the university.

This segregation of the Russians into separate schools also gives impetus to the Russianization of Central Asia. All education beyond the secondary schools is in the Russian language. That is to say, the Uzbek who wants to be an engineer, doctor, agronomist, or chemist must go to a university or institute where instruction is given in Russian. He is not barred because he is an Uzbek; the doors are, indeed, wide open to him. But in reality the Russian student has a preference. To do college work the Russian need qualify only in the Russian language, while the Uzbek must master two languages—his own and the Russian. The advantage is, therefore, with the Russian. And it shows up in the statistics. The University of Alma Ata has 3500 students and 300 faculty members. Only 40 per cent of the faculty and only 30 per cent of the student body are Kazakhs. Even at the Foreign Language Institute at Alma Ata, which is in substance the equivalent of one of our teacher training schools, only 40 per cent of the student body is Kazakh.

In short, the segregated public school system of Central Asia operates to favor the Russian and to disadvantage the native.

The administration of justice also favors the Russian. Today there is a unified system of law throughout all Russia. The same code is applied in Ashkhabad as in Moscow. Up to the 1920s this was not the case. In the beginning of the Soviet rule, the Moslem religious courts exercised their jurisdiction as they did under the czars. In both criminal and civil cases, Moslem customary law was applied. By 1930, however, that system was abolished and Russian courts were substituted. In Central Asia, as in the rest of Russia, the judges are chosen for a short term of years. That means they are hand-picked by the Communist party. In Soviet Central Asia, the party invariably selects a majority of the judges from among the native people. But the party always adds Russians to the group, making sure, of course, that the Russians are in the minority. So far as outward appearances go, the natives are in control of their own courts. But that is not the case when a Russian is a litigant. Once a Russian is a party, a vital change takes place. Soviet trial courts sit in panels of three judges. When a Russian is at the bar, a majority of the three judges are Russian. Russians sit in judgment on Russians in Central Asia just as Frenchmen sit in judgment on Frenchmen in North Africa. When, however, an Uzbek, Tadzhik, or Kazakh is on trial, he does not necessarily get the benefit of a trial before judges of his own race. I discussed the problem with lawyers in Alma Ata. Kazakhs get a court of Kazakh judges only in cases where the Kazakh language becomes an important factor in the trial, as for example where all the witnesses speak only Kazakh. Then Kazakh judges are preferred for they can better follow the case. But the Russian litigant always gets a Russian court—not as a matter of written law but as a matter of judicial administration.

One Uzbek official summed it up when he said that the Uzbeks owed their achievements to the Communist party and to their "elder brother," the Russian people. The "elder brother" has, indeed, played a decisive role in Central Asia. He has been alert to see that his protégé developed no independent traits or characteristics. And day in and day out he has followed the example of other colonial powers and discriminated against the native.

In spite of nearly forty years of repressive Soviet practices, the flame of nationalism still burns in Central Asia. One would have to become a member of the community, speak the language, and earn the confidence of the people to have the true measure of its strength and vitality. But that it exists is plain. One never finds it in the printed page or in conversation. But occasionally I detected it.

I was tendered many feasts by farmers and by factory workers.

At these banquets there were many toasts—to health and happiness, to peace and friendship, to Bulganin and Eisenhower. I made a special point of raising toasts to these Asian people, their history, and their heroes. In Ashkhabad I emphasized the Turkish tie; in Stalinabad the Persian influence; in Uzbekistan, the great Timur and his halls of learning. Each time I watched the faces of my native hosts. Without exception my toast brought a transformation. It tapped deep wells of memory, and there came flooding to the surface emotions long suppressed. It was evident that the force of nationalism, which above all else the Soviets fear, is still a factor in the affairs of Central Asia.

This does not mean that revolt is imminent or that an independence movement has any real chance of success. Those who think so are engaged in wishful thinking. The liquidations in Central Asia have robbed the movement of its leaders. Moreover, these suppressed people have no political tradition, for prior to the Communists they lived in a feudal society under khans and emirs. The watchful eyes of the Communist party and of the MVD make certain that no new leadership will arise. The Communist party in Central Asia is relatively small; but it is a hard, solid core of the tried and the true. It is everywhere, as I have said—on every collective farm, in every university, in each factory, in government at all levels. It is there to indoctrinate the people with the "true faith" and to detect "deviationists." The MVD is also omnipresent. The MVD is an army as well as the police. It has tanks and airplanes and a ground force too. It has offices in every district in Central Asia. In Kazakhstan alone the MVD has 200 stations, the equivalent of one for every county in Texas. These district offices are tied together with a network of telephones, radios, and teletypes. Because of the MVD and the Communist party, no revolt from within Central Asia is in the realm of probabilities.

The suppression of nationalism in Central Asia dates back at least as far as a speech by Stalin on March 10, 1921, when he stated

MOSCOW

The Kremlin, Moscow, is our White House, Capitol, and Supreme Court all combined.

A third of the workers in the Stalin plant at Moscow are women.

Greenhouse tomatoes at a collective farm near Moscow are boxed for shipment.

The manager of the Stalin plant in Moscow tells the author that his assembly line is as good as any in Detroit.

MOSCOW

The guard changes at
the Lenin-Stalin tomb,
Moscow, every four hours.

The Baptist Church at
Moscow has a Sunday
congregation of 1500.

Rabbi Solomon Shliffer
of the Choral Synagogue,
Moscow, is the head of
an active Jewish community

that the Soviets had discarded the slogan "national determination" and substituted for it a new one, "the right of nations to political secession." The right to secede was adopted, Stalin announced, because it is "a revolutionary slogan" aimed at the colonies of Great Britain, France, America, and Japan. There is, of course, great irony in it.

England gave India and Pakistan a degree of political maturity and ultimately turned them loose as independent nations. America nurtured the Philippines for several decades and then granted them complete independence. Russia has no such program for her subjugated peoples.

The contribution of the West to underdeveloped countries and feudal areas has been primarily political and spiritual—the self-determination of peoples, racial equality, the free ballot, due process of law, freedom of conscience. Russia's contribution to Asian life, though primarily materialistic, has also been political to a degree. She has emancipated women not only from the Moslem veil but also from a subservient place in society. In all my traveling in Central Asia, I saw no more veiled women than I could count on the fingers of two hands. In Samarkand, Bukhara, Frunze, and Tashkent there were a few; and they were heavily veiled with black cloth woven from horsehair. But they are the exceptions. The Moslem women of Central Asia are as free with their dress as Russians and Americans. Equal rights for women have been applied in Central Asia, as throughout Russia, with a vengeance. Russia's contribution to Asian life is, however, essentially materialistic. The Marxist influence has exalted the economic and deprecated the spiritual. Russia today is bent on raising the standard of living of her peoples and strengthening the Communist international domain through ideological and economic ties. One can be sure, therefore, that Russia's Central Asian empire is not destined for political independence, but there to stay.

The natives of Central Asia are slowly but surely being Russianized. A new generation is being reared which has little chance to know even its own history. Moreover, the Russians have infiltrated the country and its government so deeply and they are now so necessary to the operation of Central Asia's vast industrial plant, that the political emancipation of Central Asia is a lost cause. Even the chances of these people getting more political autonomy and more cultural freedom within the Russian federation seem very remote.

Of course the Turks, Persians, and Mongols who make up the bureaucracy in Central Asia all praise the Soviets for the reconstruction of this area. Though the masses are silent, I occasionally broke through the barrier. And when I did I learned that there were many natives who feel greatly oppressed. I will never forget an interview in some railroad yards with a group of Kazakh workers. There were three of them; and they were employed as cleaners of passenger cars. They had on their heads not turbans or the circular karakul hats typical of their ancestors, but the heavy dark caps that mark the Russian worker. They wore rough brown mackinaws and greasy dark trousers, running into knee-high boots. The boots—frayed and decrepit—were the only visible link they had with their ancestors except, of course, their round Mongol faces and high cheekbones. I was the first American they had ever seen, and they were filled with curiosity. Their questions came fast. Finally it was my turn.

"How do you like it under the Communist regime?" I asked.

Each looked over his shoulder to make sure no one was listening. Then the oldest one—a man of about fifty with a wisp of a black mustache—whispered:

"Well, we exist."

I mentioned this episode to a Russian, and he countered by asking if our railroad yards might not also contain decrepit characters who, if asked how they fare in the United States, might not give the same answer. I had to concede that perhaps he was right.

But I went on to say that in America there were no people longing for their own nation and for independence from Washington, D.C., that the United States was denying no people their national aspirations. He countered by saying that we Americans had been cruel and unfair to the American Indians, that they were being denied their "nationalist" ambitions. I admitted that in the past we had not always been fair and honorable in our dealings with the Indians but that in recent years we were making amends by giving them restitution in cash for their lost claims. I also told him that there was no separatist movement among our Indians. He answered by saying that that was also true of most Central Asians, that if I took a poll of young Central Asians I would find them in step with the Russians, not pulling against them.

That, I think, is fair comment. The national aspirations in Central Asia are mainly nurtured by the older people who, once having known the zeal of nationalism, keep it proudly alive in their hearts.

CHAPTER **11**

THE NEW RUSSIAN STRATEGY

I finished my Russian journey with several convictions. First, the Russian people want peace. Second, the Kremlin is anxious to avoid war. Third, the ultimate aims of communism have not changed. Fourth, Russia has moved into a position of increased strength as a result of her change in policies. Fifth, peaceful coexistence will involve a degree of political competition which to date we have never experienced in international affairs.

The Russian people are in the mood for friendship with Americans. Both the Russian people and the Russian officials want peace. They want to avoid war, for they realize, I think, the horrors of the atomic and hydrogen bombs. They want peace so that they can enjoy the dividends of the society which they have created. The desire for consumer goods is strong. Cars, refrigerators, washing machines, sewing machines, television—these are the things the Russian people want. They also want more and better clothes and shoes. They are fed nutritiously, and they eat heartily, perhaps because they once starved. But they do not have the variety of food they crave. They do not have the steaks and chops they want. Their houses are inadequate. They want roads and airports and sewage-disposal plants. They want, in other words, the comforts of life. They have pulled in their belts before; and they can do it again. But they want relief from austerity. The industrial plant that can give them that relief has been built. The industrial plant, if devoted to peace, not to war, can turn out a veritable plethora of goods.

The agricultural economy, though inefficient, has firm foundations. There is today enough to eat. There can be an abundance of good foods in a few years if the agricultural economy is given priorities.

The desire for a higher standard of living—for better food, for more of the comforts of life—has created a political ground swell of vast proportions, so strong that it cannot be ignored even in a dictatorship.

Under Stalin, Russia was a one-man dictatorship. Since his death there has been an important change. Today Russia is run not by one man, but by a committee. That committee is made up of the eleven men in the Praesidium. No one of them is supreme; they act as a group. A major weakness in the Soviet system is the absence of any machinery for transferring power peacefully and smoothly from one group to another. Therefore, someday one man may emerge to seize the paraphernalia of government and assume Stalin's role. That, however, is not likely in the near future. The present group lived under Stalin and knew the horrors of his rule. They are relieved at his passing and today openly denounce him.

The committee now in control of Soviet Russia is representative of the new aristocracy that has come into existence since the October Revolution. This aristocracy is talented, elite, and dedicated to the *status quo*. They won their honors under the Soviet system and are indebted to it. They cherish the freedom which Stalin's death brought them. They thrive under new contacts with the outside world.

This group is composed of ministers, their deputies, and the vast army of experts hidden in the Soviet bureaucracy. It also includes engineers, mathematicians, agronomists, dancers, singers, musicians, artists, writers, professors, judges—in fact, the whole host of the intelligentsia. This new aristocracy realizes as much as we do the horrors of thermonuclear warfare. They want to exploit the Soviet system for themselves and their children. They have pride in it; they want to see it improved; they now have a vision of a great and prosperous Russia under socialist auspices.

I talked with many members of this bureaucracy and sensed a measure of their enthusiasm. They even deny that communism is an international conspiracy managed from Russia. They even deny that the Communist parties in foreign lands have any relationship to the Communist party in Russia. They stoutly deny that Russia is the training camp for communism in its foreign operations. They swear that the Comintern, which was dissolved on June 10, 1943, was never re-established. They maintain that the Cominform, which was created in September 1947, is nothing but a propaganda or educational agency. They go on to say that "non-interference" of an "economic, political, or ideological character," which Russia promised India in June 1955, is also promised every nation. I must have shown my lack of belief. For these protagonists of the Soviet system would quickly add that while they do not support overseas political operations of the Communists, they are wholly sympathetic with all the Communist parties in every country. As Ivan Benedictov, Minister of State Farms told me:

"Of course, we are in sympathy with every Communist party in every nation. We have common aims. When a Communist party wins in an Asian country, we naturally are encouraged. For we like to see our way of life succeed."

From my interviews with the bureaucracy, I became convinced

that the new Russian aristocracy believes that a dramatic increase in the standard of living inside Russia is the greatest momentum that can be given the Communists in other lands.

If Russia can get peace even for a decade, she can substantially raise her standard of living. By that very act she will create tremendous pressure on Asia and Africa and on Europe too. There are some democratic regimes in Asia, viz., Burma, India, Israel, Japan, and the Philippines. Some of them have the problems of food production, birth rate, and industrialization ahead of them. Many Asian countries are still under feudal regimes. Some like Korea and Vietnam have been torn and divided by war. Malaya, a colony, is about to be free. Indonesia is in transition. Almost all of the Asians have low standards of living—from $150 to $300 a year per worker. A Russian's annual income is higher. Money income alone does not measure it accurately, since so many services, such as medical care, are free. But if the average wage is taken at $600 a year (4800 rubles) at least one fifth should be added for those free services. That makes, roughly, $720 average annual income for the Russian, as compared with $150 to $300 for the Asian. That means that Asians will be increasingly vulnerable as neighbors to a Russia that is both peaceful and prosperous. A rising standard of living in Russia will be a powerful attraction. Even the masses of Italy and France may also be tempted by a Russia that is both prosperous and smiling. Though Russia today has a standard of living below most of the countries of Europe, tomorrow her standard may be even higher than theirs, if Russia has peace.

The Russian economy has been devoted primarily to war. If it can be turned to peace it can, during the next few decades, revolutionize the bleak areas of the world. That, I think, is the vision of the new Soviet aristocracy.

Stalin shook the world with war and threats of war. Fear of Russia was the mucilage binding NATO together. It was the basis of many co-operative actions and programs among the Western nations. Those same co-operative compacts might not have been possible in face of a smiling Russia. A smiling Russia may, indeed, make the maintenance of them difficult.

Certain of Russia's objectives are a matter of record. On November 26, 1940, while Russia and Germany were partners, Molotov sent a historic message to the German Foreign Office concerning a four-power pact between Germany, Russia, Italy, and Japan. Molotov stated that Russia was willing to accept the proposed draft of the pact on certain conditions. Some of the conditions related to withdrawal of German troops from Finland, the renunciation by Japan of oil and coal concessions in northern Sakhalin, and the conclusion of a mutual assistance pact between Russia and Bulgaria. Two other conditions clearly disclosed some of Russia's long-range ambitions. One of those conditions called for "the establishment of a base for land and naval forces of the U.S.S.R. within range of the Bosporus and the Dardanelles by means of a long-term lease." The other condition declared that "the area south of Batumi and Baku in the general direction of the Persian Gulf is recognized as the center of the aspiration of the Soviet Union." Not many days later—on December 18, 1940, to be exact —Hitler issued his directive for Operation Barbarosa that on June 21, 1941, headed the Nazi armies toward Moscow.

There is reason to believe that Russia's main interests still lie in the direction of the Indian Ocean, the Persian Gulf, and the Mediterranean Sea. There are great riches in those areas; and those waters are highways to Africa.

Many assumed that the Geneva Conference meant that Russia had discarded her former ambitions. Any such assumption was unfounded. Geneva signified Russian agreement only on the stalemate in thermonuclear warfare. Russia went to that conference in an agreeable state of mind. But agreeableness does not mean agreement on everything or on most things. Geneva meant only that the Great Powers agreed that the nations of the world should not be threatened with a thermonuclear war and therefore that no people need fear such a war. Geneva left open every other political issue. Geneva did not mean that any basic settlement of other issues had been made or could be made. It certainly did not mean that Russia's dreams had changed.

The new Russian attitude means a new Russian strategy, one that can be infinitely more effective than Stalin's. He was an evil person who generated the fear that united the free world against him. The new Russian strategy is more disarming. It is to use oats, not a whip, to drive the horses, as an old Russian proverb counsels.

Under Stalin, Russia worked clandestinely in foreign lands. Under the new regime she is no longer an outsider conspiring with an internal underground. She is now an open and skilled player in the game of power politics. Today Russia is everywhere with missions and programs.

She is now in the Mediterranean, the Middle East, Africa, Asia, and Latin America on countermoves against the position of the West. Her strategy is roughly as follows:

First is the matter of *economic aid*. Russia now can launch the most ambitious Point IV program the world has seen. She has the resources for that program. And equally important, she has the engineers, agronomists, and other scientists to supervise and direct it. She can move into underdeveloped nations with programs for agriculture, hydroelectric power, steel production, medical care and public health, atomic energy—in fact with any program that involves the application of modern technology. She has already extended that kind of aid to Argentina, Afghanistan, and India. Her offers are out to other nations, including Egypt. She now plans to build atomic energy plants for "friendly" nations. She has technical missions in various Asian countries, advising on oil exploration, mining, and hydroelectric power.

We can expect an active Russian Point IV program backed by vast resources and great ability.

Our economic aid has often been hitched to a military alliance. Soviet Russia will impose no such condition. She will use economic aid to pry nations loose from their military alliances. She will say, "Your military alliances only provoke us. We'll protect you when necessary. Be neutral in the conflict between East and West and we will finance you."

The appearance of Russia in Asia, Africa, and Latin America as a supplier of capital has broken the monopoly of the West. Competition is now wide open; and those nations that need development can be expected to take full advantage of their new choice.

Second is the matter of *military aid*. Russia has a huge supply of war materials that are obsolete to her but highly useful in the political chess game going on in Asia, the Middle East, and Africa. When Russia exploited Egypt's attitude toward Israel, she set a precedent that can be applied over and again in these troubled regions. Russia can go further and train army and air corps officers for political conquests as well as for military duty. She can use the offer of military aid to build Communist alliances that will extend her influence and power over several continents. Here, too, Russia has broken the monopoly of the West and stands ready to compete with us.

Third is the matter of *trade*. Russia uses trade not only to make rubles, but also to make political conquests. She is in the business of trade for politics as well as for profits.

Burma has a rice surplus. Other nations have surplus crops that depress their economies. The new Russia will purchase these surpluses for machinery, equipment, and raw materials that are needed by the selling nation for industrial development. The new, emerging countries of Asia and Africa need steel, machine tools, oil-drilling material, and almost endless supplies of machinery and factory equipment. Russia is at last ready and able to furnish these materials in considerable quantities on either a barter basis or a cash basis.

Russia has commodities and products to sell at a cutthroat price or even to give away as the occasion may demand. Her aim is to use trade to establish dependent areas which cannot afford to be hostile. Yugoslavia and Finland are examples. When Yugoslavia broke with Russia, the Yugoslav economy was heavily dependent on the Soviet Union. It is estimated that about 50 per cent of Yugoslavia's trade was with Russia at that time. The economy of any nation would collapse if that close a cord were cut. It was only liberal Western aid that saved Yugoslavia. Finland, too, has moved into a dangerous position vis-a-vis Russia. Russia used the reparations she exacted from Finland to lace her into the Soviet economic block. She required Finland to build a metal industry and to pay Russia in its products. The costs of that metal industry were high, since the volume was too low to get the benefits of mass production. The high costs prevented Finland from selling to the West. That meant that Russia and her satellites were the only market for Finnish goods from that plant. The Finnish metal industry was built up until it employed 80,000 workers. To shut that industry down would be to rock the Finnish economy and perhaps send the nation spinning towards communism. So when the period of reparations was coming to a close, Russia foisted a trade agreement on Finland, under which Finland supplies steel products to Russia, Czechoslovakia, and Poland and receives in return various products including the small Russian car, the Moskvitch, that the Finns dislike. Under this trade agreement, Russia pays high prices. Those high prices serve a political end. By 1954 the Soviet Union had managed to get 34 per cent of all of Finland's trade—a dangerously high percentage because of the leverage it creates on the Finnish economy. By 1955 that percentage had dropped to 27 per cent. Finland is quietly and firmly anti-Communist. But a nation tied so closely to Russia by vital trade must lead a discreet political life, especially when she is contiguous to the Soviet Union.

Fourth is the matter of *diplomacy*. Lazar M. Kaganovich, member of the Praesidium, recently told the Soviet people that "If the nineteenth century was a century of capitalism, the twentieth century is the century of the triumph of socialism and communism." Soviet diplomacy is now dedicated to that cause the world over. The new regime in Russia has forsaken Stalin's conspiratorial silence. The aim of Russian diplomacy, like that of Russian economic aid, military aid, and trade, will be to get new allies, to neutralize other nations, and to pry countries loose from existing alliances against Russia. She obviously wants a united Germany freed from NATO. She obviously uses fear of Israel to woo the Arabs. She obviously caters to Afghanistan and to India to obtain staging grounds for operations against Pakistan, in either the military or political sense or both. She has an affirmative program designed to set the feet of other nations on the Communist path. The program will have strong appeal in Asia and Africa. Those continents are mostly in the same underdeveloped stage Russia was in forty years ago. Russia today points to the tremendous progress she has made and tells these other nations, "See what we have done in less than four decades. You can do the same if you want to follow our example. Why not follow us rather than the United States? We did in a generation what it took the United States a century and a half to achieve." This can be powerful talk in the wastelands of the earth. It is especially powerful talk in Asia because Asia is predominantly socialist in philosophy. The capitalism that Asia knew was highly exploitive, not the healthy, responsible type we have known in America. Moreover, the present political leaders of Asia absorbed more of their ideas of economics and politics from Soviet Russia and Red China than from the West. For these and other reasons, the socialists have made a profound impression upon Asia's intelligentsia. The Russian experiment in socialism makes a much greater impact on the Asian mind than it does on ours. When Russia shows that her socialist society is flourishing, Asians are truly impressed.

Fifth is the matter of *Communist attitudes and politics.*

The Russians have a missionary attitude that is part of the proselytizing that goes with communism. One finds in current Soviet literature the theme that there is "no greater happiness in life than to fight for communism." That is the gospel preached to all the youngsters. The generation born and raised since the October Revolution has been thoroughly indoctrinated in it. This missionary attitude has many other forms. On my visit to the Tashkent radio station the staff boasted to me about the warm reception their broadcasts received in the United States. I asked them how they knew their programs had a high rating here. They said they had a file of letters written by admirers. I asked if I could see the file. A lady returned in a few minutes with the file. In it was one letter from a man who lives on Boscobel Place in the Bronx, New York City. One boaster or convert in the Bronx was enough to make the faithful in Tashkent as hopeful as the pastor who starts his revival meeting.

We have never fully understood the true nature of the link between Communist Russia and the peoples of other lands. We have thought of communism only as a conspiracy. Though it is a conspiracy, it is cast in terms of brotherhood. It is the old, old theme of one for all and all for one. It has for many the same universal appeal as Thomas Jefferson's creed, "All men are created equal" and "endowed by their Creator with certain inalienable rights" including "life, liberty, and the pursuit of happiness." The Russian call to revolution reaches peoples of every race and color. Its universal base was put in eloquent terms by a Soviet author at the Second All-Union Congress of Soviet Writers in December 1954:

"Who, at the top of his voice, told all mankind: 'No matter how hard it may be for you, no matter how difficult the struggle, you will be victorious, you will never be alone, you will meet friends, and they will not forsake you'?"

That is a powerful rallying cry to the poor and the oppressed. It is not the cry of the sentimentalist. It is backed by solid political organization. The Communists have a genius for political discipline and the use of authority that comes from discipline. American labor knows as well as anyone how effective that discipline can become in a political campaign. For American labor took long, bitter months to rid itself of the Communist influence. But this discipline, and the authority it carries, has a power in Asia and Africa that we of the West have never appreciated.

Asia and Africa are mostly feudal domains where the wealth and the power have traditionally been held by a few men or by a few families. The masses have been engaged in agrarian activities under the supervision or control of a tribe, a family, or a landlord. The people are accustomed to the authority of some superior. The Asian has had close ties to a priest or to an elder of the family. He has had a church, a family, a village to which he belonged and where he was welcome. Those groups did not give him much opportunity. He lived at the low level of subsistence and never had a chance for advancement. Nevertheless he found security in those groups. He was not an outcast. He had a sense of belonging. The groups that demanded his loyalty had authority too.

At times the Asian is bewildered when that authority and security are removed.

Before entering Russia, I visited farms in Iran where farmers for the first time in history owned their own lands. No longer were they under a tribe or a landlord. No longer was there a man to tell them what to plant, when to plow, when to sow, when to reap. They were completely on their own; and many were dazed by the experience. They desperately needed some guiding hand to direct them, some new discipline to take the place of the old. The same is true in the cities. In the new industrialization programs for Asia and Africa, labor is moving off the farms to the new plants and factories. These new wage earners have also known discipline and security. They feel the need for both. With out authority and security they drift. Asia and Africa today ar filled with the uprooted first generation living in shanty towns— lost, bewildered, and dazed, their old moorings gone, easy prey to the fanatic. They all feel the hunger for some new authority to take the place of the older one. This is a psychological vacuum that is filled by the Communist parties in Asia and Africa.

As the Communists carry through the new programs of industrialization, they recreate the security of the tribal or village life the worker once knew. The Communist regime has discipline as well as security; it creates a sense of solidarity as well as authority. This is despotism of a high order. But to a worker emerging from the dictatorship of feudalism it is warm and friendly paternalism.

Over the years it is this pressure of the Communist totalitarian faith that will present the greatest difficulties to the Western world. Only strong nationalist leaders like Nehru of India, U Nu of Burma, Ngo Dinh Diem of Vietnam, and Magsaysay of the Philippines can compete with the Communists at that level. They alone can supply the symbolism of authority and security which the masses sorely need.

These are five ways in which a smiling, peaceful Russia will find great political opportunities within Africa, Asia, Europe, and Latin America.

The military stalemate appears to be permanent. Thermonuclear warfare is impossible if life is to go on. But a smiling, peaceful, prosperous Russia presents the most difficult international problem that America has yet faced. It will require more fluid diplomacy than we have ever known. It will, indeed, require a regrouping of our forces, a reorientation of our thinking, and a complete revision of our theory of containment, if a smiling, prosperous Russia is not to conquer the world from the inside.

The last half of this century will see the emergence of new, great powers, including China, India, Germany, and Japan. They together with Russia and the United States will make up the new Great Powers. Merely to state the fact is to expose the great weakness in our present position and the startling new alignments that will be necessary if we are not to become a rather small minority in a fast-changing world.

The tasks confronting American foreign policy will be agonizing ones. There will be the problem of preventing a majority of the new Great Powers from swinging to the Communist orbit. Military alliances will be of secondary importance. Political action will come first.

This competition is power politics in the raw. It's as old as history and as new as the ingenuity of man. The advantage moves back and forth across the board. It is not all with Russia. Russia, neighbor of turbulent Asia, has problems of a dimension we do not know. Asia is not all asset and no liability. Asia has conflicts and stresses that have plagued Russia throughout history. Nicolson in *The Congress of Vienna* writes that Lord Castlereagh in the early 1800s plotted British policy toward Russia so as to show a combined conciliation and firmness. Castlereagh knew, he wrote, that "if Europe could only gain sufficient time, the vast tide of Muscovy would be sucked back again by the Asian moon." Castlereagh proved to be right. The pull of the "Asian moon" may be even greater in the years ahead than they were in Castlereagh's day.

If we are to succeed in building close and enduring relations with the emerging Great Powers, we must start afresh. We must have affirmative programs, not merely anti-Communist ones. We must have negotiable positions, not inflexible ones. We must woo where we have been prone to castigate. We must remember that a nation is not necessarily Communist because it is socialist. We must learn to be at home in a world that is more socialist than capitalist. We must be rid of the attitude that those nations which refuse a military alliance with us are necessarily fellow travelers or dupes of the Communists.

The important decision, however, will concern our relations with Russia.

The ideological differences between Russia and America strike too deep for settlement. But even great human antagonisms tend to mellow with time, as evidenced by the history of the relations between Christianity and Islam. The new generation, while not forsaking principle, comes to the problem with gentler attitudes. While a Stalin would not listen or stay his hand, a Khrushchev might. Russia of the next generation may, indeed, have the mellowness of present-day Communist Yugoslavia. If Asia industrializes and produces a Genghis Khan with the hydrogen bomb, Russia and America might become indispensable to each other if either is to survive.

The fact that Marx, Lenin, and Stalin talked in terms of the ultimate bloody conflict between communism and the West, does not necessarily mean that tomorrow's Soviet leaders will do the same. In February 1956 at the Twentieth Congress of the Soviet Communist Party, Khrushchev, indeed, announced a revision of Marxist doctrine. He pointed to the parliamentary victory as one path to Communist success, denying both that violence is always a necessary instrument of the class struggle and that Communist countries will intervene with arms in the affairs of other nations. Though the basic theory of the class struggle is the same under Khrushchev as under Stalin, the tactics are altered. Every political theory tends to bend to expediency or necessity. No society is static. Every society is always in the process of change. The "free enterprise" we know today with all of its controls and subsidies is quite different from the "free enterprise" of our fathers. Nor can the communism that flourishes in Russia be squared with the communism of Marx or Lenin.

Attitudes also change. Even those Americans most hostile to communism often found comfort in having Communist Yugoslavia as an ally. The Americans of tomorrow may come on friendlier terms with all socialists and all Communists, not as a matter of conversion to their schools of thought but as a measure of tolerance and of practical expediency in the problem of coexistence.

That is the long-range philosophical viewpoint. The more difficult problem is what to do today. On that I think we have only two choices.

One is to continue our present policy of military preparedness and to step up our international economic program to meet Russia's new competition. Any such economic program would entail massive expenditures over a long term. This choice would involve technical and political missions of a nature we have never imagined. The aim would be to outbid Russia on all the continents. It would not be enough, however, to build dams in Egypt, mills in India, irrigation projects in Afghanistan. Capital alone is not sufficient. Political ideas and political-action programs are even more essential. For unless the overseas development programs were under healthy political auspices in the lands where they were launched, they might soon be inherited by new Communist regimes. It is plain, above everything else, that the feudal, reactionary regimes of Asia and Africa are doomed. They will be replaced either by the kind that has laid hold of North Vietnam and North Korea, or by vigorous democracies as are represented by Burma, India, Israel, and the Philippines, or by interim holding operations under a dictator, as we witness in Egypt. A vast overseas economic program has no place in the American agenda, unless it is hitched to political programs that have sturdy roots among the masses of Asia and Africa. If it is not, American billions will be lost in political debacles as serious as that which caused China to collapse.

The other choice is to make a political truce with Russia. A political truce would involve a disarmament program, a treaty of friendship and nonaggression, and an agreement on a *status quo* which each nation would defend. This is the preferable choice because it insures a measure of security and reduces the risk of wasting our resources in an endless race of armaments. A political truce would leave some problems unsolved—probably the problem of a divided Korea and Vietnam. It would leave other problems on the agenda for discussion, perhaps such matters as free elections in eastern Europe. At the same time it could be the means for a solution of the problems of Formosa or Germany or the occasion when their settlement was announced.

A political truce would recognize that, hostile as the two systems are, each exists and promises to survive. A political truce would accept competitive coexistence as the only way of life that is feasible in the atomic age. A political truce would mean that the ideological conflict that splits the world need not be forced to a decision. A political truce would put aside war as a solution and bank on the self-interest and residual good will among men to negotiate settlements. A political truce would necessitate the restoration of diplomacy in our relations with Russia—not the diplomacy of the press conference or television, but the diplomacy of quiet, unhurried talk where joint solutions of existing conflicts would be patiently pursued.

A political truce would not mean unconditional surrender by either power. It would not mean an end to proselytizing either by democracy or by communism. For no political truce could be expected to stop the bid of each side for the uncommitted people of the world.

Today the bulk of the peoples of the world are uncommitted in

243

the struggle that is going on between the Communist and democratic ways of life. The chances of saving them and the world from the deluge of communism are good. We have powerful advantages over the Communists. The Communists preach social justice and fulfill the longing for security; but as a price they fasten a harsh regime on a people. To the Communists, humanity as an abstraction is more important than human beings. To the West, human beings are more important than theory. The right of self-determination, the dignity of man, his freedom of conscience and expression, his right to worship as he chooses, his claim to due process—these rights rank even higher than man's right to security. They constitute our democratic faith. They give the West a great advantage in the competition—if we will only think in terms of people, their fears, their needs, and their dreams.

INDEX

Abdul Said Mir Alim (last Emir of Bukhara), 44–46

Abdurakhmanov (former Kirgiz leader), 216

Afghanistan, 44, 47, 51–52, 76, 101, 115, 161, 187, 210, 233, 236, 242

Afghans, 209. *See also above*

Agricultural Bank, 68, 87

Aitakov (former Turkmen leader), 216

Akmolinsk (Kazakhstan), 32, 97

Alamedin State Farm (Kirgizia), 73

Aleppo (Syria), 52

Alexander the Great, 50, 54, 168

Alexandra Theater (Leningrad), 56

Alexei (Patriarch of Russia), 196

Alexis Petrovich, Prince, 43

Alexjeva, Elizabeth (interpreter, Baku), 23, 54

All-Union Congress of Soviet Writers, 177–78, 237–38

Alma Ata (Kazakhstan), 13, 33, 38–39, 89, 99, 114, 115, 135, 155–57, 164, 170–72, 185, 189, 190, 195, 204, 210, 214, 215, 218, 219, 221, 222, 223

Alma Ata Foreign Language Institute, 189, 222

Alma Ata, University of, 13, 190, 222

American Indians, 227

Amu Darya River, 44, 211

Anatolian Turkish (language), 187

Anderson, Marian, 172

Ankara (Turkey), 17

Anushin, B. F. (Chief Justice, Regional Court, Petropavlosk), 12–13, 28

Arab(ic), 53, 55, 236. *See also* Moslem(s) *and under names of countries*

Aral Sea, 211

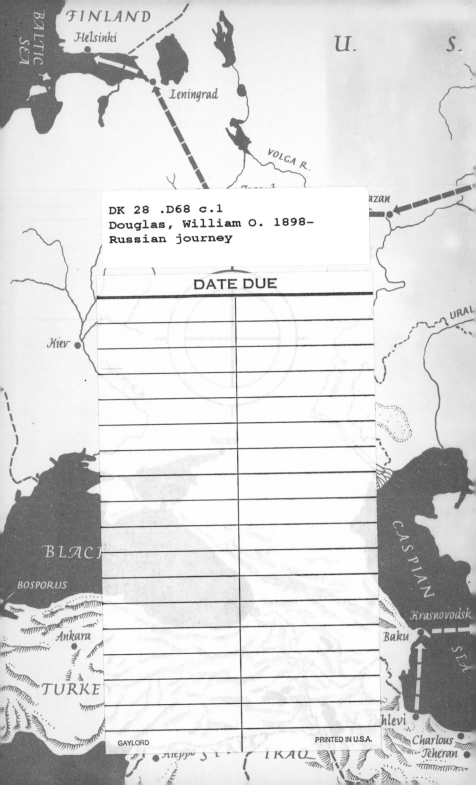

DATE DUE